Multi-Method Social Science

Reflecting the rising popularity of research that combines qualitative and quantitative social science, *Multi-Method Social Science* provides the first systematic guide to designing multi-method research. It argues that methods can be productively combined using the framework of integrative multi-method research, with one method used to carry out a final causal inference, and methods from other traditions to test the key assumptions involved in that causal inference. In making this argument, Jason Seawright considers a wide range of statistical tools, including regression, matching, and natural experiments. It also discusses qualitative tools including process tracing, the use of causal-process observations, and comparative case-study research. Along the way, the text develops over a dozen multi-method designs to test key assumptions about social-science causation.

Jason Seawright is Associate Professor in the Department of Political Science at Northwestern University and has written extensively about multi-method research, publishing in journals including *Political Analysis, Political Research Quarterly, and Sociological Methodology, Sociological Methods and Research*. He was the author or co-author of several chapters in *Rethinking Social Inquiry: Diverse Tools, Shared Standards* edited by Henry E. Brady and David Collier. He has taught courses on multi-method research design at institutes worldwide.

Strategies for Social Inquiry

Multi-Method Social Science: Combining Qualitative and
Quantitative Tools

Editors
Colin Elman, *Maxwell School of Syracuse University*
John Gerring, *Boston University*
James Mahoney, *Northwestern University*

Editorial Board
Bear Braumoeller, David Collier, Francesco Guala, Peter Hedström,
Theodore Hopf, Uskali Maki, Rose McDermott, Charles Ragin,
Theda Skocpol, Peter Spiegler, David Waldner, Lisa Wedeen,
Christopher Winship

This new book series presents texts on a wide range of issues bearing
upon the practice of social inquiry. Strategies are construed broadly to
embrace the full spectrum of approaches to analysis, as well as relevant
issues in philosophy of social science.

Published Titles
John Gerring, *Social Science Methodology: A Unified Framework, 2nd
edition*
Michael Coppedge, *Democratization and Research Methods*
Thad Dunning, *Natural Experiments in the Social Sciences: A
Design-Based Approach*
Carsten Q. Schneider and Claudius Wagemann, *Set-Theoretic Methods
for the Social Sciences: A Guide to Qualitative Comparative Analysis*
Nicholas Weller and Jeb Barnes, *Finding Pathways: Mixed-Method
Research for Studying Causal Mechanisms*
Andrew Bennett and Jeffrey T. Checkel, *Process Tracing: From Metaphor
to Analytic Tool*
Diana Kapiszewski, Lauren M. MacLean and Benjamin L. Read, *Field
Research in Political Science: Practices and Principles*
Peter Spiegler, *Behind the Model: A Constructive Critique of Economic
Modeling*
James Mahoney and Kathleen Thelen, *Advances in Comparative-
Historical Analysis*

Multi-Method Social Science

Combining Qualitative and Quantitative Tools

Jason Seawright

Northwestern University, Illinois

CAMBRIDGE
UNIVERSITY PRESS

CAMBRIDGE
UNIVERSITY PRESS

University Printing House, Cambridge CB2 8BS, United Kingdom

Cambridge University Press is part of the University of Cambridge.

It furthers the University's mission by disseminating knowledge in the pursuit of education, learning and research at the highest international levels of excellence.

www.cambridge.org
Information on this title: www.cambridge.org/9781107097711

© Jason Seawright 2016

First published 2016

Printed in the United States of America by Sheridan Books, Inc.

A catalogue record for this publication is available from the British Library

ISBN 978-1-107-09771-1 Hardback
ISBN 978-1-107-48373-6 Paperback

Contents

Figures and Tables

Figures

Tables

Acknowledgments

As with any lengthy academic project, the composition of this book has been supported by a wide variety of individuals and institutions. Discussions with my graduate school mentors — David Collier, Ruth Berins Collier, Henry E. Brady, and David Freedman — were invaluable throughout the development of this project. Other colleagues, including Jeb Barnes, Andrew Bennett, Thad Dunning, Colin Elman, John Gerring, Diana Kapiszewski, James Mahoney, Stephen C. Nelson, Benjamin I. Page, Andrew Roberts, and Nicholas Weller, have generously read and given helpful comments on some or all of the book. While they may well disagree with key ideas in this book, it is inarguable that these colleagues have made the final product better.

I would also like to thank years of participants at the Institute for Qualitative and Multimethod Research at the Maxwell School of Public Policy at Syracuse University and at the Summer School in Social Science Data Analysis at the University of Essex, who have given feedback on this book in many preliminary incarnations. I am also grateful for the comments, suggestions, and support offered by participants in the INPUT seminar series at Northwestern University's Political Science Department.

Finally, I want to thank my family for their encouragement and support, and for putting up with what must at times have been exasperating conversations about methodology and the philosophy of science.

1 Integrative Multi-Method Research

The social sciences are in the middle of a boom in multi-method research. An increasing number of books and articles combine techniques from different methodological families within a single study. In conjunction with this trend in application, there has been a marked increase in methodological debate regarding the merits of and best practices for multi-method designs.

This book advances the proposition that well-designed and well-executed multi-method research has inferential advantages over research relying on a single method. I argue that multi-method research can test assumptions that are generally untested in single-method research, thereby transforming key issues of descriptive and causal inference from matters of speculative assertion into points of empirical debate. Yet in order to realize these advantages, multi-method research must be designed from the start with a clear focus on testing assumptions – a priority that informs decisions about case selection, statistical analysis, and the substantive targeting of qualitative inquiry.

While multi-method research has potential advantages for diverse goals, including concept formation and refinement (e.g. Pearce *et al.* 2003), description (Campbell and Fiske 1959; Eid and Diener 2006), and applied policy evaluation (Smith and Lewis 1982; Greene, Caracelli, and Graham 1989), this book focuses on designing multi-method research for causal inference. This emphasis is not intended as a slight against the other families of goals just listed. After all, these goals are deeply interrelated. Good conceptualization and description in particular are essential components of successful causal inference; causal claims, in turn, are routinely central to work in normative theory and policy evaluation. Instead, causal inference is emphasized because it has been the primary focus of sustained debate regarding multi-method social science, with some scholars arguing that multi-method work has no advantages for this goal vis-à-vis single-method designs (Beck 2006; Ahmed and Sil 2009; Kuehn and Rohlfing 2009; Beck 2010). Hence, showing how multi-method research can improve causal inference is more urgent than demonstrating its less-contested role in other domains.[1]

Multi-method designs are not a panacea for the challenges of causal inference. Even the best designs will leave some issues unaddressed, and some common designs arguably have little advantage in comparison with single-method designs. Nonetheless, when carefully constructed and executed, multi-method research can make a major contribution to the social sciences. This book is intended to help scholars design, execute, and evaluate such research.

1.1   The Multi-Method Boom

Multi-method research involves combining data-gathering and -analyzing techniques from two or more methodological traditions. Examples of multi-method research thus include studies that combine survey data with laboratory experiments, focus groups with participant observation, statistical analysis of a corpus of text with careful qualitative interpretation of a selected handful of texts, and so forth. Out of the wide range of possible multi-method combinations, this book focuses on designs that combine quantitative and qualitative methods[2] in support of a single causal inference. This focus is adopted in part because it has been the central theme of most debates regarding multi-method designs, and in part because the very significant differences between the families of methods being combined render particularly vivid both the challenges and the advantages of multi-method approaches.

Issues of how best to combine methods to form the basis for a causal inference have become a central concern in the social sciences

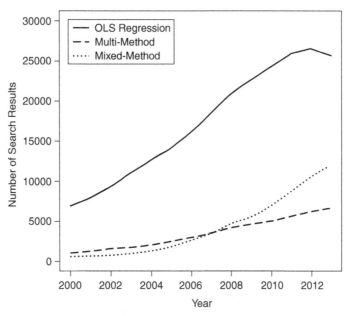

Figure 1.1   Google Scholar Search Results Related to Multi-Method Research.

in light of recent growth in the application of such methods. As a rough measure of the development of multi-method techniques, consider the number of Google Scholar search hits for the terms "multi-method" and "mixed-method." Figure 1.1 shows the number of scholarly texts that contain these two search texts for each year between 2000 and 2013. By way of comparison, the figure also includes the trend for the phrase "OLS regression" (without quotation marks) during the same period.[3] All three search categories show increasing numbers of hits over time – a result that no doubt reflects a combination of increasing digitalization, an increase in the number of venues for scholarly publication, and trends in methodological usage. Relative comparisons are, perhaps, most informative. During this period, the number of references to multi-method research grew from 14% of the references to OLS regression, to 26%. References to mixed-method research grew far more impressively, from 8% to 47% of the number of search results for OLS regression. These suggestive data, combined with qualitative indicators such as the publication of textbooks (e.g.

Greene 2007; Teddlie and Tashakkori 2009; Creswell and Plano Clark 2011) and the launching of a specialized journal, *The Journal of Mixed Methods Research*, specifically devoted to the methodology of multi-method research, indicate quickly and substantially growing scholarly interest in, attention to, and application of research designs combining qualitative and quantitative strategies.

1.2   Integration, not Triangulation

While multi-method research is evidently experiencing a surge of popularity, there are reasons to worry about whether multi-method applications are in fact producing more grounded, justified, and persuasive inferences than studies using a single method. These concerns arise from the "triangulation" framework (Webb *et al.* 1966; Jick 1979; Tarrow 1995) that has for some decades served as the prototypical research design for multi-method social science. Simply put, triangulation designs involve asking the same question of causal inference using two different methods, and checking that the same substantive conclusions are produced by both. The metaphor is to the geometric technique of estimating distance by measuring the angle of sight toward an object from two different vantage points.

Triangulation in the social sciences has major flaws. One is well-known and widely discussed: what conclusion should be drawn when the two methods produce different findings? Unfortunately, the list of intellectually plausible responses to such an outcome is all but unbounded. For example, a scholar could reasonably conclude that both findings are correct but capture different aspects of the phenomenon of interest; that one method or the other displayed fundamental limitations in the analysis; that the divergence provides evidence against the credibility of the assumptions involved in both methods; that the outcome involves a contrast in terms of scope or relevant populations for the two methods; or that the failure to triangulate simply leaves the inference in a state of uncertainty. In decades of writing about triangulation, no definitive guidance has yet emerged about how to respond to divergent findings between the multiple methods in a study.

In my view, this frequently discussed limitation of triangulation designs is a product of a deeper incoherence in their conception. What, in fact, does it mean to say that a qualitative and a quantitative and/or experimental study ask and answer the same research question? In a very general sense, the answer is, perhaps, clear: if both methods produce causal inferences in which a particular concept is important, then there is some degree of overlap in the results. Yet because qualitative and statistical approaches produce results that are different in kind, it is only possible to assess such convergence very abstractly. If a variable has an effect estimate that is positive and statistically significant in some analysis, and a related variable also seems to play an enabling causal role in an analysis of sequences of events within a single case, then that variable has positive support from both methods. This requires essentially ignoring the magnitude of the quantitative effect estimate, as well as qualitative inferences about sequence and context that go along with the discovery of a role for this one variable – effectively, everything but the sign of the inference must be disregarded. At any more detailed level of analysis, it becomes difficult or impossible to decide whether qualitative and statistical results correspond.

For example, if a scholar does a cross-national statistical analysis relating various hypothesized explanatory variables to the outcome of civil war, and then conducts case-study analysis of the dynamics of civil war or its absence in some of the cases used in the statistical part of the study (see, for example, Fearon and Laitin 2003, 2008), then it is clearly true that we have a quantitative and a qualitative study of the outcome of civil war. If one finds "positive" results on related variables from the statistical analysis and the case studies, then there is an overlap, and the triangulation design has made a connection.

Yet if the question is taken more seriously, this connection becomes far more tenuous. The easiest way to see the problem is to ask what it means to decide whether the quantitative and qualitative component of a multi-method design agree. For example, in Fearon and Laitin's logit analysis of civil wars, the logged percentage of a state's territory that is mountainous has a coefficient of 0.219 – an estimate that is significantly different from zero (Fearon and Laitin 2003). What kind of finding from a case-study analysis of Colombia would confirm this estimate? What would contradict it? Colombia is, of course, a mountainous country with a history of endemic civil war. Geographically, the relevant point is that three major Andean mountain ranges run through the center of Colombia, running the length of the country and housing most of its heavily populated areas, as well as its capital city. Furthermore, in terms of civil war and related forms of political violence, Colombia has a long and regrettable record, including a substantial number of wars in the nineteenth century, as well as La Violencia between 1948 and 1958, and the current civil war, which has been ongoing at one level of intensity or another since the 1960s (LeGrand 2003). So far, so good (for the quantitative finding, if not for Colombia), one might suppose.

With a closer examination, though, the apparent agreement between case study and statistical result becomes mired in dilemmas. At some historical moments and for certain components of the conflict, the mountainous regions of Colombia have in fact been host to key events in the civil war. For example, an early event in Colombia's ongoing conflict involved a military attack on a de facto autonomous republic of leftists in the high Andean community of Marquetalia (Arenas 1972). In a very different phase of the conflict, the M-19 revolutionary movement was based in mountainous regions of Colombia and carried out several of its most famous actions in the city of Bogotá – itself in the mountainous region (Duran et al. 2008). A great many other examples could also be provided, of course.

At the same time, the mountainous areas near the national capital at Bogotá have often been among the safest areas and the zones with strongest state presence in the country. Furthermore, mountain-free regions in the southeast and along the Caribbean coast have also served as important areas of refuge for anti- and non-state armed actors, thereby facilitating and prolonging the civil war. For instance, through the 1990s the FARC guerrillas had their primary bases in the jungle regions of southeastern Colombia. Thus, case-study consideration of Colombia would have to suggest that mountainous terrain plays a supporting causal role at some points and for certain actors in the Colombian conflict, but is not a relevant consideration at other points. Further research would likely illuminate how and why terrain matters for some aspects of Colombian political violence but not others.

How does this line of inquiry compare with the estimated coefficient of 0.219? It seems that the best one can say is that the two results do not obviously contradict each other; but nor are they clearly mutually supportive. Does Colombian history show too much of a role for terrain in light of a statistical coefficient that is significant but substantively moderate? After all, the current civil war began in part because anti-state actors had created refuges for themselves in the mountains; a conceivable counterfactual is that less rugged terrain would have prevented these key actors from organizing in the first place. On the other hand, perhaps the case suggests that the coefficient is too large; armed actors have at times found the jungles and other regions as hospitable a refuge as the mountains, so various forms of difficult terrain may be substitutes in a way that the statistical results fail to demonstrate. Or perhaps these competing considerations are just what the value of 0.219 implies?

I think it is in fact impossible to decide whether the case study and the logit coefficient agree. Furthermore, this is not a problem specific to Colombia; any case study would face similar issues of interpretation. The fundamental problem is that the qualitative and quantitative methods are not in fact asking the same question, even though they focus on the same topic. The statistical analysis estimates the difference in conditional probability of civil war associated with a given contrast in geographies across countries, while the case study asks whether there is within-case evidence consistent with the proposition that terrain features helped enable or prevent various components of a particular civil war. These *questions* are fundamentally different, and so it is essentially useless to ask whether the *answers* are the same.[4]

The practical result of a triangulation perspective on multi-method research is the proliferation of studies in which scholars effectively carry out two separate analyses sharing a broad topic and theoretical orientation but with no serious intellectual interaction at any level of detail. Factors that "matter" to some extent in both studies are emphasized, while the actual meaning of inferences drawn in each study, as well as any contrasts in results, is neglected. Such loose forms of multi-method design often do not substantially persuade their target audience. More seriously, there is no obvious reason why they should. I cannot find either a serious argument – beyond the flawed triangulation metaphor – or an empirical demonstration that causal inference is more likely to succeed when it is done twice with different tools and non-comparable results within a single book or article.

Multi-method research can be much more powerful than the triangulation design. In this book, I advocate a contrasting family of multi-method designs, which I will refer to as integrative multi-method research. Integrative designs are multi-method designs in which two or more methods are carefully combined to support a single, unified causal inference. With such a design, one method will produce the final inference, and the other is used to design, test, refine, or bolster the analysis producing that inference.[5]

For example, the scholar may use a regression-type model to produce the final causal inference, drawing on case-study research to test and adjust key assumptions about measurement, omitted variables, causal interactions, and pathways. Here, the final product is a causal effect estimate drawn from a statistical coefficient, as in a purely quantitative study. Yet that coefficient comes from a model designed, refined, and tested in light of serious qualitative analysis. Both methods contribute substantially to the overall inference, even though the final product comes from one and not the other. Integrative designs may also ultimately rely on case-study methods to produce a final causal inference. In such designs, quantitative analysis is often used to test especially important, sensitive, or elusive steps in the case study's causal chain connecting the initial cause to the outcome of interest; if these analyses support the existence of a causal effect at key points, then the overall claim regarding the set of connections from cause to effect is strengthened, and the case study inference becomes more robust.

The central idea of integrative multi-method research is to use each method for what it is especially good at, and to minimize inferential weaknesses by using other methods to test, revise, or justify assumptions. This is in contrast to triangulation designs, in which whole inferences – fully dependent on both the strengths and the weaknesses of each method – are carried out and then somehow compared and combined. Integrative designs thus use multiple modes of inference to substitute strengths for weaknesses, whereas triangulation designs compare whole causal inferences whose individual strengths and weaknesses are the same as those of single-method designs. For this reason, a well-constructed integrative multi-method design will yield a more robust and higher-quality causal inference than either a triangulation design or a single-method design using only one approach. Furthermore, with integrative designs the issue of how to reconcile very different kinds of inferences from quantitative and qualitative analysis does not arise, because these methods are deliberately used from the very beginning to ask different kinds of questions about separate issues related to the causal inference. While the final causal findings from an integrative study will depend on the answers to all of these questions, they are not a direct combination of those answers; one method influences the final inference by shaping the way the other is used, while the second method generates the final causal inference.

Much existing work on multi-method designs emphasizes research sequences, differentiating designs by whether qualitative and quantitative components are simultaneous or sequential and – if the design is sequential – also by which method is used at each stage (Tashakkori and Teddlie 1998: Chapter 3; Teddlie and Tashakkori 2009: Chapter 7; Cresswell and Plano Clark 2011: Chapter 3). The integrative approach requires a sequential design – if qualitative and quantitative research are carried out in parallel, then it is extremely difficult for the findings of one component to inform design decisions involved in the other. In an integrative research sequence, one method provides an initial summary of current knowledge about a problem of causal inference. An alternative method then tests the assumptions behind that initial summary, ideally discovering new material that can be incorporated into an improved version of the first analysis. In turn, the assumptions behind that improved analysis can be tested and improved with a new round of multi-method research. Thus, in contrast to the linear sequences or parallel designs typical of triangulation-based research, integrative multi-method designs involve an indefinite cycle of discovery and refinement.

1.3 The Origins of Proportional Representation: An Integrative Example

Integrative multi-method research designs can be implemented within a single study, perhaps by a single author, but they can also play out across debates among scholars; integrative designs are a wonderful tool for evaluating and critiquing others' research, as well as for strengthening one's own causal inferences. For example, beginning with Boix's (1999) essay on the origins of proportional representation (as opposed to single-member district) electoral systems, the *American Political Science Review* hosted a decade-long debate about the politics of electoral institutional choice. Boix's initiating argument draws on classic theories in comparative politics and a simple game-theoretic model to argue that proportional representation results when the electoral left is powerful and the right is politically fragmented; a regression analysis serves as the primary empirical test of the hypothesis.

Cusack *et al.* (2007) argue, against Boix, that proportional representation is instead caused by an elective affinity between that system and politico-economic arrangements in which workers' skill formation is coordinated between employers and representatives of labor. This argument is tested using a triangulation multi-method design; somewhat methodologically loose qualitative argumentation based largely on historical primary sources (Cusack *et al.* 2007: 379–83) is offered alongside a functionally independent regression analysis (Cusack *et al.* 2007: 383–87).

For present purposes, it is far more interesting to note that this rejoinder employs integrative multi-method strategies within the quantitative section of the analysis. In reaction to Boix's regression analysis, Cusack *et al.* draw on case-based considerations to argue that some cases did not in fact receive the treatment of interest at the time Boix claims; for example, in the Netherlands the 1913 election was at least two-thirds as inclusive as the 1918 election that Boix focuses on, and therefore arguably the proper focus for analyzing the first elections with mass suffrage (Cusack *et al.* 2007: 383). Correcting for the instances of possible measurement error that the authors identify based on case-study evidence somewhat weakens Boix's key statistical finding, thus making the political economy-based alternative explanation perhaps more credible.

A subsequent intervention in the debate, by Kreuzer (2010), adopts a completely integrative multi-method design. Drawing on the secondary historical sources cited by Cusack *et al.*, as well as other relevant materials, Kreuzer conducts qualitative analysis of each of the 18 countries that appear in the statistical analysis (Kreuzer 2010: 371–74, 385–87). This qualitative work examines the quality of measurement for each component of Cusack *et al.*'s key explanatory variable – a critical issue because, as will be discussed below, causal inference using regression typically depends on the assumption that the hypothesized cause is measured correctly. A subsequent regression analysis using a version of the independent variable rescored to capture Kreuzer's qualitative arguments, demonstrates that the implications of these interesting measurement issues for causal inference are quite minor in this context (Kreuzer 2010: 373–74).

However, Kreuzer mounts a far more impressive challenge to Cusack *et al.*'s causal inference on the basis of a second integrative research design element: a case-by-case consideration of whether there is qualitative evidence consistent with the causal pathway that Cusack *et al.*

hypothesize to operate between the cause and the effect (Kreuzer 2010: 374–78). After all, a standard assumption in interpreting regression results is that causally meaningful, as opposed to merely descriptive, regression findings correspond to the existence of a series of steps that carry some form of causal impetus from the treatment through to the outcome (Brady 2008). By using qualitative evidence to check for evidence consistent with the existence of such a pathway in each relevant case, Kreuzer thus carries out a test of a key causal-inferential assumption. As it turns out, Kreuzer finds significant gaps in the relevant evidence, implying that the regression results should not be given a causal interpretation.

One need not decide this debate in Kreuzer's favor to appreciate the impact of his direct qualitative tests of quantitative assumptions in moving the conversation forward. The cyclical movement between quantitative analysis and qualitative tests of assumptions here raises issues related to measurement and causal pathways – but also settles the measurement concerns as low priority issues while focusing attention squarely on the question of whether a series of causal steps in fact exists that is capable of connecting the treatment to the outcome in the cases of interest. In their reply to Kreuzer, Cusack *et al.* (2010: 399–401) carry on the multi-method dialogue with a fairly in-depth discussion of three German states, arguing that close within-case analysis provides compelling evidence of the existence of a plausible causal pathway. This kind of relevant, novel evidence in relation to the assumptions of the initial quantitative analysis clearly deepens and enriches the causal debate – even if the audience perhaps leaves the conversation still unsure about the true causal patterns at play in countries' choice of electoral institutions. Integrative multi-method design facilitates this sort of empirical deepening of debates in ways that ensure the relevance of the new evidence to the underlying causal inference. When designed carefully, it can also address issues that go beyond the questions of measurement and pathways considered in this example.

1.4   Overview of the Book

Having dealt with these important, but nonetheless fundamentally preliminary, considerations regarding the reasons why we might expect inferential gains from integrative multi-method research, the rest of this book will deal with more concrete issues, showing the advantages of integrative multi-method designs through argumentation, example, and the development of a range of research designs. Multi-method research in principle includes any analysis that draws on evidence from more than one technique, such as purely quantitative research that uses both cross-sectional regression analysis and survival analysis. However, this book will focus on one important subset of multi-method designs: those that feature combinations of qualitative research with either a quantitative observational component or an experimental component. These combinations, in a sense, maximize the difference in assumptions between the methods to be considered, and therefore – following the argument of the last section – have the highest level of expected gain from multi-method, as opposed to single-method, research.

Chapter 2 answers a major criticism of multi-method research: the claim that qualitative and quantitative modes of research address fundamentally different concepts of causation and therefore produce inferences and research agendas that are effectively incommensurable (for an engaging recent statement of this perspective, see Goertz and Mahoney 2012). This book emphasizes a different perspective: that qualitative and quantitative research involve different tools and ask fundamentally different questions, but that those tools are used to address, and those questions interrogate, a shared core understanding of causation. In the terms of Brady and Collier (2004), that conception of causation represents a key "shared standard" between qualitative and quantitative research. Furthermore, it is an essential ingredient for multi-method research, because it ensures that qualitative and quantitative inquiry share an ultimate object of study on the basis of which integrative designs can be built. Appendix A extends this argument by showing that a suitably expanded version of the leading statistical framework for thinking about causation – the potential-outcomes framework – accommodates a wide range of qualitative agendas and insights, and can serve as one systematization (possibly out of a number of essentially equivalent alternatives) of the unifying objective of causal understanding.

Chapter 2 goes on to argue that regression's contribution to causal inference is routinely overstated in discussions of multi-method design. Regression and related techniques have a great deal of value as tools for descriptive summary of multivariate data, and can be very useful as a way of providing a final summary of causal inferences justified through other information, such as an experimental research design or unusually strong prior knowledge. These important roles notwithstanding, it remains essential to bear in mind that when a regression-type analysis produces a causal inference, most of the work has been done outside of the regression. In particular, causal inferences based on regression rely on strong assumptions about measurement, as well as about the absence of confounding variables and post-treatment bias. These assumptions generally cannot be thoroughly tested by regression-type methods, and thus require multi-method evidence.

Chapters 3–4 constitute a unit on multi-method designs involving regression. Whereas Chapter 2 argues that regression is less central to causal inference than some multi-method literature suggests, Chapter 3 tries to show – against some skeptical scholars who regard multi-method research as fruitless because the qualitative component of such designs adds nothing – that case studies can play central, direct or indirect, roles in causal inference. Case studies can sometimes effectively clinch a causal inference by uncovering fortuitous and decisive pieces of information: events or situations that allow a real-world comparison of two cases to stand in for the key causal counterfactual, discoveries about causal processes that make a large effect seem highly likely or all but impossible, and so forth. Yet such decisive discoveries are somewhat serendipitous; scholars should remain open and attentive toward them while carrying out case-study research, but since they are somewhat unpredictable they usually cannot form the basis for an a priori research design. However, case studies can reliably and predictably play other essential roles in causal inference, including roles that improve on existing regression-based inferences: testing measurement quality, evaluating the plausibility of hypothesized causal paths, and searching for evidence of omitted variables. These contributions that have the capacity to improve on existing regression analyses, in conjunction with the occasional major breakthrough, justify assigning case studies an important role in multi-method causal inference.

When scholars wish to use case-study methods to test or refine the assumptions involved in a regression analysis (drawn from their own research or from a literature that they wish to address), how should they choose cases to study? Chapter 4 briefly reviews a menu of case-selection techniques, including traditional qualitative approaches, techniques based on regression diagnostics, and tools drawing from matching methods. The chapter then argues that extreme-case selection on independent variable and deviant-case selection are generally the two best options in relation to a set of common case-study goals: checking the quality of measurement on the key independent or dependent variable, searching for omitted variables and interactions, and testing or building hypotheses about causal pathways.

Chapter 5 moves a step away from regression analysis, addressing the best ways to combine case studies and statistical matching methods. The chapter discusses designs that use paired comparisons between matched cases to discover omitted variables, measurement problems, and information about causal pathways. Although the set of relevant issues is the same as for regression analysis, and thus multi-method evidence is needed regarding measurement, confounders, and post-treatment bias, matching facilitates particularly clean multi-method research designs because of the inherent focus on paired (or sometimes grouped) differences among cases.

Continuing the movement away from standard regression studies, Chapter 6 considers designs that combine qualitative research and natural experiments. First, the chapter uses the potential-outcomes framework to characterize three families of natural experiments: (A) the true natural experiment (in which "nature" randomly or as-if-randomly assigns the independent variable of interest), (B) the regression-discontinuity design (a useful subtype of the true natural experiment), and (C) the instrumental variables natural experiment (in which a cause of the independent variable is randomly or as-if-randomly assigned).[6] For each family, the key assumptions for causal inference are discussed, with special emphasis on the way that all three designs rely on assumptions about a random or as-if-random assignment process. A central multi-method design for the chapter is one in which case-study research focuses squarely on this crucial assignment process, as well as on the linkage between the independent variable and the outcome of interest.

Chapter 7 explores ways to combine true, randomized experiments with qualitative approaches. It uses the potential-outcomes framework to review the strengths and limitations, in terms of causal inference, of laboratory and field experiments. The key assumptions for causal inference with experiments involve experimental realism and limits on the possible interactions among cases; thus these are special areas of attention for multi-method design. Case-study techniques can thus be used within an experimental design to enrich findings, provide tests of key maintained assumptions regarding the quality of measurement and experimental realism, and provide a complementary alternative to assumption-heavy quantitative approaches to mediation analysis.

Chapter 8 reverses the relative roles of quantitative analysis and case studies, discussing research designs that use quantitative or experimental elements to strengthen a causal inference ultimately made through case studies. Three designs are analyzed. First, one stereotype involves the idea that quantitative research should be used to test the generalizability of qualitative and case-study findings. There are significant obstacles to this procedure, involving interpretation, measurement, and testing hypotheses about causal pathways. A second design offers more: quantitative or experimental components test one or more key links in the case study's causal chain, thereby becoming a tool for process tracing. The final design uses causal effect estimates from statistical components to measure the outcome variable for a comparative-historical analysis. This design reconceptualizes causal heterogeneity – a frequent obstacle to inference and generalization in the potential-outcomes framework in general – as an invitation to deeper investigation.

Throughout these chapters, the analysis focuses on methods of analysis and tools for causal inference – both qualitative and quantitative. Much less will be said about methods for gathering evidence; choices regarding these tools obviously depend substantially on the pragmatics of the research at hand. Work on individual decision-making and psychology in current societies invites the use of techniques such as surveys (Fowler 2013), simulated, closely observed decision-making scenarios (Camerer 2003), and automated or manual coding of relevant texts (Grimmer and Stewart 2013) on the quantitative side; as well as in-depth interviews (Guest *et al.* 2012: 113–71), focus groups (Cyr 2016), and participant observation (DeWalt and DeWalt 2011) on the qualitative side. By contrast, research focusing on organizational dynamics in a past economic system might require systematic collection of archival and government indicators on the quantitative side and in-depth work with primary-source texts on the qualitative side. Obviously, good multi-method research depends on the skillful execution of these research practices. Yet the most challenging problems of multi-method research design involve how to construct and carry out causal inference using the results of these techniques, rather than the relatively straightforward set of tasks related to choosing context-appropriate tools for gathering evidence. We now turn our attention to these challenges of multi-method causal inference.

Notes

1 For discussions of the role of multi-method research in description and measurement, see Campbell and Fiske 1959; Axinn and Pearce 2006; Eid and Diener 2006, and much of Brewer and Hunter 2006. For a dissenting voice, see Ahram 2013.

2 These terms have been used to point to a series of partly independent distinctions (Collier *et al.* 2003). Their use in this volume is a way of differentiating between a

cluster of methods that generally analyze a large number of cases, focus on cross-case comparison, and use statistical tests, and a second cluster that usually analyzes many fewer cases, focuses on within-case analysis and process-tracing, and rarely uses statistical tests.

3 Obviously, all three searches will return false positives in which the term is used in a sense other than that intended here. It is unclear how much of a problem this is; inspection of the first several pages of search results in each case revealed at least some false positives, as well as a marked preponderance of search results using these terms in a relevant methodological sense.

4 One might argue that, with full causal knowledge of all the processes that produce civil war, we would eventually be able to derive connections between the answers to these two categories of questions. This claim is of course possible, but could only be shown to be true if we in fact came to possess full causal knowledge – at which point neither the statistical analysis nor the case studies would be needed for purposes of causal inference.

5 The suggestion that multi-method designs should use one design component to test and improve the inferences that can be drawn from the other has been made in various discussions of multi-method design. For example, Lieberman (2005) provides a design that sometimes uses case studies to test and improve assumptions in a regression analysis, and Dunning (2012) suggests designs in which qualitative work tests the assumptions involved in using natural experiments. There are also many applied examples, some of which will be discussed in this volume. The discussion here builds on these developments. Integrative multi-method designs as discussed here are a distinctive and very structured subset of Caracelli and Greene's (1997) integrated (as opposed to component) mixed-method designs.

6 This typology of natural experiments is partially drawn from Dunning (2010).

2 Causation as a Shared Standard

The central thesis of this book is that causal inferences based on careful integrative multi-method research designs have advantages over similar inferences that rely on only one method. A necessary first step in making this argument is showing that many applications of qualitative and quantitative methods in the social sciences share an underlying notion of causation. If causation in these two methodological traditions is fundamentally not the same sort of relation, then there is good reason to worry that they cannot contribute to a joint causal project. Indeed, given such fundamentally divergent worldviews, it is unclear that the methods could even contribute to testing each others' assumptions – the central theme of integrative multi-method research designs.

I argue below that the potential-outcomes framework, in which causal effects are characterized as the difference between what actually happens in a given case and what would have happened had that case been assigned to a different treatment category, can serve as that notion.[1] After introducing this concept, I argue that stereotypically qualitative and quantitative causal thinking can be seen as sharing an underlying conceptual structure.[2] The potential-outcomes framework is used to explicate causal models and hypotheses throughout the book.

Existing work on the potential-outcomes framework has produced clear insights into the challenges of causal inference.[3] Most famously, authors have pointed to the fundamental problem of causal inference: because it is impossible to observe both what does happen to a case in reality and what would have happened to that case had the independent variable been assigned a different value, no direct empirical observation of causation at the case level is possible (Holland 1986).

Prior research also provides detailed findings regarding the assumptions necessary to get around this problem and make causal inferences in experiments, natural experiments, and quantitative observational studies (e.g. Morgan and Winship 2007). The last segment of this chapter reviews those findings with respect to regression-type analysis of observational studies, paying special attention to the assumptions about control variables necessary for regression-based causal inference. In particular, this literature shows that scholars need independent evidence that the regression does not suffer from confounders, colliders, or post-treatment bias. While these assumptions are not sufficient for causal inference, they are necessary and provide key openings for integrative multi-method research design.

2.1   The Potential-Outcomes Framework

The central argument of this book is that, for purposes of causal inference, there are gains to be had from integrative multi-method research designs, i.e., research in which diverse techniques are carefully designed to compensate for each others' weaknesses in testing a well-developed causal hypothesis. This position conflicts with some strands of argumentation in the literature on how quantitative and qualitative methods should interact. Some scholars argue that, in principle or in practice, qualitative evidence adds little to competent quantitative research (Beck 2006). The concrete research designs and illustrative examples presented throughout the remainder of this book should serve as an extended counterargument to these positions.

However, some scholars (notably Ahmed and Sil 2009, Chatterjee 2009, and to an extent Goertz and Mahoney 2012) offer a more fundamental objection: multi-method research designs that combine qualitative and quantitative tools may be unproductive because these families of methodological tools employ fundamentally divergent conceptions of causation. If this is true, then qualitative and quantitative tools genuinely cannot collaborate in making a causal case. After all, each tool would have a proprietary understanding of what counts as causal. If qualitative and quantitative methods focus on different aspects of a shared inferential project, all is well. However, if the two traditions have essentially incommensurable concepts of causation, evidence, inference, and so forth, then it is clearly problematic to combine contributions from qualitative and quantitative research practices in a single causal inference.

I argue that such concerns about fundamental, philosophical incompatibility or incomparability between qualitative and quantitative approaches to causality should usually be seen as unpersuasive. I will make this case by arguing that there is a language for causal claims that can comprehensibly represent the central ideas of at least most qualitative and quantitative causal claims. After all, if qualitative and quantitative ideas about causation can be seen as emphasizing different aspects of a broader unified conception of causation, then it follows that thinking about causation within the two methodological camps is not incommensurable. In developing this argument, it will first be helpful to think more carefully about what it means to say that one thing causes another. Imagine, for example, that a researcher is interested in the relationship between parents seeing a particular public service announcement and deciding to take their children to be vaccinated. What does it mean in this context to claim that seeing the announcement causes a higher vaccination rate?

A possible, and intellectually important, answer is as follows. For a given family, we can envision a scenario in which the parents see the public service announcement. We can also imagine a very similar scenario in which researchers intervene to prevent the parents from seeing the public service announcement. Suppose that we could observe these scenarios playing out in parallel, with each scenario taking place in something like a parallel universe in which a perfect copy of the family lives out its life unaware of the other universe.

One way of defining the causal effect of the public service announcement for this family involves comparing the parents' decisions about vaccination in each of these parallel scenarios. Either the parents vaccinate their children in the scenario in which they see the announcement, or they do not. The same is true for the scenario in which the parents do not see the announcement. The causal effect of the announcement on vaccination for this one family may be characterized as the difference between the vaccination decision made in the scenario where parents see the announcement and the vaccination decision made when the announcement remains unseen. If the parents' decision is the same whether or not they see the announcement, then there is no causal effect. On the other hand, if the children are vaccinated in one scenario but not the other, then the announcement affects the vaccination decision.

This example presents the key features of the potential outcomes theory of causation (Neyman 1923/1990; Rubin 1974), a framework for thinking about causation that – I will argue below – can be used as the basis for a common language that captures core concerns of both qualitative and quantitative causal thinking. Let us briefly introduce a formal language for representing the components of this framework. Suppose that the hypothesized cause of interest takes on two values; following experimental tradition, we will refer to one of these values as a treatment and the other as a control. Thus, in the vaccination story, a family where the parents see the public service announcement receives the treatment, while a family where the parents do not see the announcement receives the control. There is also an outcome, Y, which the analyst measures for each of a set of cases. For one arbitrary case, labeled i, the analyst considers two scenarios. If the parents in family i see the announcement, then the analyst observes their vaccination decision conditional on seeing the announcement, which is often labeled as $Y_{i,t}$ to emphasize that this is the value that the outcome takes on for case i in the scenario in which that case is exposed to the treatment. If, by contrast, the parents in family i do not see the announcement, then the analyst observes their vaccination decision conditional on not seeing the announcement, denoted as $Y_{i,c}$.

From the point of view of the potential-outcomes framework, the effect of the potential cause on the outcome for case i is simply the difference between $Y_{i,t}$ and $Y_{i,c}$. If these two versions of the outcome are the same, then there is no causal effect for that case. If they are different, then the causal effect for that case is the difference. It bears emphasis that this is a theoretical definition of causation, and not an empirical estimator. After all, as will be emphasized below, the difference between two potential scores on the dependent variable that serves as the core concept of a causal effect in the potential-outcomes framework inherently entails comparison between two alternative versions of the same case, and thus is not particularly simple to put into direct statistical service.

Any causal effect defined in terms of the potential-outcomes framework depends centrally on a crucial substantive assumption, the stable unit treatment value assumption (Rubin 1980), commonly given the equally unintuitive acronym, SUTVA. This is the assumption that $Y_{i,t}$ and $Y_{i,c}$ adequately characterize the possible values of the dependent variable within the context of the study. SUTVA can fail in a variety of ways, but the two most important are probably if (a) the treatment in fact takes on more than two values because of causally relevant heterogeneity in its administration, or (b) treatment assignment in case j affects the outcome in case i. If either of these two SUTVA failures arises, then $Y_{i,t}$ and $Y_{i,c}$ are not uniquely defined. Instead, each of these labels represents a family of possible outcome values, and the value actually observed depends on extraneous circumstances. Thus, when SUTVA fails, there is no single causal effect for the case in question, and the potential-outcomes framework is inapplicable. We will return to this assumption, and consider designs for testing it, in Chapters 7 and 8.

The potential outcomes approach to thinking about causation, while in itself relatively simple, becomes more intellectually intricate when it encounters the centuries-long philosophical and statistical literatures on causation and causal inference.[4] A full understanding of these debates is, of course, unnecessary for the present text; however, touching briefly on some key philosophical ideas related to the potential-outcomes framework will help illuminate the ways in which this approach can accommodate causal ideas of concern to both qualitative and quantitative thinkers in the social sciences.

In a recent essay that attempts to draw pragmatic lessons about causal inference for social scientists from the philosophical and statistical literatures about causation, Brady (2008) identifies four families of philosophical thought about causation, involving special attention to patterns of regularities across cases, counterfactuals involving specific cases, manipulations of cases, and mechanisms linking causes and effects. As a way of exploring the extent to which the potential-outcomes framework incorporates a broad range of themes in thought about causation, it is useful to ask how the framework approaches the points of central emphasis within each perspective.[5]

Brady's first philosophical approach to thinking about causation, the "Neo-Humean" or regularity approach, involves attempts to specify the set of patterns that must hold true across cases in order for a relationship of causation to exist. Causation may entail, for example, the cause, X, being descriptively sufficient[6] for the occurrence of the outcome, Y; descriptively both necessary and sufficient for Y; or an insufficient but necessary part of a condition that is itself unnecessary but sufficient for Y. With respect to this last pattern of regularity, Mackie (1974: 67) suggests that "causal regularities as known are commonly of this sort," and goes on to argue at length that causal inference should be carried out by comparing cases with an eye to discovering such patterns. More recently, Baumgartner (2008) has defended a somewhat more elaborate regularity account, building on the general flexibility allowed by Boolean algebra.

Similar ideas are, of course, widely discussed in the social sciences. For instance, the econometric concept of Granger causality posits that X causes Y if past values of X statistically predict the present value of Y after conditioning on the past history of Y and a general set of control variables (Granger 1969, 1980). Attempts to specify a set of criteria that regression-type analyses must meet in order to possess causal interpretations also often fit this mold.

Critics argue that observed regularity is neither necessary nor suffi-cient for causation (e.g. Cartwright 1979, 1989; Irzik 1996; Hausman 1998: 36–54; Ward 2009). Such a pattern is not necessary, because other causally relevant variables may disrupt the observed connection between the potential cause and the outcome of interest. Likewise, observed regularities may not be sufficient, because they might not altogether rule out problems involving the direction of causation or the possibility that X and Y share a common cause rather than causing each other. Such issues notwithstanding, this family of thought regarding causation usefully raises the point that causal models, to be useful, must posit meaningful cross-case regularities – at the very least for a carefully defined set of cases.

The potential-outcomes framework fulfills this role in a variety of ways. Least realistically, if evidence or a theory can somehow exactly pin down $Y_{i,t}$ and $Y_{i,c}$ for a set of cases, the potential-outcomes framework can then provide precise predictions about relationships between the cause and the outcome across those cases. More plausibly, if approximate average magnitudes of $\bar{Y}_t$ and $\bar{Y}_c$ can be described for a given population of cases, then the potential-outcomes framework specifies regularities in terms of the comparison between treatment and control groups when treatment is randomly assigned. Of course, far more complex patterns of regularities must be defined when, for example, treatment is confounded by some other variable. However, this complexity is not a weakness: it makes the potential-outcomes framework responsive to a wider range of causal situations than simpler regularity accounts. In particular, as argued in detail below, the potential-outcomes framework can readily incorporate specific patterns of causal regularity of interest to qualitative as well as quantitative social scientists.

Brady considers a second tradition, in competition with the regularity approach, that describes causal claims as fundamentally characterizing differences between what happens in the real world and what would counterfactually have happened in the most similar other world in which the cause did not take place. Although associated especially with Lewis (1973a, 1973b, 1979, 2000), counterfactual definitions of causation date back at least to Hume who – just after offering a regularity-based definition of causation that serves as an inspiration for the work grouped as Brady's first approach – suggests that one object causes another when it is true that "if the first object had not been, the second never had existed" (Hume 1748/1999: 146).

Counterfactual approaches to causation differ from regularity approaches in specifying that causal claims inherently require knowledge that goes beyond the pattern of observable data across a set of cases. After all, special prior causal knowledge of one kind or another is needed in order to determine which counterfactual world is in fact most similar to the real world, and the determination of the most similar world that did not happen is necessary for determining the causal relevance of an event or variable in a given case. This complex prerequisite of causal knowledge is a virtue in that it highlights the difficulties entailed in causal inference; however, it faces the serious challenge that it is not always feasible to decide which counterfactual is the best or most relevant, even when significant prior causal knowledge is available. Furthermore, unless supplemented in some way, counterfactual approaches remain vulnerable to problems of confounding or reverse causation (Brady 2008: 237–38). These weaknesses notwithstanding, a wide range of thinkers would agree with Lewis that:

"we do know that causation has something or other to do with counterfactuals. We think of a cause as something that makes a difference, and the difference it makes must be a difference from what would have happened without it" (Lewis 1973b: 557).

The linkages between the philosophical counterfactual approach to causation and the potential-outcomes framework are self-evident. Clearly, the potential outcomes approach captures the insight that causation requires information that goes beyond the easily observable. Indeed, Holland (1986) famously characterizes this need for additional information as the fundamental problem of causal inference. In the context of the potential-outcomes framework, the point is easily made: it is possible to empirically observe either $Y_{i,c}$ or $Y_{i,t}$, but never both. One or the other parameter has to be inferred, either from theory or from comparison of some kind across units. Hence at least one central notion from the counterfactual approach to causation is rather completely incorporated into the potential-outcomes framework, and as such made central to quantitative discussions of causal inference in the social sciences. Counterfactuals have independently been a long-standing focus of interest in qualitative methodological reflection about causal inference (e.g. Tetlock and Belkin 1996). Thus, once again, the potential-outcomes framework connects key concerns across these two traditions.

The third philosophical approach to causality that Brady discusses involves manipulation. When researchers have manipulated the hypothesized cause, and a change results on the outcome of interest, "the factor that has been manipulated can determine the direction of causality and help to rule out spurious correlation. The manipulated factor must be the cause" (Brady 2008: 239). In some accounts (e.g. Gasking 1955), such manipulation is inherent to the definition of causation; other accounts emphasize the importance of manipulation in discovering causes. Even if we allow that manipulation is not inherent to causation, it seems evident that many people's ideas about causation entail the hypothesis that deciding to change the cause should lead to a difference in the outcome (e.g. Lakoff and Johnson 1999: 170–234).

Rubin (1986), the central figure in the development of the potential-outcomes framework, and Holland (1986) discuss the potential-outcomes framework as requiring manipulation for causation. In practice, this stipulation has largely been treated in the potential outcomes literature as being a tool for determining which kinds of claims are causal and which are not – rather than a deeper, fundamental component of the understanding of causation (Brady 2008: 252–53). If the potential-outcomes framework involves counterfactual comparisons but not manipulations, then it may not be fully robust against confusing common cause or reciprocal causation situations with causal links from X to Y.

On the other hand, it seems a reasonable extension of the potential-outcomes framework to read the counterfactual comparisons it posits as entailing either manipulations or hypothetical manipulations along the lines discussed by Woodward (2003).[7] That is to say, accounts of causation using the potential-outcomes framework can be employed even when the cause is not in fact manipulated by deliberate human action; however, the potential outcomes account of such situations should be taken to describe what would have happened if a specific manipulation had been employed. Such a friendly amendment helps more completely specify the kind of counterfactual intended in the comparison between $Y_{i,t}$ and $Y_{i,c}$; one symbol represents the outcome that would happen if a manipulation is carried out, and the other represents the outcome that happens if there is no manipulation.

This emphasis on manipulation may seem foreign or unhelpful to qualitatively oriented readers – and, perhaps, quantitatively oriented readers who work mostly with purely observational data. But it should not usually be a special source of concern. After all, for most causes that interest social scientists, the cause takes on the value that it does because some person or people at some point in history made decisions that led the cause to take on that value. Discussions of manipulation as part of the potential-outcomes framework highlight such decisions, potentially connecting quantitative thought about causation with long-standing qualitative and social theoretical concerns regarding the role of agency in social explanation (e.g. Giddens 1979: 49–95).

Voters acquire information about candidates, for example, both because someone decides to make it available to them (e.g. a campaign worker by knocking on their door and giving them a speech and a pamphlet), and because they choose to pay attention to it. An easy hypothetical manipulation of a given voter's level of information about a candidate involves the proposition that the campaign worker decided not to knock on that voter's door. What is different in the world in which the campaign worker makes that decision, as opposed to the decision to knock? This kind of question (or parallel ones in other domains of research) is familiar to virtually all scholars engaged in causal inference, even if the hypothetical human manipulations (or, in other frameworks, the relevant exercise of agency) required to think about more macro-level causal relationships are often historically remote or a bit heroic.

In contrast with the three approaches just discussed, the potential-outcomes framework as typically discussed does not directly address the central concerns of mechanisms and capacities approaches to causation, which together constitute Brady's fourth philosophical approach to causation. These accounts focus attention on the arrangement of entities, components, actors, etc., that in sequential action connect the independent variable with the dependent variable in the context of a single causal problem or a defined set of similar problems. From a mechanisms or capacities point of view, the essence of causation is the existence of an arrangement of relatively modular causal components (in the mechanisms account) or the inherent causal capacities of the entities involved in a given situation. From either point of view, X causes Y in a particular situation exactly when that situation is characterized by an arrangement of elements that have properties that fit together in such a way that they can convey the causal action of X through to Y.

While the potential-outcomes framework does not emphasize such arrangements of elements, it does nonetheless share a central concern of several authors who contribute to the mechanisms and capacities approaches: singular causation as the essence of causality. In Cartwright's words:

Singular causal claims are primary. This is true in two senses. First, they are a necessary ingredient in the methods we use to establish generic causal claims. Even the methods that test causal laws by looking for regularities will not work unless some singular causal information is filled in first. Second, the regularities themselves play a secondary role in establishing a causal law. They are just evidence – and only one kind of evidence at that – that certain kinds of singular causal fact have happened. (Cartwright 1989: 2)

Causation in a given case is fundamental for approaches that emphasize mechanisms and capacities, because the arrangement of components or entities that links X and Y need not be identical in every case, or indeed in any two cases. If these arrangements differ, then the direction and magnitude of the causal connection between X and Y may also differ. Such a deep commitment to the possibility of causal heterogeneity is also a defining trait of the potential-outcomes framework, in which all definitions of causation build out from case-specific causal effects. This core concern with heterogeneity is thus a major point of compatibility between this tradition and the potential-outcomes framework. Recent extensions of the potential-outcomes framework also allow scholars working within this tradition to represent and analyze causal processes involving a sequence of mechanisms or capacities, as will be discussed in the section on causal pathways below. It is perhaps self-evident that this openness to causal heterogeneity and to elaboration of causal pathways is a deep connection between the potential-outcomes framework and the causal concerns of qualitative researchers.

One should not, of course, claim that all causal ideas could be feasibly discussed within the context of the potential-outcomes framework. There may well be causal mechanisms or arrangements of causal capacities for which no manipulation exists that could define the counterfactual outcome at the heart of the potential-outcomes framework. It may even be true that, for some causal arrangements, not even a hypothetical manipulation will do, because any manipulation involves a fundamental alteration of the arrangement of capacities. So the potential-outcomes framework should probably not be seen as a universal causal language. Furthermore, some of the causal ideas that can be represented within the potential-outcomes framework become complex and cumbersome. Last but not least, it would obviously be absurd to claim that the potential-outcomes framework captures the full scope and content of any of the philosophical approaches to causation; instead, the potential outcomes setup quite evidently pays attention only to selective, central considerations, and abstracts away from many of the details.

However, the far more modest argument advanced by this chapter is that the potential-outcomes framework can accomplish a great deal of work in synthesizing and rendering mutually intelligible ideas about causation in qualitative and quantitative social science. While there are causal ideas and intuitions that do not fit, or fit awkwardly, with the potential-outcomes framework, I argue that the central causal intuitions and claims of social scientific writers in qualitative and quantitative traditions fit nicely with the broad version of the potential-outcomes framework discussed here. For quantitative work, this perspective is familiar and perhaps needs no additional emphasis (see, e.g. Morgan and Winship 2007; Angrist and Pischke 2009). Qualitative approaches to causation in the social sciences draw especially on themes connected with three of the philosophical traditions just discussed: regularity approaches (Ragin 1987, 2000; Mahoney 2004), counterfactuals (Tetlock and Belkin 1996; Lebow 2010), and mechanisms and pathways (Collier *et al.* 2004; George and Bennett 2004; McKeown 2004). As argued above, the potential-outcomes framework either directly incorporates, or is open to central concerns of, each of these approaches. The appendix to this book extends the argument by showing that a set of common and important qualitative causal models in the social sciences are in fact fairly straightforward to represent in that framework.

2.2   Regression and Causal Inference

Thus far, this chapter has argued that most qualitative and quantitative work in the social sciences shares a broadly compatible conception of causation. This argument is made by showing that most of the key elements of causation important to methodologists working in both traditions can be translated cleanly and coherently into the potential-outcomes framework. The implication is not that the potential-outcomes framework is therefore the one true conception of causation or that it is adequate for characterizing all meaningful social science relationships. Instead, the point is a more modest, if still useful, one: a great deal of thought about causation in the social sciences involves a shared core conception, and that conception fits well with the potential-outcomes framework. Thus, causation will be treated vis-à-vis potential outcomes throughout this book as a way of acknowledging this widely shared concept of what most social science causes are like. What, then, can this framework teach us about the prospects for causal inference using regression-type models on observational data?

Arguably, most causal inferences in the social sciences, from Yule's (1899) pioneering work on welfare policy and rates of poverty in England to the present, have relied on regression-type analysis of observational data. Furthermore, regression has been the central quantitative tool for most work to date on multi-method research, serving as the basis for Lieberman's (2005) nested analysis and Coppedge's (2005) nested inference, and receiving 29 mentions – more than any other individual quantitative technique – in Tashakkori and Teddlie's (2010) handbook of mixed-method research approaches in the social and behavioral sciences. As such, close consideration of multi-method designs – combining regression analysis with qualitative techniques – is in order here, and will be the topic of the next chapters.

Here, we apply the ideas about causation from the first part of the chapter and begin analyzing multi-method designs involving regression by discussing the assumptions that can sometimes connect regression with causal inference. In particular, regression may work for causal inference when there are no confounding variables, when the set of control variables includes no colliders or post-treatment variables, and when measurement of the treatment variable in particular is accurate. These assumptions do not guarantee the success of a regression-based causal inference, but such inferences are all but impossible without meeting these prerequisites. The next chapter explores ways that case studies can contribute to testing these assumptions, as well as the assumptions involved in direct qualitative causal inference. Subsequent chapters consider case selection after regression and also roles that regression can play within primarily case-study research.

The objective of adding a case-study component to an integrative multi-method design using regression analysis for the final causal inference is to increase our confidence in that causal inference relative to what we can know from a regression alone. In order to think systematically about how case studies can meet this objective, it is important to begin by figuring out exactly what kind of contribution to causal inference is produced by regression analysis in non-experimental contexts. To this end, this chapter discusses what regression coefficients can mean in relation to the potential-outcomes framework.

Successful causal inference using regression requires not only the assumptions directly connected with the potential-outcomes framework, but also the assumptions that enable successful descriptive and statistical inference. These assumptions, routinely discussed in conjunction with the Gauss-Markov theorem that provides the classical statement of regression's value, can be tested in part using well-known regression diagnostic tools, and can readily be reviewed in any standard regression textbook.

For present purposes, the most important of these assumptions is that the variables of interest are measured correctly. If the dependent variable is randomly mismeasured, the amount of harm to the overall causal inference is minimal, because the measurement error can simply become part of the regression's error term. However, regression has no such capacity to absorb measurement error in the right-hand-side variables, i.e., the hypothesized cause and any included control variables. If these variables are mismeasured, the resulting causal inference will be biased. Hence, inference – descriptive, statistical, or causal – based on a regression analysis generally depends on an assumption that all variables, but particularly the right-hand-side ones, are correctly measured. Beyond this initial condition, the potential-outcomes framework identifies further, and sometimes less obvious, assumptions needed to causally interpret regression results.

2.3   Regression and the Potential-Outcomes Framework

In many ways, regression analysis fits awkwardly with the potential-outcomes framework.[8] For one thing, regression is not naturally a tool for causal inference. It was originally developed as a way of handling measurement error in astronomical observations; in that context, regression's role was strictly descriptive, in that it was limited to removing inaccuracies related to imperfections in lenses, atmospheric disruptions, and human error from descriptions of the planets' orbits (Stigler 1986). Clearly, a great deal of conceptual distance lies between a role for regression as a technical fix for measurement error on the one hand, and a conception of regression as a tool for estimating the counterfactual causal effects of hypothetical manipulations on the other.

Nonetheless, there are special circumstances in which regression estimates can be sensibly connected with causal ideas drawn from the potential-outcomes framework. Suppose, as a starting point, that the independent variable of interest is dichotomous, with assignment to the treatment or control condition neither under the control of the researcher nor conveniently randomized by some other actor or process. Let us label the score on this independent variable for case i as D_i. Furthermore, let us stipulate that $D_i = 1$ when the case is in the treatment condition and that $D_i = 0$ otherwise.

By definition, it is true that Y_i, the observed value of the dependent variable for case i, is equal to $Y_{i,t}$ whenever $D_i = 1$; otherwise, $Y_i = Y_{i,c}$. In more mathematical terms,

$$Y_i = Y_{i,c} + D_i(Y_{i,t} - Y_{i,c}) \tag{2.1}$$

Equation 2.1 says nothing new; it is simply a formal expression of the idea that we see one potential outcome if the case is in the treatment condition, and the other if not. Nonetheless, the equation begins to resemble a regression model. It has a dependent variable: the observed value of Y_i. It has an independent variable: D_i. There is an intercept

($Y_{i,c}$) and a slope ($Y_{i,t} - Y_{i,c}$); conveniently, that slope corresponds with the causal effect of treatment for case i.

Unfortunately, this model cannot be estimated. The problem is that both the slope and the intercept in Equation 2.1 are case-specific. This means the regression would have to estimate two values for each data point, which is of course impossible without a great deal of additional information. Conceptually, this captures the fact that case-specific causation requires evidence about both what would happen in the case under the treatment and what would happen in the same case under the control – and therefore goes beyond what is ever empirically available.

The situation seems less hopeless if we rewrite the right-hand side of Equation 2.1 in terms of population averages and case-specific deviations from those averages:

$$Y_i = E(Y_{i,c}) + D_i E(Y_{i,t} - Y_{i,c}) + [Y_{i,c} - E(Y_{i,c})] + D_i[(Y_{i,t} - Y_{i,c})$$
$$- E(Y_{i,t} - Y_{i,c})] \tag{2.2}$$

The first two terms in Equation 2.2 simply substitute the population averages of $Y_{i,c}$ and ($Y_{i,t} - Y_{i,c}$) for their case-specific values. This may be helpful, because – treating these values as the intercept and slope of a regression – there may now only be two parameters to estimate, and potentially many more cases with which to estimate them. This is a familiar move in causal inference: if we cannot readily access causation at the case level, we instead move to the level of the population.

However, regression's value as a tool for estimating these population values depends crucially on the two terms in square brackets at the end of the equation. These two terms represent case-specific deviations from population averages. The first term represents case i's difference from the average on $Y_{i,c}$, while the second term represents that case's difference from the average on the effect of treatment. If regression is to be a useful tool for estimating the population causal parameters in the first two terms on the right-hand side of Equation 2.2, then these last two terms will have to be treated in combination as the error term, and will have to meet some conditions. To discuss those conditions, it will be useful to give shorthand names to the last two terms of the equation:

$$\epsilon_{i,1} = [Y_{i,c} - E(Y_{i,c})] \tag{2.3}$$

$$\epsilon_{i,2} = D_i[(Y_{i,t} - Y_{i,c}) - E(Y_{i,t} - Y_{i,c})] \tag{2.4}$$

In order for regression to successfully estimate the first term in Equation 2.2, $E(Y_{i,c})$, it must be the case that the sample is such that the average across all cases of $\epsilon_{i,1} + \epsilon_{i,2}$ is approximately equal to zero. The simplest way for this to be true is if both $\epsilon_{i,1}$ and $\epsilon_{i,2}$ are separately equal to zero on average.[9] If the sample being analyzed is representative of the population (or perhaps contains the entire population), then $E(\epsilon_{i,1}) = 0$ by definition.

However, the same cannot be said about $E(\epsilon_{i,2})$, because that expression consists of the case-specific deviation from the population average treatment effect *multiplied by D_i*. To see how this can create complications, let us set up a simple example. Suppose that the cases of interest are high school students preparing to take a college admissions exam (Powers and Rock 1999). The independent variable is whether each student chooses to enroll in an after-school test-preparation program, and the dependent variable is the student's score on the admissions exam. Then $\epsilon_{i,2}$ represents a student's exam-score gain due to the test-preparation program, relative to the rest of the students, multiplied by that student's choice about whether to participate in the program.

It seems possible that students have some private information about how much the program will help them, individually, and that they act on the basis of that private information. Consider the worst-case scenario, in which students choose to enroll in the program if and only if they know that their personal benefit from the program will be greater than the average for the school. If this is true, then D_i will be equal to 1 whenever $[(Y_{i,t} - Y_{i,c}) - E(Y_{i,t} - Y_{i,c})] > 0$, and will be equal to 0 otherwise. Hence, $\epsilon_{i,2} \geq 0$ for all i, and – assuming that at least one student chooses to participate in the program – the sample average of $\epsilon_{i,2}$ will be strictly greater than zero. In this example, students' prior information serves as a confounding variable, i.e., a variable causally connected with both the independent and the dependent variable that distorts the causal inference of interest. When confounders are present, estimating $E(Y_{i,c})$ may not be straightforward.

The requirements for successfully estimating the slope in Equation 2.2, $E(Y_{i,t} - Y_{i,c})$, are even more problematic. In effect, successful inference about this slope using regression requires that D_i be statistically unrelated to $\epsilon_{i,1} + \epsilon_{i,2}$.[10] Yet this condition will usually not be met, because D_i appears in the formula for $\epsilon_{i,2}$; obviously, D_i is not statistically unrelated with itself. Causal inference based on the simple bivariate regression implied by Equation 2.2 can essentially only work if (1) $Y_{i,t}$ and $Y_{i,c}$ are each constant across all cases, which would imply that $\epsilon_{i,1} = \epsilon_{i,2} = 0$ for every case, or (2) D_i is by some fortuitous accident completely unrelated with either $Y_{i,t}$ or $Y_{i,c}$, such that the treatment group is for all intents and purposes a random sample from the same population as the control group – and therefore the study happens to be equivalent to a randomized experiment.

Usually, neither of these special exceptions holds, and therefore the causal parameters of interest cannot be estimated using a bivariate regression. Of course, this will not come as much of a surprise to the reader; few social scientists put much causal stock in bivariate regressions. Instead, the standard regression analysis in the social sciences includes some collection of control variables:

$$Y_i = \beta_0 + \beta_1 D_i + \beta_2 W_{i,1} + \beta_3 W_{i,2} + \cdots + \beta_k W_{i,k} + \delta_i \qquad (2.5)$$

Equation 2.5 represents a standard multivariate regression; the connection with Equation 2.2 is that the dependent variable and the first independent variable are the same. The W variables are added to the model in the hope that they will somehow break the statistical connections between D_i and $\epsilon_{i,1} + \epsilon_{i,2}$. In spite of the additional parameters, attention remains focused on the slope connected with D_i which – we hope – may provide some information about the effect of treatment on the outcome. For purposes of estimating the slope for

D_i, the multivariate model in Equation 2.5 is really the same as the following adjusted bivariate regression:[11]

$$Y_i - E(Y_i|W_{i,1}, W_{i,2}, \ldots W_{i,k}) = \beta_0 + \beta_1[D_i - E(D_i|W_{i,1}, W_{i,2}, \ldots W_{i,k})]$$
$$+ \epsilon_{i,1} + \epsilon_{i,2} - E(\epsilon_{i,1} + \epsilon_{i,2}|W_{i,1}, W_{i,2}, \ldots W_{i,k})$$

This adjustment is obviously somewhat complex, and it may help or hurt in terms of causal inference. The simplest scenario in which the adjustment is known to help is if the W variables contain all the non-random immediate causes of D_i. If this is true, then $[D_i - E(D_i|W_{i,1}, W_{i,2}, \ldots W_{i,k})]$ retains only purely random variation in the treatment variable and therefore ought to be unrelated with the adjusted version of $\epsilon_{i,1}$ and $\epsilon_{i,2}$.

More generally, a nearly necessary condition for causal inference is that the set of W variables contains at least one variable somewhere along every causal path connecting D_i and Y_i via a confounding variable. That is to say, whenever there is a variable Z_i that has a causal effect on both D_i and Y_i, we assume that the set of W variables includes at least one measure of Z_i, of some variable on the causal path between Z_i and D_i, or of some variable on the causal path between Z_i and Y_i. If some confounding path is not blocked by a variable in W, then part of the variation in $[D_i - E(D_i|W_{i,1}, W_{i,2}, \ldots W_{i,k})]$ will be caused by the confounder, Z_i. Furthermore, because Z_i is by definition also causally connected to at least one of the potential outcomes of Y_i, $\epsilon_{i,1}$ and/or $\epsilon_{i,2}$ will be statistically related to Z_i. Thus, even after adjusting for W, D_i will be related to $\epsilon_{i,1}$ and $\epsilon_{i,2}$.

That is to say, when at least one confounding path is not blocked by a variable in W, the regression-based causal inference will be biased – and will be misleading unless there happens by coincidence to be an equal and offsetting bias. Because social scientists cannot design research based on the expectation of coincidence, we must instead assume that we have identified all confounding causal pathways and included at least one control variable somewhere along each path. Through much of the rest of this book, this assumption that there is a control variable corresponding to each confounding variable will be a key opportunity to add qualitative insight into regression-based causal inference.

Although controlling for all confounders is necessary for causal inference, including variables in W can hurt in a variety of ways. If any of the W variables is caused to any extent by the treatment of interest and also causes Y, then this multivariate regression adjustment will subtract out part of the effect of D on Y, and the resulting inference will be misleading. The reason is that, when the multivariate regression calculates $[Y_i - E(Y_i|W_{i,1}, W_{i,2}, \ldots W_{i,k})]$, the adjustment removes all variation in Y_i that can be predicted based on the W variables. If one of the W variables is caused by D_i, even in part or only in some cases, then part of the relevant causal effect is removed from the data and $\epsilon_{i,2}$ will be distorted in ways that produce bias. Hence, a second key assumption is that no variables in W are part of any causal path from D_i to the outcome of interest.

Adjusting using a W variable may also create new problems of causal inference if that variable is what scholars have referred to as a collider. A collider variable is any variable that is caused by two kinds of other variables, one statistically connected with the treatment and another statistically connected with the outcome. Including a collider as a control, variable induces bias in the regression even if the model previously produced a perfect causal inference (see Elwert and Winship 2014); we can therefore note in passing the assumption that none of the variables in W are colliders. Furthermore, if one or more factors that cause both D and Y are not included in the set of W variables, then the multivariate inference adjusting for those W variables seems about as likely to be better or worse in comparison with the inference from a bivariate regression (Clarke 2005).[12]

2.4   Conclusions

This chapter has argued that the idea of causation has a broadly shared core, and thus that qualitative and quantitative scholars are talking about the same kinds of phenomena when they develop causal theories and make causal inferences. Furthermore, this chapter has argued that there are special circumstances in which regression analysis can provide useful estimates of something like an average treatment effect. Yet it has also argued that these circumstances are unusual and may be difficult to identify. After all, the key conditions for causal inference, using either bivariate or multivariate regression, involve a great deal of knowledge that goes beyond what regression analysis can itself justify. Deciding whether a given regression has any causal meaning involves, at a minimum, addressing measurement quality and ensuring that all confounders are addressed through appropriate control variables, that no control variables are themselves caused by the treatment, and that no issues arise due to colliders. Even if these assumptions are somehow guaranteed to be true, causal inference is not thereby completely secured, and scholars are justified in suspending their belief in the causal inference until they are provided with evidence about the existence (or absence) of evidence for a causal pathway consistent with the results of the regression.

The next chapter will explore some ideas about how case-study research can help test these kinds of conditions permitting causal interpretations of regression estimates, but one major message of this chapter is simply that there is something of a mismatch between regression analysis as a tool and causal inference as an objective, particularly but not exclusively for the kind of heterogeneous, case-specific causal effects of interest in the potential-outcomes framework – and, as argued above, in much qualitative research. Thus, a central argument of this book, developed primarily in the later chapters, is that multi-method designs can be far more valuable if the quantitative component of the design is not based primarily on regression analysis or related techniques. The near-total focus on combining regression and case studies in the multi-method literature to date seems to represent something of an error of emphasis.

Nonetheless, given that regression will probably remain a prominent feature of the social science toolkit for some time to come, it is important to ask whether and how case-study research can contribute to strengthening causal understanding in the wake of regression analysis. Such research sequences, beginning either with an influential regression analysis from the literature or with a scholar's own regression work, are a common form of multi-method research, and a systematic understanding of the specific contribution of case-study work in such setups may offer opportunities to design and implement them more productively.

Notes

1 King, Keohane, and Verba (1994: 76–84) introduced this long-standing concept to debates about qualitative and multi-method research.

2 See also Gerring 2005 and Mahoney 2008.

3 An insightful review and discussion is provided by Freedman (2006).

4 In addition to the themes considered in the text below, there is some debate about whether accounts of causation such as that offered by the potential-outcomes framework are adequate to deal with problems of preemption and overdetermination (Lewis 1986; Brady 2008). Preemption, of course, involves a situation in which two independent sufficient causes of the outcome are present in a case. One acts first, and the other second. To borrow a morbid but popular philosophical example, suppose that Hitman 1 shoots his target in the head, and that in the case that Hitman 1 chooses not to shoot, Hitman 2 shoots the same target in the head two seconds later. What is the causal effect of Hitman 1's action on the target's survival? In the case that Hitman 1 shoots, the target dies due to a gunshot to the head; the same is arguably true in the case that Hitman 1 refrains from shooting. Hence, it may be the case that the potential-outcomes framework defines the causal effect of Hitman 1's action to be 0, a result that is significantly at odds with any common-sense understanding of causation. Overdetermination is a related situation in which two independent sufficient causes of the outcome happen simultaneously. Here, Hitman 1 and 2 shoot the unfortunate target in the head at the same instant. Once again, it appears as if the causal effect of either hitman's actions under the potential-outcomes framework is 0, even though it seems evident that both Hitman contribute causally to the target's death. Woodward (2003: 85–86) argues that a hypothetical manipulationist framework for thinking about causation, which I regard as a friendly amendment of the potential-outcomes framework and which I largely take for granted in the discussion below, resolves these concerns by dissolving them into a rather straightforward set of patterns of counterfactual dependence.

5 Brady (2008: 249-67) also juxtaposes the potential-outcomes framework – there discussed as the "Neyman-Rubin-Holland Theory" – with the various traditions of philosophical thought about causation. In this chapter, I argue that a flexible, friendly reading of the potential-outcomes framework, while obviously not

absolutely inclusive, incorporates many more of the key ideas behind diverse approaches to causation than appears to be the case in Brady's presentation.

6 By descriptively sufficient, I mean that all instances where $X = 1$ are also instances where $Y = 1$, with no implications regarding counterfactuals or manipulations. A parallel definition applies for the idea that a variable may be descriptively necessary.

7 Cartwright (2007: 80–151) argues, and I think rightfully so, that not all situations that should be taken as causal have the kind of structure necessary for manipulations, whether hypothetical or not, to make sense. The kinds of causal systems for which even hypothetical manipulations make little sense represent a clear exception to this chapter's argument that most kinds of causes discussed in the social sciences can be treated within the potential-outcomes framework.

8 For more technical and detailed discussion of the material introduced here, see Morgan and Winship (2007: 61–85) and Berk (2004).

9 One might devise situations in which $\mathrm{E}(\epsilon_{i,1}) = -\mathrm{E}(\epsilon_{i,2}) > 0$, but these are generally quite artificial.

10 The technical requirement is that $E(D_i[\epsilon_{i,1} + \epsilon_{i,2}]) = 0$.

11 This assumes that the W variables are modeled using the correct functional form, or alternatively that they are treated nonparametrically.

12 Even when the adjustment helps, the result estimates a treatment effect that weights cases unusually. Cases for which D_i is highly predictable given information about the W variables will make little contribution to the effect estimate, while cases where D_i is unpredictable or surprising will make a bigger contribution (Angrist and Pischke 2009: 68–112). This kind of differential weighting of cases is built into the multivariate regression estimator, but it is conceptually somewhat undesirable. In principle, we want an estimate of the treatment effect for all cases, rather than one preferentially weighted toward cases where treatment assignment was surprising or unpredictable. This drawback to multivariate regression estimates is part of the rationale for the matching methods discussed in a later chapter.

The assumptions described above are needed, even as new complexities arise, when the treatment of interest is not dichotomous. The simplest case arises when there is a set number, greater than two, of discrete treatments, i.e., when the independent variable is categorical but not dichotomous. Here, a simple extension of the potential-outcomes framework suffices. Suppose that there are four levels of the treatment. For example, an individual stopped by the police may have been given an informal warning, a formal warning, or a ticket, or may have been arrested. The outcome of interest is how many police stops the individual has in the 6 months after the treatment. We can represent each of the treatment conditions as a score on D_i; for convenience, let us represent them numerically, with an individual who receives an informal warning denoted by $D_i = 0$, a formal warning represented by $D_i = 1$, a ticket by $D_i = 2$, and an arrest by $D_i = 3$.

For each individual, there is a unique potential outcome under each of these treatments. Thus, instead of simply discussing $Y_{i,t}$ and $Y_{i,c}$, we must now consider $Y_{i,0}$, $Y_{i,1}$, $Y_{i,2}$, and $Y_{i,3}$. As a result, the set of treatment effects that might be estimated grows substantially: we might be interested in learning about the average difference between $Y_{i,1}$ and $Y_{i,0}$, but also about the averages of $Y_{i,3} - Y_{i,1}$, $Y_{i,2} - Y_{i,0}$, $[Y_{i,0} + Y_{i,1}]/2 - [Y_{i,2} + Y_{i,3}]/2$, and so forth.

Two basic regression setups have been proposed for multilevel treatments. The first estimates effects in a pairwise manner. The idea is really quite simple: to estimate the average difference between $Y_{i,1}$ and $Y_{i,0}$, discard all cases where $D_i = 2$ or $D_i = 3$, and then estimate the treatment effect of interest using the remaining cases using the same kind of dichotomous-treatment regression discussed above. A degree of extra complexity arises because such a setup requires multiple regressions, each of which may require a unique set of conditioning variables in order to succeed, and also because the process of discarding cases may limit the generality of the resulting estimate.

A second setup involves estimating a regression with the following structure:

$$Y_i = \beta_0 + \beta_1(D_i = 1) + \beta_2(D_i = 2) + \beta_3(D_i = 3) + \beta_4 W_{i,1} + \beta_5 W_{i,2} + \cdots + \beta_k W_{i,k} + \delta_i$$

$$(2.6)$$

Here, if the inference is successful, β_0 is an estimate of the average value of $Y_{i,0}$. Furthermore, β_1 serves as an estimate of the average value of $Y_{i,1} - Y_{i,0}$; β_2 and β_3 have similar meanings. If it can be made to work, this approach is convenient in that it provides a unified estimate of most causal effects that we might care about.

On the other hand, Equation 2.6 is harder to estimate successfully than a set of pairwise regressions between treatment categories, because the assumptions involved are somewhat stronger. Because the equation is simultaneously dealing with each level of treatment, successful inference will require that a single set of included W variables block off statistical relationships between each treatment level indicator and the error term. Returning to the setup regarding the effects of warnings, tickets, or arrests at police stops, for example, it is necessary that the W variables include all immediate causes of getting arrested, of getting a ticket, of getting a formal warning, *and* of getting an informal warning; this is obviously even harder than including all of the immediate causes of any pair of these treatments.

Things become more problematic still in the common circumstance that the independent variable of interest in a regression is continuous. Here, D_i can take on infinitely many values; since each possible value of the treatment creates a new potential outcome, this implies that each case has infinitely many potential outcomes. Hence, there is no limit to the number of relevant treatment effects that need to be estimated. It is clearly unreasonable to attempt to estimate an infinity of treatment effects, and so some simplification is needed. One helpful approach is to specify a function that shows, using x to represent any valid value that D_i can take on, what the potential outcome for that case is when $D_i = x$:

$$Y_{i,x} = f_i(x) \qquad (2.7)$$

This is often called a dose-response function or a response schedule (Freedman 2005). The function f_i in Equation 2.7 is specific to the case i, and therefore can perfectly represent the potential outcomes for that case; unfortunately, the case-specific nature of the function also makes it impossible to estimate without extensive counterfactual information. If analysts have additional information about the f_i functions, for example that the differences in those functions across the cases of interest depend only on the values of a set of known variables and an error drawn randomly from a symmetric distribution, it may be possible to write down a shared function f with a finite set of parameters that could be estimated from the data. Then regression can be used to estimate those parameters and complete the description of f_i. The kind of a priori causal knowledge necessary to specify such a shared function with the same causal meaning as the case-specific function Equation 2.7 is unusual, to say the least, in the social sciences.

3 Using Case Studies to Test and Refine Regressions

The last chapter talked about the contributions regression can make to causal inference, as well as about the fact that too much is sometimes expected from regressions. Regression analysis cannot by itself resolve key issues of causal inference. Instead, causal inferences that use regression always depend centrally on additional information that comes from some other source. Such information may involve knowledge that the treatment was experimentally designed, evidence that a credible natural experiment took place, insights that specify a complete and causally justified set of control variables, and so forth. Regardless of the specific form of additional information used to justify using a regression for causal inference, the central point remains: regression can never be a stand-alone basis for causal inference. Instead, it is an incredibly useful tool for summarizing data – and by extension a powerful way of simplifying and quantifying the results of causal inferences that derive their justifications from some other source.

This reframing of the role of regression in justifying causal inference resets the parameters of the debate over the role that qualitative analysis can play in multi-method research. Because regression analysis cannot itself settle causal questions, there is no point in asking whether there is any meaningful role left for case-study work in the wake of a regression. Instead, the question we must face is this: can qualitative research bridge the gap between the descriptive statistical summaries provided by regression and the complex counterfactual knowledge necessary for causal inference?

On rare occasions, it may be true that qualitative research can provide the bolstering information necessary to clinch a causal argument, in conjunction with regression analysis. Usually, however, case-study analysis will fall short; causal inference can simply require too much knowledge that is difficult to acquire in an observational context. Nonetheless, qualitative research when skillfully combined with regression analysis can identify the next step forward toward successful causal inference.

In this chapter, I characterize four essential contributions that qualitative research can make to causal inferences that depend centrally on regression analysis. First, I discuss the value of case studies that are fortunate enough to turn up evidence, usually involving interrupted time series, that helps bound or identify the causal counterfactual for one or a few cases. I then discuss more universal ways that case-study research can help with multi-method causal inference: improving or validating measurement of the treatment and the outcome, building or testing hypotheses about causal pathways, and providing evidence regarding potential omitted variables. For each of these qualitative contributions, I show how the information in question contributes to making causal inferences in conjunction with regression. I conclude by discussing how scholars can refine a regression analysis to benefit from such qualitative insights.

3.1   Identifying a Case's Causal Counterfactuals

Once in a while, case-study research can turn up unusual but valuable kinds of evidence that effectively shortcut the process of causal inference. Such evidence works by providing empirical information about the value of both $Y_{i,t}$ and $Y_{i,c}$. Case-study research of this sort may pinpoint the exact causal effect for a given case, or may only provide bounds; either kind of information can be informative for thinking about overall causal effects (Glynn and Quinn 2010).

One common way for a case study to provide information about both causal counterfactuals is for the case to offer a striking before/after comparison. In such case studies, it is important to verify that the only causally relevant change between the time of the first and the second decision is the treatment variable. If other variables are changing as well, then the second decision does not measure $Y_{i,t}$, reflecting instead some other causal quantity. A classic and highly useful, if probably incomplete, inventory of problematic varieties of changes between the first and second measurement in such case-study designs is given by Campbell and Stanley (1963; see also Campbell and Ross 1968).

A fascinating example of a case study that uses comparisons before and after an unexpected change in the independent variable is Card's (1990) analysis of the Miami labor market before and after the Mariel Boatlift, in which Cuba unilaterally deported a substantial number of citizens to the city. Card takes advantage of the shock to the local labor market that results from accommodating this sudden influx of migrants – who, importantly, do not arrive in Miami because of expectations about the local labor market. Card compares distributions of wages across demographic groups in Miami before and after the boatlift, and also compares between Miami and economically comparable cities that were not affected. Generally, he finds little evidence of differences in wages. While the comparisons involved use statistical data, the logic of the causal inference here represents a core qualitative design. The causal inference is credible because the comparison can meet the criteria for good comparison outlined by Campbell and Stanley.

Case studies can also help pin down a causal effect by relating counterfactual outcomes to plans formed regarding a single decision before and after the availability of information relevant to that decision. That is to say, a first plan was formed before a communication or piece of information representing the treatment became available, while a second was made afterwards. Here, a comparison between the initial and the final plan may reveal the two causal counterfactuals associated with the treatment (Collier *et al.* 2004: 256–57). The success of such a strategy will depend on details of the context, which scholars should examine.

While a wide range of specific empirical patterns can allow case studies to provide evidence regarding the value of both $Y_{i,t}$ and $Y_{i,c}$, such patterns are nonetheless more a fortuitous discovery than something to be expected in a given case study. In most non-experimental studies, many things change at the same time as the treatment of interest, making this research design inapplicable. Furthermore, very often the context simply provides no robust clues about the value of either $Y_{i,t}$ or $Y_{i,c}$ until after the treatment takes place. The other issues identified by Campbell and Stanley above can also arise. Thus, helping identify both causal quantities for a single case is a signal contribution of case studies when it occurs, but it usually cannot be planned for or counted on.

3.2   Validating Measurement

Measurement quality is widely regarded as an important issue in causal inference, for quantitative as well as qualitative scholars. Major quantitative debates regarding measurement have arisen in conjunction with literatures that seek to make causal inference about the causes and effects of democracy (e.g. Bollen 1993; Alvarez *et al.* 1996; Bollen and Paxton 2000; Casper and Tufis 2003; Treier and Jackman 2008; Munck 2009; Pemstein *et al.* 2010), as well as in debates over the best way to measure legislators' ideological positions (e.g. Heckman and Snyder 1997; Hill *et al.* 1997; Poole and Rosenthal 1997; Burden *et al.* 2000; Jackman 2001; Clinton *et al.* 2004; Carroll *et al.* 2009; Clinton and Jackman 2009). The task of measuring political regimes has of course spawned substantial qualitative debates as well (see discussion in Collier and Levitsky 1997; Munck 2009). The existence and prominence of these debates in literatures driven by causal inference suffice to demonstrate that both qualitative and quantitative scholars regard measurement as a key issue in causal inference – although the traditions bring substantially different sets of tools to bear in evaluating measurement quality (Seawright and Collier 2014).

One of the widely acknowledged distinctive strengths of case-study research is that it allows researchers to evaluate, adjust, or create measures based on a great deal of often case-specific information. While this property of case studies is intuitive, it is nonetheless worthwhile to think about why case-study research can improve measurement. Social science measurement involves an interaction between a complex social reality and scholars, concepts and measurement tools. This interaction can be usefully schematized as follows (Adcock and Collier 2001). Scholars adopt or create a measurement instrument in light of their conceptualization, and they introduce that instrument into social reality. A causal interaction between selected features of social reality and the measurement instrument generates the scores or classifications that are the end product of measurement.

For example, in survey research the causal interaction between social reality and the measurement instrument often takes the form of a partially scripted conversation between an interviewer and a respondent. The respondent hears a question, goes through one or another process of interpretation, recall, judgment, and editing, and then responds (Tourangeau *et al.* 2000). The response, which becomes a survey measure, is thus a product of a causal interaction between the survey text and a social dynamic involving the interviewer and the respondent.

An indicator is the central product of the interaction between social reality and the measurement instrument, but it need not be the only one. A resourceful researcher can capture other pieces of evidence related to the causal process by which measurement takes place, using those data as clues regarding possible sources of measurement error (Mahoney 2010: 125–28). Likewise, evidence of components of social reality that are relevant to, but in fact happened to be uninvolved in, the measurement process can be collected to evaluate that process. Case-study research allows flexible attentiveness to the accumulation of such evidence, allowing an evaluation of the extent to which a given indicator captures the relevant information or was perhaps distorted by features of the process leading to the final scoring for the case.[1]

In a survey-based design, case-study research can attend to the expressions of certainty, self-justification, confusion, and so forth that occur as part of the survey interview – if those remarks are recorded or otherwise preserved. For example, Chong (1993) uses unusually complete records of 30 respondents' expressed thought processes while they answer a survey battery to analyze the kinds of attitudes, knowledge, and other considerations that are involved in the causal process leading to survey response regarding civil liberties. Similar close attention to accumulating evidence about the process of measurement and the aspects of social reality not included in the measurement process has long been central to more traditional macro-level case-study contexts as well, as we shall see below.

This is in contrast to a variety of quantitative measurement traditions that rely on one or a relatively small number of pieces of information per case, and that generally attend more closely to the overall properties of measurement across a sample or population than to case-specific correspondence between indicators and broader sets of relevant evidence (Seawright and Collier 2014). Because good description is an essential component of good causal inference, case-study work that serves to validate or refine measurement can make an important contribution to multi-method causal inferences.

From a potential-outcomes perspective, in-depth verification or correction of measurement makes two important contributions. First, scholars may discover that the treatment variable was misclassified for a case: the case really received the treatment but was measured as having received the control or vice versa. When, for example, case i really receives the treatment but is misclassified as having received the control, any causal inference using that case may be distorted. After all, because of the misclassification the scholar analyzes the observed value, $Y_{i,t}$, as if it were $Y_{i,c}$. This is a harmless mistake if the treatment has no causal effect for case i, because then the two quantities in question are equal. Otherwise, such a mistake will change treatment effect estimates, although the degree of change depends on the size of the causal effect in case i and also on the overall number of cases in the analysis. When causal effects are large – i.e., when the cause in question matters most – causal inferences can be dramatically improved by correcting such measurement errors.

A second important contribution arises when case studies correct distortions in the measurement of the outcome for case i. In most causal inferences, each case's score on the outcome contributes directly to the estimation of treatment effects. Hence, eliminating errors in the measurement of the outcome straightforwardly improves causal inference.

As an example of the role that in-depth research can play in improving measurement, consider Fourcade's (2009) analysis of differences in the structure and practices of the economics profession in the United States, Britain, and France.[2] A first approach to measuring the professional structure of economics in each country might be to collect data, from national census records or surveys, about the number of professional economists in each country. Such an approach yields the surprising result that France lacks economists, whereas the United States has many and Britain has some; in contrast to the Anglophone countries, "'economist' does not exist as a valid occupational title" (Fourcade 2009: 14) in France. Instead, in France, being an economist is an identity that specialists within the state bureaucracy as well as nonspecialists adopt in arguing over the direction of public policy and the proper content of intellectual debate. Evidence for the claim that nonspecialists have access to the economist identity comes from opinion pieces and letters to the editor where the author self-identifies as an economist (Fourcade 2009: 14), discussion of a protest movement in which students write an "Appeal of Economists to End Uniform Thinking" demanding a shift in focus away from mathematical theory and toward real-world policy issues (Fourcade 2009: 185), and the wide diffusion of popular economic discourse through generalist newspapers, books, and *clubs de réflexion* (Fourcade 2009: 232–34). Likewise, extensive documentary and interview evidence is provided to show that professionals in the state and mathematically oriented theorists in academia are involved in French economics and publish in influential journals even if they are not economists by occupational title (Fourcade 2009: 185–235). Thus, in contrast to a simple quantitative measure showing economics to be a weak or even nonexistent profession in France, Fourcade provides a range of context-dependent qualitative evidence supporting the view that French economics involves a divided, heterogeneous, and conflict-laden but nonetheless large intellectual community. This case-based measurement demonstrates that census-based quantitative measurement showing France to have zero (or even merely few) economists reflects substantial measurement error.

Such findings about measurement error, whether involving the treatment or the outcome variable, differ in importance. The most valuable discoveries regarding measurement error not only improve classification and measurement for one or a few cases, but also generate hypotheses about the sources of measurement error that may apply to a broader set of cases. Such hypotheses can improve measurement across the board, either by helping scholars devise improved measurement instruments that are not subject to the identified sources of error or by facilitating after-the-fact adjustment to remove the effects of errors. Thus, case-study knowledge of this sort may result in generalized gains for causal inference. Because general hypotheses about the sources of measurement error are so valuable, case-study scholars should, when possible, attempt to discover not only that a case is mismeasured but also why the error arises.

Sometimes, case-study research will yield no useful insights into the sources of measurement error. Instead, the finding will simply be that one or a few cases are incorrectly scored and should be recoded. Even such limited and case-specific findings can be highly important for causal inference when the cases in question make a disproportionate contribution to causal inference. Fixing the scoring of high-leverage cases can remove important sources of bias from the overall treatment effect estimate even though no broader knowledge about measurement results.

Third, and least valuable, are case studies that correct measurement errors for cases that make a minor contribution to the overall treatment effect estimate. Such case studies generate no new insight into the measurement process itself, and also do little to improve the causal inference at hand. It is noteworthy that the difference between this kind of finding and the more important finding that significantly alters the case-study inference need not be evident in the case-study research itself; rather, this critical difference is generally discovered in the context of multi-method research.

How common is the use of examining measurement to improve causal inference within the existing case-study literature in the social sciences? Is this a marginal practice or a core technique? In fact, careful consideration of measurement is one of the central contributions of much qualitative research to causal inference, although many of the studies in question do not explicitly frame their analysis in this way.

While close consideration of measurement decisions can play a central role in case-study research of many kinds, its relative contribution is especially clear in research that is designed around systematic cross-case comparisons of a relatively small set of cases with attention to a uniform set of variables. This mode of case-study research has been variously described as using the method of structured, focused comparison (George 1979, George and Bennett 2004: 67–72); Mill's methods of agreement and difference (Mill 1891/2002: 253–84) as understood in qualitative social science; nominal or ordinal strategies of comparative analysis (Mahoney 1999); and intuitive regression (Collier, Mahoney, and Seawright 2004). These practices are unified by their comparative inattention to building detailed evidence regarding causal paths, with the emphasis shifted to the tasks of coding and comparing cases on a fixed list of variables reflecting the outcome of interest, the key causal hypotheses, and important alternative explanations.

The comparisons produced by these methods represent a very weak tool for causal inference. Designs of this sort are vulnerable to confounding in just the same way as regression, because the methods' deprioritization of causal process leaves them without any obvious way to distinguish between a factor that causes the outcome, a factor caused by a cause of the outcome, and a factor caused by the outcome. Furthermore, as Lieberson (1992) among others has argued, these designs are more vulnerable to error due to random chance or coincidence than are regression-type designs. After all, while it would be incredibly unlikely for 600 cases to align themselves purely at random in such a way that all the cases with $Y = 1$ also had $X = 1$ and all other cases had $X = 0$, such a chance outcome would not be especially noteworthy for a sample of four cases.

There is, however, a far more powerful argument to be made against the idea that qualitative cross-case comparisons provide special leverage for causal inference. The key to this argument is recognizing that qualitative and quantitative cross-case comparisons involving a fixed set of variables are two approaches to the same underlying problem: drawing patterns of association out of data and distinguishing genuine connections from merely apparent ones. Once this commonality is recognized, we can immediately conclude that a statistical approach to a given comparison will be as good as, or better than, a qualitative approach to the same comparison. The reason is that regression and other quantitative techniques for cross-case comparison have a variety of optimality theorems. For example, the Gauss-Markov theorem for OLS regression (Greene 2000: 244–45) shows that technique to be the best linear unbiased estimator, and in some cases the best unbiased estimator, for the kind of comparison it carries out. Thus, no estimator – qualitative or quantitative – can systematically beat regression in terms of both precision and accuracy for regression-type relationships. Qualitative regression-like comparisons may aspire to be as good at cross-case comparisons as regression-like models in terms of these two goals, but not better. Furthermore, they can easily be worse.

For readers of work in these case-study traditions, there is an immediate tension between this argument and experience. How could the densely textured, often book-length argumentation and analysis typical of such work be interchangeable with – or even less informative than – a single regression table? Such qualitative work focused on cross-case comparisons can indeed make a contribution to causal inference over and above what any regression-like analysis could offer, but that contribution involves evidence regarding the measurement of difficult-to-capture or error-prone treatment and outcome variables.

This suggestion is consistent with the relative emphasis on measurement vis-à-vis explicit comparison in many such volumes.

For example, the central substantive chapters of Goldstone's (1991) case-study analysis of relationships between demographic dynamics and the occurrence of social and political revolutions each have a formal three-part structure. The first part involves an exploration of the literature and evidence regarding demographic and economic trends in a given country during a pre-revolutionary period. The second provides an intensive process-tracing description of the outcome, with careful emphasis on causal contributions from demography and economic developments. The third part engages in comparative analysis. Thus, the first section of each chapter focuses narrowly on measurement: its central goal is to describe the demographic and economic trends in each country as accurately as possible. The second part is a mixture of work on causal pathways, along the lines discussed in the next section, and attention to measuring the outcome. Only the final part of each chapter is devoted to the sort of explicitly comparative analysis that is formalized in techniques such as Mill's methods. This example's unusually clear structure makes evident a pattern that applies much more broadly: comparative case-study research in the social sciences often spends a majority of its attention and research effort on refining and justifying the measurement of cases. Yet if this is correct, we must conclude that one high-profile branch of case-study methodology involves research with the central causal-inferential goal of justifying or improving measurement. Surely, then, we can see this as a distinctive contribution of qualitative research more generally to the enterprise of causal inference.

3.3   Testing or Discovering Hypotheses about Causal Pathways

A second commonplace about case-study research is that it is useful for exploring "causal mechanisms." Unfortunately, a near consensus about this property of case studies seems to rely on a great deal of ambiguity regarding the nature of mechanisms (Gerring 2007b). For some authors, causal mechanisms are the arrangement of entities and relationships that connect an initial intention or causal impulse to the result of interest. This meaning of mechanism can be illustrated by reference to actual mechanisms, as in Cartwright's discussion of the mechanical components that causally link the activation lever on a toaster with the end result of toasted bread (Cartwright 2007: 85–87). By contrast, other authors use the concept of causal mechanisms to refer to frequently repeated social processes that play roles in a variety of causal narratives or hypotheses (Elster 1989, 2007; Hedström and Swedberg 1998). To extend the toaster analogy, a causal mechanism in this sense would not be the entire arrangement of components that collects the activation lever with the outcome, but rather a single device such as a heating coil or a solenoid. A causal mechanism in the first sense thus involves a particular configuration of causal mechanisms in the second sense. Still other scholars regard a causal mechanism as an account of the causal relation at a lower level of analysis or that involves unobservable entities. These perspectives raise important issues and motivate worthwhile hypotheses regarding the nature of specific causal relations, as discussed in Chapter 2, but are not of direct concern for this chapter.

An additional difficulty regarding causal mechanisms involves the degree of generality that they should possess in order to be of social scientific interest. For some scholars, attention to mechanisms is part of a thoroughgoing commitment to the proposition that causal relations in the social world are heterogeneous. Hence, the set of causal steps between the treatment and the outcome is expected to be case-specific and completely not generalizable. A competing perspective follows on statistical traditions involving structural models in which intervening causal steps are treated as a uniform part of the theory to be tested across a set of cases.

A pluralistic approach to causation allows us to see all of these viewpoints as useful ways of highlighting specific kinds of causal relationships. Sometimes a specific debate hinges on the exact sequence of entities and causal capacities that translates a cause into an outcome; other times, attention may focus more on the pervasiveness of a single kind of causal linkage. Certain theories will indeed posit uniform sequences of causal steps between treatments and outcomes – and no doubt, there are social realities that correspond with some of these theories. In other domains, heterogeneity will be the rule. From a pluralistic perspective, these issues become part of the substance of specific scientific debates, and not matters to be settled by methodological fiat.

In discussing these issues, I will adopt the term "causal pathways" to refer to arrangements of entities, relationships, and causal capacities that convey an initial causal impulse of some sort forward to an outcome for one or more cases. This position allows causal pathways to be universal or highly case-specific, to involve movement to a lower level of analysis or to remain at the same level, to entail unobservable and/or observable entities, and so forth. This focus on causal pathways is thus highly general and pluralistic regarding the kinds of causal relationships that might exist, while also providing a language for articulating ideas about variables, processes, and so forth in the middle of causation. It is also directly compatible with the potential-outcomes account of causal mediation discussed in the Appendix.

Scholars have long argued that qualitative research has distinctive tools for building evidence about causal pathways, a set of tools variously discussed as involving process tracing (Einhorn *et al.* 1979; George 1979; Ford *et al.* 1989; George and Bennett 2004: 205–32) or the analysis of causal-process observations (Brady and Collier 2004; Mahoney 2010). From either perspective, the argument is as follows. Causation in the social world tends to involve a long sequence of decisions, actions, institutional patterns, and so forth that connect the treatment to the outcome. That sequence generates a collection of real-world records and evidentiary traces that case-study researchers can gather. Some of this gathering will involve interviewing actors to recover their memories and understandings of events; in other circumstances, the most important records will be documents, objects, and so forth.

Because these pieces of evidence are generated by the same causal process that connects the treatment to the outcome, they can provide clues to the existence and nature of that causal process. Interpreting causal-process observations involves a dialogue between evidence and theory. Given a set of potentially viable theories of the causal process, the usefulness of various possible causal-process observations can be evaluated using the following intuitive Bayesian logic (see also Bennett 2008).

The key question is: how likely is it that we would see the set of causal-process observations that we actually collected if each theory is correct? If the evidence is equally likely under each theory, then the evidence is useless. As an extreme example, the discovery that each of our interview subjects breathes in oxygen and breathes out carbon dioxide would be essentially certain under virtually any social science theory, and would therefore tell us nothing about the relative value of each theory. At the opposite extreme are pieces of evidence that would be all but certain to be so under one theory and all but impossible if any competitor accurately described the causal process; observing such a piece of evidence would strongly confirm – indeed, would be a nearly totally compelling argument – that a single one of the available theories best characterizes the causal process.

In practice, of course, evidence is rarely either so useless or so decisive. Instead, evidence may be equally likely under multiple theories, or may even be highly unlikely under all theories. The central point remains: evidence is useful when it is more likely under some theories than under others. When this criterion is met, the theories that make the evidence seem more likely in relative terms are supported; the others, weakened to some extent.

All of this is of course rather abstract. In the present context, the kinds of theories we are considering involve claims about both the causes of an outcome and the causal process that leads to that outcome. The best pieces of evidence for process-tracing purposes, then, will be evidence that should almost certainly be present if one theory of the causal process is correct, and that should be hard to account for under any other theory. Measurement quality is therefore an important aspect of evaluating causal-process observations: if the observation in question could easily be mismeasured, then other theories can easily account for the observation and its evidentiary value is low.

In addition to measurement issues, the quality of a causal-process observation also depends on the complexity and credibility of the network of auxiliary causal theories that are needed to connect the observation with the main theory or theories of the causal process that are being tested. In some contexts, these auxiliary theories are quite basic or almost self-evidently true. For example, a common category of causal-process observations relies on the fact that a particular piece of information did not become available until after a key decision to conclude that this particular information had no causal effect on the decision. The inference seems self-evident, but on closer inspection relies on a set of causal understandings. For example, the causal-process observation is only more likely under the theory that the information in question had no effect than under alternative theories if the decision-makers in question have neither telepathy nor mental access to future events. While these causal theories are essential to the value of the causal-process observation, they are also so heavily supported and widely accepted that they are usually not worth discussing.

Two other auxiliary causal theories for causal-process observations of this kind are less trivial. The first involves the hypothesis that the decision-makers and, perhaps, a network of other actors conspired to alter the available evidence to make the historical record appear as if the information in question was unavailable at the time of the decision, even though it in fact played a central causal role in that decision. The hypothesis of such manipulation cannot in general be disregarded; unlike the theories in the previous paragraph, it violates no basic principles of reality. Furthermore, actors may sometimes have strong motives to falsify the record of their decision-making process, particularly if the actual process involved considerations that were illegal, unethical, or socially unacceptable. Scholars who rely on this kind of evidence to support their hypothesized causal process thus need to consider whether any of the actors involved had the motive and capacity to alter the pool of available evidence.

Another, generally more important auxiliary causal theory for such causal-process observations rules out the alternative that, even though the information itself was unavailable, the decision-makers possessed sufficient clues to successfully forecast the information and made the decision on the basis of that forecast. In order for the causal-process observation of this kind to do the work that is needed of it, such an alternative must be ruled out – either through general considerations or through specific evidence. If it can be shown through recourse to other causal theories that the kind of information in question is unpredictable in general, then the alternative interpretation is ruled out and the causal-process observation has greater value. The same result can be achieved using case-specific evidence, if such evidence reveals either that actors had no expectation regarding the information in question or that their expectation was incorrect. Either of these lines of argument would make the causal-process observation less likely under alternative hypotheses – therefore rendering it more valuable evidence in favor of the hypothesis of interest.

One family of issues that can render causal-process observations relatively less useful applies to so many common case-study practices as to deserve a brief separate discussion: issues related to the reliability of people's accounts of their own decision-making process. Case-study researchers routinely gather evidence by asking actors to retroactively report their own reasoning regarding a decision process, a technique that Van Evera discusses as the Delphi method (Van Evera 1997: 70–73). While such evidence is attractive and widely used, it is also problematic. The issue is that people often do not know the real causal process behind their own decisions, and their explanations of that process will often be post hoc rationalizations rather than reliable reports. This conclusion is a straightforward deduction from the many studies in cognitive psychology showing that people are overconfident in their own decision-making and are subject to strange, unconscious biases and distortions (Kahneman *et al.* 1982; Kahneman and Tversky 2000; Gilovich *et al.* 2002). This argument is explicitly developed in a classic paper by Nisbett and Wilson (1977) summarizing a wide body of research in which people turn out to have limited insight into their own decision-making, and cognition more generally. In these studies, "the accuracy of subjective reports [about reasoning and causation in people's own decision-making] is so poor as to suggest that any introspective access that may exist is not sufficient to produce generally correct or reliable reports" (Nisbett and Wilson 1977: 233). Instead, they argue, people's reports of their own decision-making are often the result of applying a priori folk causal theories to their own memories of the situation. Thus, self-reported reasons for decisions may represent common-sense social scientific theories, rather than the kind of independent evidence that can serve as a powerful causal-process observation. Counterintuitively enough, causal-process observations that less directly reveal decision-making processes – involving, for example, information flows or the structure of debates within an organization – are more likely to be useful in ruling out some theories and supporting others than causal-process observations based on people's own explanations of those decisions.

Real-life applications of process tracing almost always rely on a mixture of strong and weaker causal-process observations. For example, Prasad's (2006: 43–97) fascinating analysis of neoliberal economic policy initiatives in the United States under Reagan uses a collection of interesting and persuasive observations to build a case for her theory of elite decision-making and interactions during that process. She is particularly interested in showing that the policy initiatives were caused neither by collective action on the part of corporations nor by a consensus among professional economists in favor of the policies. To that end, the analysis focuses on information showing that businesses favored only some of the policies that were undertaken, that many or most economists doubted the wisdom of key elements of Reagan's neoliberal package, and that the actual decision-making process behind budget cuts was low-information and was carried out largely by administration actors with few ties to business and little knowledge of economics.

For example, a particularly telling and important source of evidence regarding the budget-cut decision process comes from an interview between a journalist and David Stockman, Reagan's director of the Office of Management and Budget. In the interview, Stockman describes selecting economic projections for political reasons, talks about the chaotic and under-institutionalized nature of the budgetary process, and mentions that Reagan resisted cutting funds for the military or for retirement programs. Prasad carefully considers possible explanations for this evidence other than correspondence with Stockman's actual experience of the decision-making process, focusing in particular on the hypothesis that Stockman may have strategically misrepresented events for political gain. As a counterargument, process-tracing evidence is offered to show that the interview in fact came at a high political cost for Stockman (Prasad 2006: 88–90), a fact that makes the alternative hypothesis of strategic misrepresentation much less plausible. This explicit attention toward, and analysis of, evidence regarding perhaps the most compelling alternative theory of the evidence makes the contents of this interview a powerful collection of causal-process observations.

By contrast, the portions of Prasad's account that involve mass political attitudes and decision-making rely on far weaker causal-process observations. Prasad's overall theory connects the degree of class antagonism inherent in a country's pre-1980s economic policy package with the extent of neoliberal economic reform after 1980. Mass opinion and decision-making serve as the key step in the theorized causal process: antagonistic economic policy creates discontent among the middle classes and therefore creates "the potential to ally the majority of voters with market-friendly policies" (Prasad 2006: 38), a potential that political entrepreneurs exploit to bring about neoliberal reform. Key claims about the masses here include that citizens subjectively perceive antagonism in the policies that Prasad describes as objectively dividing the interests of social classes, that such perceived antagonism creates a desire for policy change, and that voters supported Reagan and other neoliberal politicians because those leaders implemented policies that satisfied such desires. An opponent of this account could offer a number of plausible alternative hypotheses: voters may not even be aware of most economic policies, they may perceive economic policies more in terms of the national interest than in class terms, or they may vote largely on the basis of identities other than class; or they may vote largely on the grounds of identities and issues outside of the economic domain. The analysis provides some evidence that voters were favorably disposed toward tax cuts in 1980 and earlier, providing marginal percentages from Gallup surveys and discussing California's Proposition 13 and other state-level citizen votes to limit taxes (Prasad 2006: 45–46). Yet the analysis never shows evidence of an individual-level set of associations among perceiving antagonistic economic policies, supporting policy change, and subsequently rewarding politicians who implement neoliberal reforms – let alone a set of causal connections along these lines. Hence, in comparison with the argument regarding political elites, the process-tracing evidence regarding mass behavior is far more open to alternative explanations and therefore less powerful.

Such a mixture of strong and weaker causal-process observations is common and perhaps even universal in case-study research. It is difficult at best, and probably in fact unmanageable, to consider the set of plausible alternative explanations for each piece of evidence presented in a complex case-study narrative. In the face of such trade-offs, scholars routinely and defensibly choose to focus on some aspects of the narrative but not on others, with the result that even very strong case-study research typically includes weak or contestable components. For present purposes, the important point is that the weaker and stronger observations can be systematically distinguished by considering the degree of difficulty involved in accounting for those observations if an alternative causal hypothesis were true.

In a multi-method context combining case studies with regression, two applications of process tracing are particularly important. The first involves collecting causal-process observations to examine the causal path connecting the treatment with the outcome. This application of process tracing has been widely discussed in the existing literature on multi-method research, and could be said to represent the core of the received wisdom regarding what case studies can contribute to causal inference (Roberts 1996; George and Bennett 2004).

In particular, it is useful to check that there is within-case evidence consistent with the existence of a causal effect of the direction and magnitude estimated by the regression. The best multi-method research uses process tracing not only to show evidence of the existence of a pathway consistent with the overall theory, but also to suggest that the pathway could plausibly account for as much of a causal effect as the regression found. When the regression has shown an especially large causal effect, researchers should look for causal-process observations that reveal a major connection between the treatment and the decision processes or other causal phenomena of interest.

A genuinely large causal effect typically coincides with high consistency and low contingency in the linkages between treatment and outcome across cases. A highly consistent causal process is one in which the same basic steps occur in the same sequence connecting the treatment and the outcome across many or most cases. A causal process has low contingency if few or none of the causal steps involve factors that are idiosyncratic to a given case, highly unpredictable, or coincidental. Large causal effects can arise with low-consistency causal processes when there are many equally efficacious but theoretically distinctive paths that can connect a treatment with an outcome. However, it seems likely that in most cases where many possible paths exist connecting treatment and outcome, some of the possible paths will be more causally efficacious than others. If this is so, then sets of cases where there is variety in the causal paths will have lower causal effects than cases where the causal path more consistently involves the most causally efficacious arrangements – variety will tend to water down the large effects from the most efficacious arrangements. Hence, a finding of inconsistent causal paths across a set of cases can call a large treatment effect estimate into doubt, while evidence of consistency will support the large effect estimate.

A similar logic applies regarding contingency. A causal process involving high contingency may bring about large effects in a few cases, but by definition it is unlikely to do so for most cases. Hence, averaging across a reasonable sample will tend to water down the effects from the handful of cases where the causal effect is large due to the fortuitous coincidence of contingent elements. By this reasoning, finding that the causal process connecting treatment to the outcome is highly contingent raises concerns about a large treatment effect estimate, while causal-process observations consistent with a low-contingency causal process can bolster that large estimate.

More generally, multi-method scholars should check that within-case evidence about the causal process in key cases is consistent with both the theory being tested and with any regression results that are to be used as evidence in favor of that theory. This kind of research has long been at the heart of multi-method research. Yet there is an additional research design objective, related to causal processes, that is even more intimately related to the assumptions of regression-based causal inference: checking for post-treatment bias.

As discussed in the previous chapter, regression-based (and, more generally, multivariate statistical) causal inferences are distorted when control variables are included that are affected by the main treatment of interest. Such analyses suffer from "post-treatment bias," i.e., they produce a causal inference in which the main causal effect of interest is mis-estimated because one of the pathways by which the treatment affects the outcome is inappropriately excluded from the analysis (Rosenbaum 1984). In general, regression-type studies cannot resolve the question of whether a control variable induces post-treatment bias, so this is a prime opportunity for a qualitative contribution to the causal inference.

The best design for testing the assumption of no post-treatment bias is to examine all available evidence about the causal pathway connecting the treatment to the outcome. Yet here the focus is not on evaluating whether the causal pathway is consistent with the kind of causal effect estimated by the regression analysis. Instead, the goal is to search for moments in which control variables in the regression analysis appear as causal steps connecting the treatment and the outcome. A scholar may well use the same evidence as in the kinds of research discussed up to this point in this search.

If evidence is found that a control variable from the regression may be part of a causal pathway connecting the treatment and the outcome in at least one case, then the control variable is probably inappropriate. Alternatively, if no evidence is found of post-treatment bias in a given case study, the result provides only weak support for the assumption that there is no such bias. In particular, scholars should worry that one or more control variables appear in the causal pathway for some subset of cases – and that the case that was analyzed simply was not one of those. Hence a collection of multiple, diverse case studies focused on causal pathways provides much better evidence in support of the assumption than a single study can.

As an example, consider Ward *et al.*'s (2015) analysis of how globalization affects the content of political party competition. Using data on a wide range of countries from 1961 to 2010, these scholars use a series of time-series cross-sectional regressions to estimate the relationship between economic integration and party polarization on economic and other issues. The results suggest that globalization increases polarization on non-economic issues but tends to produce consensus on economic issues. Of particular interest here is the fact that the key regression models include a country's overall level of economic inequality as a control variable (Ward *et al.* 2015: 1240, 1245, 1249).

Does the inclusion of economic inequality create post-treatment bias in the relationship between economic globalization and party polarization? The central issue in answering this question is determining whether globalization has a causal effect on inequality; after all, the inclusion of inequality as a control variable implies that Ward *et al.* believe it to have a causal effect on polarization.

Fortuitously enough, Keyder (2005) provides us with a case study of the economic effects of globalizing economic integration on Turkey in the 1980s, a context that is included in Ward *et al.*'s regression analysis. Keyder finds that globalization transforms urban life in the country's capital, Istanbul, in a variety of ways that increased inequality. Economic integration generated economic segregation within the city, with multinational businesses displacing small-scale entrepreneurial endeavors from central districts, and gated communities aimed at international and globally connected Turkish renters replacing more economically mixed residential neighborhoods (Keyder 2005: 128, 130). Economic integration more directly affected inequality by undermining Turkish industrial production and thereby pushing formerly working-class employees toward less desirable informal-sector jobs (Keyder 2005: 128–29), and by reducing Turkey's capacity to maintain its welfare state institutions (Keyder 2005: 130–31). All of this, in Keyder's view, adds up to substantial evidence of a collection of causal pathways by which globalization has greatly increased economic and social inequality in Turkey.

If Keyder's case-study analysis is correct, then inequality is an inappropriate control variable in Ward *et al.*'s analysis. Those authors then face a choice. They might delete Turkey from the analysis and present evidence that inequality is not a post-treatment variable in any other included countries; reestimate their models excluding inequality as a control variable; or argue in detail that Keyder's case-study analysis is misleading for the case of Turkey. Whichever of these options they choose, it is clear that the qualitative argument based on one of the cases in the larger regression model moves the causal debate forward by raising new issues for debate and by suggesting possible revisions to the prior regression analysis.

3.4   Searching for Confounders

While tests of causal pathways are important, both as evidence that a relevant pathway exists and as a way of testing the assumption of no post-treatment bias, the potential contributions of process-tracing evidence to testing and refining regressions are more extensive. Regression estimates of causal effects can be more credible if there is corroborating within-case evidence that a causal process exists consistent with the estimated effect; however, making a credible case that a regression result represents a causal effect also requires some evidence that key assumptions behind the regression correspond with the facts of the cases in question.

Process tracing can help with the most important assumption behind causal inference using regression: the assumption that there is no confounding. As discussed in the last chapter, confounding arises when there is a back-door causal path from the treatment to the outcome. The easiest example of such a back-door path is when there is some variable that causes both the treatment and the outcome, although more complicated variants can arise.

This assumption is so critical for regressions that scholars should use process tracing in multiple ways to explore it when carrying out multi-method research. One relevant design involves tracing the causes of the treatment. After developing useful evidence regarding the process by which a given case receives the treatment that it does, the next step in this design requires assembling causal-process observations to check whether any of the causes of the treatment are themselves components of an autonomous causal process leading to the outcome, i.e., a causal process in which the treatment does not intervene between the more distant cause and the outcome. Evidence of such a path reveals a new confounder and provides a basis for redesigning the regression, while a lack of evidence can bolster the original causal effect estimate.

Qualitative evidence of an often somewhat unsystematic nature is routinely used in quantitative studies employing natural experiments, as will be discussed in Chapter 6. Pure case-study research sometimes also considers process-tracing evidence regarding the causes of the main independent variable. For example, in Chhibber and Kollman's comparative case-study analysis of the degree to which democracies' party systems have the same format across geographic regions, an entire chapter is devoted to characterizing the score of the primary independent variable for each country across a series of periods (Chhibber and Kollman 2004: 101–60). Yet the discussion of that variable – the degree to which governing authority is centralized – is not limited to simply describing countries' traits at a particular time. Instead, the authors repeatedly offer explanatory evidence regarding the reasons for changes in the level of centralization within a country's political system; for instance they discuss the effects of court decisions on patterns of centralization and decentralization in Canada (Chhibber and Kollman 2004: 108–9, 112, 118–19). These elements of explanation for the value of the independent variable, and other similar pieces of evidence regarding the remaining cases in the study, are not emphasized in the analysis – but perhaps they should be. After all, if Chhibber and Kollman can show that patterns of centralization and decentralization of authority happen for reasons not closely connected with party-system dynamics, then their causal inference will be less threatened by possibilities of confounding; obviously, the same applies more generally. Scholars would be well advised to incorporate into their qualitative research designs a component of careful backwards process tracing, starting from the main treatment variable.

In exploring the causal prehistory of the treatment variable, scholars may sometimes discover that there is no evidence of a connection between an included control variable and the treatment. Given the risk of bias due to collider variables, as discussed in the last chapter, finding that a control variable lacks a causal connection to the treatment is grounds for worry that the variable in question should be excluded. Yet scholars should be cautious before making such a move; the variable in question may be a confounder whose effects are only felt in some cases. Hence, analysts should expect a lack of evidence of causal connection between the control variable and the treatment in several cases, as different from each other as possible within the context of the study, before removing a variable from the set of controls in this way.

Scholars should also consider a second design, giving them an additional set of chances to turn up evidence of confounding. In this design, they begin with an open-ended exploration of causal processes connected with the final outcome, particularly including any processes that do *not* involve the treatment of interest. For each of these processes, once the tracing has reached a potential causal factor with reasonable causal distance from the outcome of interest (inevitably a matter of judgment), the analysis reverses direction and the scholar collects causal-process observations for an open-ended search regarding the effects of the potential causal factor. In comparison with the design tracing causally backwards from the independent variable, this approach is less structured and therefore runs a much greater risk of missing important confounders. Nevertheless, it gives scholars a second chance at catching potentially damaging omitted variables. Furthermore, whereas tracing the process leading to the treatment variable is a somewhat unusual step in qualitative research, a broad inductive search for causal processes bringing about the outcome is not unusual, and in fact may be a particularly natural fit for case-study researchers who have been described by some scholars as culturally oriented toward completely accounting for outcomes in each case they study (Mahoney and Goertz 2006).

3.5   Refining Regressions to Incorporate Qualitative Insights

Up to this point, we have focused on ways that case studies can test and improve regression-type analyses. The discussion has shown major areas where case-study research can contribute to causal inferential tasks for which regression is ill-suited. As a concluding set of considerations, we must discuss how to incorporate such case-study findings into subsequent, improved regression analysis. Only by incorporating case-study insights into a new iteration of statistical modeling can the full potential of integrative multi-method research be realized: while multi-method scholars who begin with regression-based inference should test key assumptions driving that inference using the techniques discussed above, it is equally important that case-study findings be systematized, extended, and tested in further, appropriately designed quantitative analysis.

When the case-study finding involves measurement problems, solutions are intellectually if not always practically straightforward. When evidence suggests that a small number of cases have been miscoded due to idiosyncratic, case-specific factors, it is reasonable to correct the scoring on those cases and proceed with analysis. On the other hand, when the case studies offer a hypothesis regarding possible systematic sources of measurement error, then the best approach is to redesign the measurement process to eliminate or work around those sources of error, redo measurement, and then statistically analyze the new indicator. Obviously, this latter approach can be expensive and labor-intensive – suggesting that case-study validation of measurement may be useful at a very early stage in the research cycle. Nonetheless, neither approach raises distinctive intellectual issues.

For possible confounders, a range of well-known solutions is available, the simplest of which is to incorporate a measure of the confounder as a control variable in the regression. This can eliminate the distorting effects of the confounder under a set of complicated and hard-to-verify assumptions; on the other hand, more complex approaches such as matching rely on essentially similar assumptions (Morgan and Winship 2007: 87–122). At the very least, causal effect estimates can be made from regressions with and without the newly proposed confounders, with those results providing guidance regarding the range of possible effect sizes that might be plausible given current knowledge.

Other categories of case-study findings require more complex quantitative analysis, moving beyond the garden-variety response of adding control variables to the end of a regression equation. In particular, case-study research can sometimes complicate regression analysis by discovering heterogeneity in the causal relationship between the treatment and the outcome. Two patterns are especially relevant. In the first, case studies uncover evidence that different kinds of cases have divergent causal effects. That is to say, the qualitative evidence uncovers one or more variables that are causally and temporally prior to the treatment that seem to change the causal process and help determine the magnitude of the overall causal effect. This may arise when case studies reveal comparisons that pinpoint causal effects for certain cases; if the causal effects differ across cases, comparison of the cases may raise hypotheses about the reasons for causal diversity. Alternatively, tracing the process from the treatment to the outcome may provide evidence that a particular contextual or background variable influences the size of the causal effect.

In either case, these causally prior variables should not be added to the regression analysis as mere controls. After all, the case-study research has suggested that they systematically shape the causal connection between the treatment and the outcome – a different causal pattern from confounding, in which the other variable might cause the treatment and the outcome. Instead, the variable or variables of interest should be added to the regression model as interactions, in order to test for the causal pattern known as moderation (Baron and Kenny 1986). Interactions in regression raise a number of interpretive issues and minor complications regarding significance testing (Brambor *et al.* 2006). While an in-depth treatment of these well-known issues is beyond the scope of this text, it is worth noting that they can be resolved by a combination of simulating the causal effect of interest for each case and calculating standard errors using bootstrapping or randomization inference.

Finally, when case-study research uncovers a possible causal pathway, subsequent statistical work needs to analyze a model of causal mediation, i.e., a model in which treatment causes a mediator variable and then both of those variables may have a direct effect on the outcome. Path analysis estimates such models when there is an assumption that causal effects are constant across cases (Baron and Kenny 1986; Bollen 1989: 10–39). Under this assumption, scholars can estimate a regression of the mediator on treatment and any needed controls related to confounding in the treatment, as well as a second regression of the outcome on the mediator, treatment, the controls from the first regression, and any additional control variables necessary to eliminate endogeneity connected with the mediator. The total effect of the treatment on the outcome will be the coefficient on treatment in the second regression plus the effect of the math through the mediator, i.e., the product of the treatment coefficient in the first regression and the mediator coefficient in the second regression. Two quantities serve as important tests of the hypothesis that the mediator is part of the causal pathway: the magnitude of the path through the mediator, estimated by the product just described, and the proportion of the overall effect of treatment on the outcome that passes through the mediator (estimated as the ratio of the product to the total effect). If both of these quantities are significantly different from zero, then there is confirmatory evidence for the case-study hypothesis regarding causal pathways. More recently, Imai and collaborators have offered a reconceptualization and a set of estimators that adapt mediation analysis to the potential-outcomes framework and the expectation of heterogeneous causal effects (Imai *et al.* 2011); while these changes are essential, the underlying concepts remain essentially the same.

This chapter makes several arguments that will be central to the rest of the book. The most important is the discussion of the ways that case-study research can contribute to causal inference by exploring issues that are areas of relative weakness for regression-type research. While case studies may have many other roles, they can clearly contribute by validating or improving measurement, by testing or discovering hypotheses about causal pathways, and by searching for confounders. All three roles revolve around process-tracing modes of research. Such research can in practice be relatively unstructured; in contrast, this chapter has offered a number of concrete designs that can be adopted and adapted to maximize the contribution of case studies based on causal-process observations to multi-method causal inference. Yet one key element of these research designs has been left unspecified: how are scholars to select the cases that receive in-depth attention?

Notes

1 The reader may protest that this account unnecessarily makes the simple and obvious complex. In fact, the value of case studies for examining measurement may be obvious to most or all readers, but thinking about why case studies work this way remains important, and may help channel research efforts in useful directions.

2 It would be complicated to argue that Fourcade's work is an example of how case studies can improve measurement for causal inference. After all, the author argues that at least important components of the work are not about causation: "the expository logic in this chapter will be interpretive (trying to penetrate the categories that are relevant in each social system) and 'colligatory' rather than merely causal" (Fourcade 2009: 31). My sense is that this argument is intended to disavow readings of her analysis as demonstrating simple relationships between one variable and another, whereas the argument involves a situation produced by the conjunction of multiple reinforcing components of an overall societal system. If this is correct, then the analysis is consistent with the broad conception of causation motivating this volume, which involves a claim that things could have been otherwise had the background conditions been other than they were. Nevertheless, we need not insist on this point; regardless of whether any kind of causation is involved, Fourcade's book remains an excellent example of using in-depth case analysis to test and refine measurement.

4 Case Selection after Regression

Before a scholar can begin case-study research to test, refine, or interpret a regression analysis, a surprisingly complex prior challenge needs to be addressed: selecting cases for in-depth analysis from the comparatively large data set necessary for regression. Seawright and Gerring (2008) have proposed a set of systematic case-selection rules as a solution to this challenge. Yet the question remains, which of the several available methods should be used in a given project? Several scholars arguing in favor of deliberate case selection have focused on three of these alternatives: typical cases, deviant cases, and extreme cases on the dependent variable.[1] Others have argued for random sampling (Fearon and Laitin 2008: 764–66) or deliberate sampling intended to represent the full range of variation in the data (King *et al.* 1994: 139–46).

I argue that the existing advice is incomplete or misleading when the goal of case-study research is discovery. I develop this argument by showing that, across a wide range of goals, the alternatives with the best chances of facilitating discovery are either deviant-case selection or the rarely discussed alternative of selecting extreme cases on the main independent variable.[2] This argument is developed with reference to a variety of discovery-related goals: searching for sources of measurement error in the dependent or key independent variables; testing for or trying to discover an omitted variable, which may or may not be correlated with the independent variable of interest; exploring hypotheses about causal pathways; finding a case with a causal effect close to the population mean; and discovering substantive sources of causal heterogeneity.

Unlike much existing research on qualitative and case-study methods, this discussion is not driven by reference to examples of excellent research. In many other kinds of qualitative research practices, the analyst's judgment is a central ingredient in the application of the research tool; consequently, there is a great deal to learn from studying how judgment was employed in notably successful applications of the research tools in question. By contrast, systematic case selection is an algorithmic process: it takes a certain kind of information as an input, and then follows logical or mathematical rules to convert that input into a case. Because systematic case-selection rules reduce scholars' reliance on judgment, the statistical properties of case-selection algorithms are more important than notably successful examples of their application. For this reason, the discussion below instead relies on argumentation and statistical reasoning about case selection, rather than on prominent examples.

In practice, of course, scholars will not always rely solely on systematic case selection to design qualitative research, because considerations of data availability, the substantive prominence of cases, and other practical concerns must sometimes be balanced with selection of the case most likely to meet a given goal. Future research analyzing the balance between such considerations in practice and offering guidance to scholars for how to handle such competing priorities would be useful.

4.1   Case Selection Techniques: A Brief Overview

In making the argument that discovery is best facilitated through the selection of deviant or extreme-on-X cases, it is important to consider a broad and inclusive set of alternative case-selection rules. Inclusiveness, after all, forestalls the possible objection that the best alternatives were simply not considered. For this purpose, it is helpful that Seawright and Gerring (2008) provide a broad menu of formal rules for case selection in the wake of a regression analysis, combining ideas from qualitative methodology in the social sciences and from the statistical literature on regression diagnostics. Here, I will briefly introduce those techniques and provide the formulas or other steps necessary for implementation before continuing to the analysis of each decision rule's statistical properties with respect to the diverse set of research goals considered here. This section will also present a case-selection technique developed by Plumper *et al.* (2010), which is effectively a hybrid of extreme and most similar case-selection rules, as well as an algorithm discussed by Gerring (2007a) that is closely related to existing techniques. This will provide an inclusive, although not necessarily comprehensive, comparison set against which to demonstrate the virtues of selecting deviant and extreme-on-*X* cases. Before introducing these techniques, however, it is useful to discuss a set of research goals for which they might be used.

4.1.1   Major Goals of Case-Study Research

Researchers obviously have many goals for case-study analysis. It is impossible to give a comprehensive account of such goals, and some desirable goals such as elucidating causally relevant counterfactuals via case-study research (Glynn and Ichino 2015) are difficult to systematize given their early state of development in the literature on qualitative methods. For present purposes, it will suffice to consider a broad collection of common goals – some widely applicable in qualitative research and some more focused on case studies with a multi-method orientation. The argument below will show that deviant and extreme-on-*X* cases are best for searching for sources of measurement error (King *et al.* 1994: 152–83; Coppedge 1999; George and Bennett 2004: 220; Fearon and Laitin 2008; for applied examples of research employing case studies for measurement, see Bowman *et al.* 2005 and Kreuzer 2010), trying to identify omitted variables, which may or may not be correlated with the key independent variable (Collier *et al.* 2004; Fearon and Laitin 2008); testing hypotheses about causal paths (Collier, Brady, and Seawright 2004; George and Bennett 2004; Gerring 2004, 2007b); and discovering the substantive boundaries of the set of cases for which a particular causal relationship holds true (Collier and Mahoney 1996: 66–69; Bennett and Elman 2006a: 467–68). Two other goals, which are not focused toward discovery, will also be considered as an extension: tracing out a previously hypothesized causal process in a case where the effect of the main cause is as typical as possible (Lieberman 2005: 444–45; Bennett and Elman 2006a: 473–74); and the intellectually dubious but widely discussed objective of reestimating the overall relationship between the independent and dependent variables (Lijphart 1971, 1975; Ragin 1987, 2000; Plumper, Troeger, and Neumayer 2010).

For each of these goals, this section will introduce a statistical model representing a simplification of the situation facing a researcher, usually involving a regression with a specified flaw. I also use a simple rule for deciding whether a case was the right one to choose for a given goal. I assume, along with several qualitative methodologists, that researchers are most likely to detect features of a case that are unusual in comparison with the relevant universe of cases (Collier and Mahoney 1996: 72–75; Ragin 2004: 128–30; Flyvbjerg 2006: 224–28). For example, in a cross-national regression where overall levels of economic inequality are an important omitted variable, it would be relatively easy to notice that variable in case studies of countries such as Brazil, South Africa, or Namibia (among the most unequal societies), or of countries such as Denmark, Sweden, or the Czech Republic (among the least unequal societies). By contrast, it may be much harder to realize the importance of inequality through in-depth study of countries such as Madagascar, Turkey, or Mexico, which fall somewhere in the middle of the global distribution of inequality.[3] As a rough operationalization of this hypothesis that each case study is most likely to succeed if the quantity to be tested or discovered has an extreme value, I will in the analysis code a case selection as a success if it is at least two standard deviations away from its population mean.[4]

We must also model the issues that case-study research is intended to discover. When considering measurement error in either the dependent or the independent variable, we will adopt a standard econometric errors-in-variables framework (Cameron and Trivedi 2005: 899–920), in which the observed value of the outcome variable is the sum of the variable's correct value for the case and a random measurement error component. In other words, using Y^* to denote the error-laden observed version of the true, correctly measured variable, Y:

$$Y_i^* = Y_i + \delta_{Y,i}$$

Here, $\delta_{Y,i}$ is the measurement error and is assumed to be independent from all other quantities in the model. An exactly parallel specification is adopted for measurement error in the main explanatory variable.

For omitted variable situations, the correct regression model includes an unknown variable or variables, U_i, such that:

$$Y_i = \beta_x X_i + \beta_z Z_i + \beta_u U_i + \epsilon_i$$

However, the scholar is initially unaware of the identity of the U variable, and so estimates a worse regression, with asterisks added to denote quantities that may be affected by the omission of U:

$$Y_i = \beta_x^* X_i + \beta_z^* Z_i + \epsilon_i^*$$

Here, by algebraic substitution, $\epsilon_i^* = (\beta_x - \beta_x^*)X_i + (\beta_z - \beta_z^*)Z_i + \beta_u U_i + \epsilon_i$. Of particular note here is the appearance of U in the expression. Because successful regression-based inference requires the error term to be unrelated to the included explanatory variables, whenever U is related to X there will be bias in causal inferences connected with X.[5] Because such bias is a very common possibility, discovering U and incorporating it appropriately into the model is essentially a precondition for learning about the causal connection between X and Y (for further discussion, see Morgan and Winship 2007: 59–86).

When the goal of interest is discovering or testing a hypothesis about a variable on the causal path from the main explanatory variable to the outcome variable, the analysis below will adopt a potential-outcomes mediation model (Imai, Keele, and Tingley 2010), generalized along the lines of Freedman's response schedules concept (2009: 94–102) to allow for continuous treatment variables. In this setup, the pathway variable W_i takes on value $f_{W,i}(t)$ when the causal variable $X_i = t$. The function $f_{W,i}$ is case-specific and need not be linear, monotonic, etc. This function provides a full counterfactual description of what would have happened to the value of W in case i if all else were held constant other than the value of X; any desired causal effect can be calculated for this case by taking the differences among values of this function. Needless to say, this function is usually unknown and is at best difficult to estimate. A second function of the same general kind relates W and X with the outcome variable, Y: $g_{Y,i}(w,t)$, which characterizes the outcome that would happen in case i if X were set to t and W were set to w. The combination of these two functions specifies the causal path of interest.

The researcher who wants to discover or test hypotheses about W as a step between X and Y needs to select cases where W_i is far from that variable's mean across the population. Because W is hypothesized to be caused by X and to be a cause of Y, selection techniques that focus on either variable may prove to be helpful.

The last two goals to be considered also make use of the potential-outcomes framework for thinking about causation. Here, attention focuses solely on the effect of the main independent variable, X, on the main outcome variable, Y. If X, conceptualized as a metaphorical or literal experimental treatment, is present for case i, then the value of the outcome variable that we observe for that case is $Y_{i,t}$; if all is the same for the case other than that X is absent, then we instead observe $Y_{i,c}$. The effect of X on Y for case i is $Y_{i,t} - Y_{i,c}$, a quantity that defines a potentially case-specific causal effect. While this case-specific effect normally cannot be directly observed or easily estimated, it is nonetheless well-defined and can be the focus of attention in selecting cases.

In particular, consider a scholar who is interested in tracing the causal process connecting X and Y in a case that has as typical a causal effect as possible. It is natural to represent that goal as entailing the selection of a case for which $Y_{i,t} - Y_{i,c}$ is as close as possible to the population average, $\bar{Y}_t - \bar{Y}_c$.

Case-study researchers are sometimes interested in discovering the substantive reasons for causal heterogeneity. We will represent this goal as involving a situation in which the size of the causal effect depends on an unknown variable, P. For cases with a large and positive value of P, $Y_{i,t} - Y_{i,c}$ tends to also be large and positive; when P is negative, the effect tends to be small. Thus, there is a positive correlation between P and the causal effect of interest. Case selection will be regarded as successfully facilitating the goal of discovering the causes of heterogeneity when the cases chosen have a value of P_i that is at least two standard deviations from its mean.

Finally, when the goal is to reestimate the overall relationship between X and Y based on comparisons across the selected case studies, things are kept as simple as possible. For a paired comparison between cases 1 and 2, which is the design analyzed throughout, the result of the reestimate is taken to be:

$$\frac{Y_2 - Y_1}{X_2 - X_1}$$

This is simply the slope of the line segment connecting the two points. The next section will use these simplified models of case-study research goals to argue that deviant and extreme-on-the-independent-variable procedures are usually the best ways to choose cases. First, however, it is essential to review the case-selection techniques in question.

4.1.2   Techniques for Choosing Cases

Past discussions of case selection in the social sciences have rarely offered detailed arguments connecting techniques with the kinds of goals discussed above. Lieberman (2005), for example, connects two case-selection practices with discovering causal pathways, identifying omitted variables, and improving measurement – but does not argue that either technique is connected with any of these goals in particular.

Seawright and Gerring (2008) characterize techniques in broad terms as exploratory or confirmatory, and only sometimes connect specific techniques with particular goals. Other authors, including King *et al.* (1994) and Fearon and Laitin (2008), justify their case-selection advice as a way of avoiding specific threats such as selection or confirmation bias. Thus for the most part the state of the debate is one in which a large number of techniques exist, but only fragmentary arguments have been made about the goals that can be achieved by each.

To improve this situation, a first necessary step is to offer a specific definition of each case-selection technique. The stylized scenario to be considered here is one in which, before selecting cases, a scholar has carried out a regression analysis in which an outcome of interest, Y, is predicted by a hypothesized cause, X, and generally also a set of control variables, $\mathbb{Z}$.[6] This regression is taken to represent the available knowledge about the relationship in question.[7] In setting up these regressions, problems of descriptive or causal inference are not fatal. After all, the discussion here presumes that the goal of the case-study research is discovery; finding such problems when they exist is thus an objective of the research rather than an obstacle to it. On the other hand, a subpar regression that does not incorporate the best current descriptive and causal knowledge is likely to produce case studies that rediscover existing knowledge. Thus, it is important to make the regression starting point as good as possible.

While slope estimates are typically the focus of attention in applied regression analysis, other regression-related quantities matter more for case selection. "Fitted values," typically written as $\hat{Y}$, reflect the best guess for the score on the dependent variable for each case, if for some reason we did not have those scores and only had access to the regression results and the information in X and $\mathbb{Z}$. The regression residuals, represented in vector form as e, are the difference between the actual values of Y and the fitted values; these represent the component of the outcome that the regression cannot successfully predict. Cook's distance scores (Cook and Weisberg 1982) measure the extent to which the overall regression results would change if that one case were deleted

Table 4.1 Techniques for Choosing Cases.

Selection Rule	Implementation
Random	Select case(s) randomly with equal probability from the entire data set.
Typical	Select case(s) to minimize $|Y_i - \hat{Y}_i|$.
Deviant	Select case(s) to maximize $|Y_i - \hat{Y}_i|$.
Influential	Select case(s) to maximize the DFBETA connected with X_i.
Extreme X	Select case(s) to maximize $|X_i - \bar{X}_i|$.
Extreme Y	Select case(s) to maximize $|Y_i - \bar{Y}_i|$.
Most Similar	Select paired case(s) that such that $X_{i,1}$ is "high" and $X_{i,2}$ is "low" while minimizing the overall difference between $\mathbb{Z}_{i,1}$ and $\mathbb{Z}_{i,2}$.
Most Different	Select paired case(s) that minimize $|X_{i,1} - X_{i,2}|$ while maximizing the overall difference between $\mathbb{Z}_{i,1}$ and $\mathbb{Z}_{i,2}$.
Contrast	Select paired case(s) that maximize $|X_{i,1} - X_{i,2}|$ while minimizing the overall difference between $\mathbb{Z}_{i,1}$ and $\mathbb{Z}_{i,2}$.
Pathway	Select case(s) for which $|Y_i - \hat{Y}_i|$ is made as much smaller as possible by including X in the regression.

from the analysis. A similar score, called the DFBETA (Belsley *et al.* 1980: 13), indicates the extent to which a single, selected coefficient would change if one given case were deleted from the analysis.

The case-selection techniques discussed in this paper are summarized in Table 4.1 using the notation just mentioned. It is beyond the scope of this analysis to offer a detailed introduction to these techniques; however, a brief review may be helpful. Random case selection involves choosing cases with equal probability from the entire data set (Fearon and Laitin 2008).

Typical cases are those that fit the regression well. Such cases can be identified by selecting those for which the regression's fitted value is as close as possible to the observed value of the dependent variable. Deviant cases, of course, are just the opposite, and can be found by choosing cases for which the fitted value is as far as possible from the observed dependent variable. Extreme cases can be found either on the dependent variable or on the key independent variable of interest;

these are simply cases that are as far as possible from the mean on that variable.

Past discussions of influential cases (Seawright and Gerring 2008) focus on those for which Cook's distance is especially large. Such cases are influential in the obvious sense that they have an unusually large influence on the regression analysis. However, Cook's distance will sometimes highlight cases that mostly affect coefficients for control variables rather than the coefficients for the independent variable of central causal interest. A more targeted version of influential-case selection uses the DFBETA for the coefficient connected with the most important independent variable.

Three selection rules rely on matching methods (Rubin 2006). Most similar cases involve finding pairs of cases for which the main independent variable differs – i.e., is above some specified threshold for one case and below it for the other – but for which the control variables in $\mathbb{Z}$ are as similar as possible. Most different cases are pairs in which difference on the independent variable is minimized but difference on the $\mathbb{Z}$ variables is maximized. Contrast cases involve a combination of most similar cases and extreme cases on the main independent variable: the pair of cases is selected to maximize the difference between them on X while minimizing the difference on the $\mathbb{Z}$ variables.

Finally, Gerring (2007a) discusses a pathway case approach, in which the analyst chooses those cases for which the regression residual is most reduced in magnitude by the inclusion of the main independent variable of causal interest, in comparison with the residual from a regression model that is identical other than in omitting that main independent variable.

Each of the techniques introduced above has both scholarly advocates and sources of intuitive appeal. Nonetheless, the analysis below will show that deviant cases and extreme cases on the independent variable offer the best chance of making discoveries across a wide range of case-study goals. Specifying those goals is the next necessary step in the argument.

4.2   Why Deviant and Extreme-on-the-Independent-Variable Cases Are Usually Best

How should scholars select cases to maximize the probability of case-study success? This section provides statistical guidance. Two techniques mostly dominate the others: selection of cases that are deviant or that are extreme on the main independent variable perform better than the other approaches introduced above across a variety of scenarios. Which of these two options is best depends on the particular objectives of the study. Furthermore, typical-case selection is only useful for the goal of tracing causal processes in a case that has a causal effect as close to the population average as possible; for case studies designed to facilitate theoretical discovery, typical cases are generally counterproductive.

Most case-selection rules involve maximizing the absolute value of some quantity – i.e., picking the cases for which some combination of variables is far from zero. Thus at various points in the argument below, understanding the application of a given case-selection rule to a particular goal involves knowing what it means to maximize the absolute value of a sum of random variables, of the form $s_i = |a_{1,i} + a_{2,i}|$, or possibly with even more elements in the sum. It will be important to know, with case-selection rules that choose cases with the highest value of s_i, what will tend to be true of the values of the a_i variables for selected cases. To simplify what is a surprisingly complex topic, cases for which the absolute value of a sum of independent variables is extreme are also relatively likely to have extreme scores on the variables that make up the sum. If some variables in the sum have a higher variance than others, the high-variance variables are especially likely to take on extreme values when the absolute sum is very large, but the low-variance variables also have an above-chance tendency to be extreme. Finally, the probability that any one variable will take on an extreme value in cases where the absolute value of the sum is extreme declines in the number of variables included in the sum. These patterns will be critically important in understanding the properties of case-selection rules.[8]

4.2.1   Deviant Cases

The received wisdom regarding case selection is that deviant cases are good for finding omitted variables. This claim is problematic, but deviant cases can be more broadly useful. This case-selection rule also has value as a way of finding sources of measurement error in the dependent variable; in a regression model, such measurement problems are often pushed into the error term, and therefore can be discovered via close study of cases with extreme estimated values on that error term.

Furthermore, and perhaps a bit surprisingly, deviant cases can be a useful way to discover new information about causal pathways connecting the main independent with the main dependent variable. This point will be developed formally below, but intuitively the reason is that cases may vary in terms of the size of the causal effect of X on Y. Cases with unusually large effects will often also have unusually extreme values of variables along the causal pathway. Because such cases are causally unusual, they will tend to have large error terms, as well. For the same reason, deviant cases are a useful way of discovering unknown sources of causal heterogeneity.

Let us begin by analyzing the traditional strength of deviant-case selection: identifying possibly relevant omitted variables. Deviant-case selection, of course, maximizes the absolute value of the estimated error term from a regression, i.e., the residual. This means that deviant-case selection will increase the probability of finding a relevant omitted variable when the omitted variable is strongly related to the residual. The residual and the omitted variables will be weakly related, and therefore deviant-case selection will fail, in either of two scenarios. First, deviant-case selection fails when the omitted variable has little or no relationship to Y_i and is thus not an important confounder. Alternatively, deviant-case selection can fail if the omitted variable can be too powerfully predicted by X_i; thus, unfortunately, this technique will tend to fail if the confounder is strongly related to the main causal variable. This second scenario forces the conclusion that deviant-case selection is limited in its ability to help find the most important confounders. It will work for moderate scenarios in which the omitted variable is quite causally relevant for explaining Y_i but not too closely related to X_i.

Turning now to less widely discussed patterns, deviant-case selection can also help scholars discover sources of measurement error in the dependent variable. Consider the relationship between the regression residual – whose absolute value is, of course, maximized in deviant-case selection – and measurement error in Y. When there are a large number of cases, the estimated residual from a regression predicting Y converges to the measurement error plus the residual from the regression using Y when measured without error. Choosing that residual to be as far from zero as possible will thus increase the probability of choosing cases with large amounts of measurement error (as well as cases with large residuals in a version of the regression without measurement error, an unwanted side effect). For this reason, deviant-case selection can help discover sources of measurement error in the outcome variable.[9]

A further surprising result is that deviant-case selection has value for the goal of choosing cases with extreme values on a pathway variable. When treatment assignment is independent of the potential values of Y, conditional on any included control variables, then the residual of a regression of Y on X will in part measure the extent to which a given case has a causal effect of X_i on Y_i that departs from the population average (Morgan and Winship 2007: 135). Given the pathway setup introduced above, there are three ways this can arise. First, X_i may have an unusual effect on the causal pathway variable for this case, which in turn has about the usual effect on Y_i. Second, the causal pathway variable may have an unusual effect on Y_i for this case. Third, X_i may, in this instance, have an unusual direct effect on Y_i, net of the causal pathway of interest. The second and third of these patterns will be unhelpful in terms of selecting cases with unusual values of the causal pathway variable; the first, however, will tend to help. Thus, deviant-case selection can help in finding out about unknown or incompletely understood causal pathways.

The same basic logic also allows deviant-case selection to uncover evidence of unknown sources of causal heterogeneity. Recall that the source of heterogeneity is by definition correlated with the magnitude of the main causal effect. As argued in the last paragraph, cases for which the effect of X_i on Y_i is quite different from the population average also tend to have regression residuals that are large in absolute value. Hence, selecting based on the regression residual has a reasonable chance of turning up cases for which P_i is far from its mean, and therefore facilitating case-study discovery of that source of causal heterogeneity.

However, there are some goals for which deviant-case selection is simply not helpful. Consider first the goal of discovering sources of measurement error in X. Usually, scholars assume that measurement error is independent of systematic variables and is not terribly large in variance. Under those assumptions, deviant-case selection is only marginally useful in finding sources of measurement error in X; the only contribution comes because a portion of that measurement error will end up in the residual. However, the value is limited because only part of the measurement error's variance is combined with the whole variance of the true residual, resulting in indirect and watered down case selection.

For some research goals, deviant-case selection is outright harmful. Suppose that the goal is to find a case where the effect of X on Y is close to the population average. As discussed earlier, deviant-case selection increases the probability of selecting cases with extremely atypical causal effects, and therefore works *against* this goal.

The second goal for which deviant-case selection is counterproductive involves replicating the overall slope estimate. Intuitively, a bivariate slope estimate based on a pair of cases can be described as involving the following fraction:

$$\frac{(\text{True slope} * \text{Difference on } X) + \text{Difference on Error Terms}}{\text{Difference on } X} \quad (4.1)$$

A slope reestimate will work well if the difference between the selected cases in the error term is small relative to the difference on X. Deviant-case selection picks cases to maximize the absolute value of the error terms for both cases. If the two cases have error terms with the same sign, this will not distort slope estimates much. However, about half the time the two cases will have opposite signs, which in combination with large absolute magnitudes means that slope reestimates will be badly off track. Hence, deviant-case selection is not a reasonable approach to reestimating the overall slope.

To summarize, deviant cases are valuable for several kinds of discovery: learning about sources of measurement error in the outcome, discovering information about the causal pathway connecting X and Y, and finding out about sources of causal heterogeneity. The technique also has some limited value for discovering confounders. The value of this case-selection rule has been underestimated and misunderstood in the literature to date, which has mostly emphasized its potential contribution in terms of omitted variables.

4.2.2   Extreme Cases

There are two variants of the extreme-cases strategy: extreme cases on the independent variable, X, and the more frequently discussed extreme cases on Y. This section argues that choosing cases with extreme values of X_i is a valuable and underrated strategy, and is more broadly applicable than selecting cases with extreme values of the dependent variable, Y_i. Indeed, I will argue that, for goals where extreme cases on Y can be helpful, deviant cases are often superior.

Consider first the project of discovering sources of measurement error; here, success requires selecting cases in which the variable of emphasis (X or Y) is especially badly measured. Choosing cases as far as possible from the mean on X^* (i.e., the X variable measured with error) is by definition the same as maximizing the combination of the true value of X and the measurement error. Hence, as long as the measurement error is not negatively correlated with the true value, extreme-case selection on X increases a scholar's chances of finding cases with a good deal of measurement error.

Obviously, this argument applies equally to the task of finding measurement error on Y using extreme-case selection on the outcome variable. However, and perhaps somewhat surprisingly, deviant-case selection will typically outperform extreme-case selection on the dependent variable for the task of finding measurement error on that variable. This is because the regression filters out some of the true variance on Y, leaving a residual whose variance is more heavily composed of measurement error than the original variable.

When the goal of case-study research is to discover omitted variables, extreme-case selection on the dependent variable can have real value. Y_i can be represented as a combination of three components: the part of Y_i that can be systematically predicted within the regression, the unexplainable part of Y_i that has nothing to do with the omitted variable in question; and the part of Y_i that cannot be predicted within the regression but can be predicted by the omitted variable. If the omitted variable is independent of the included variables, the first two of these components are completely irrelevant, but the third component represents the whole effect of the omitted variable. On the other hand, if the omitted variable is related to X_i or some other included variable, then the first component will be contaminated by the omitted variable – and thus will also contribute to finding the omitted variable. Thus, extreme-case selection on Y works well when the stakes are highest.

Extreme-case selection on X is also a good idea when the stakes are highest. If the omitted variables are not confounders, i.e., are independent of the included variables, then extreme cases on X should be altogether unhelpful. After all, X by assumption contains no information about the omitted variables. Obviously, when the omitted variable is correlated with X_i, the success rate of an extreme-case selection rule on X will depend directly on the strength of the correlation. Since omitted variables matter most when they are strong confounders – and therefore substantially related to X – this technique should have an advantage when it matters most.

In contexts where the emphasis in the case-study research is on discovering or demonstrating the existence of a pathway variable causally connecting X and Y by selecting cases with extreme values on that pathway variable, extreme-case selection on X can be a very strong approach. When the average effect of X on the pathway variable is large, the average case where X takes on an unusual value will obviously have an unusual value for the pathway variable W. Hence, when the key independent variable is an important cause of the outcome and the pathway of interest captures a large share of the overall effect, extreme-case selection on X is a good idea.

Extreme-case selection on Y will also work well when the pathway variable, W, explains much or most of the variation in the outcome – because in these contexts, extreme cases on Y are likely to be cases where W is high, as well. Deciding whether extreme-case selection on the dependent variable is ever the best approach requires some analytic thought. Suppose that Y takes on an extreme value because W also takes on an extreme value. This can happen in one of two ways. First, W may take on an extreme value because its cause, X, also takes on an extreme value. In this case, selection on X should be more or less as useful as selection on Y. Second, W may take on an extreme value even though X does not, because of some kind of unobserved uniqueness in the case in question. If this is so, then deviant-case selection is likely to pick up the case in question. Either way, whenever extreme-case selection on Y is useful for finding pathway variables, it is to be expected that either selection on X or deviant-case selection would be about as good.

When scholars wish to discover unknown sources of causal heterogeneity, extreme cases are less useful than deviant cases. In the first place, extreme cases on the independent variable are altogether unhelpful here. After all, the *value* of X_i should generally tell us little about the *causal effect* of X_i on Y_i, and in fact the two quantities are usually assumed to be independent.

Extreme cases on Y are more relevant, but still not as good as deviant cases. Intuitively, when the effect of X_i for a given case is unusually large or small, and when X_i takes on an unusual value, mathematically Y_i also has to take on an unusual value. Unfortunately, Y_i can also take on an unusual value even when the causal effect for the case is perfectly average – if X_i also takes on a sufficiently unusual value. Deviant-case selection deals with this possibility because the residual for case i accounts for the value of X in that case. Thus, deviant-case selection captures the good of extreme cases on Y for this goal while also eliminating one scenario in which the latter procedure fails.

For the goal of reestimating the overall slope between Y and X, extreme-case selection on X is once again a useful approach. Maximizing the difference between selected cases on X_i increases the two systematic components of the slope ratio in Equation 4.1 as much as possible while leaving the error component unaffected, thereby tending to get the right answer. Maximizing the difference between selected cases on Y_i will also be productive, in that it tends to maximize the systematic component of the numerator, and indirectly increases the size of the denominator to the extent that X and Y are correlated. However, this approach will underperform in comparison with extreme-case sampling on X, because maximizing the difference between selected cases on Y_i also tends to maximize the difference between the selected cases on their error terms.

When the research requires finding a case with a causal effect close to the population average effect, neither variety of extreme-case selection is useful. Under the common assumption that values of X_i are independent of treatment effect sizes, extreme values of X_i are exactly as likely to have approximately average causal effects as any other case. On the other hand, cases with extreme values of Y_i are by definition cases that have an extreme value of at least one potential outcome, and therefore are more likely to be cases with extreme causal effects than cases with average effects.

Overall, extreme-case selection on X is a powerful, underappreciated approach to choosing cases for in-depth analysis. This is a strong approach for discovering measurement error, examining causal pathways, and reestimating overall slopes, and it can also be useful in some omitted-variable scenarios. Case-study scholars should seriously consider adding this approach to their applied repertoire.

4.2.3   Random Sampling

The argument so far has shown that deviant and extreme-on-X selection rules can help achieve most of the goals under analysis here; extreme cases on Y have some value but should be less central. The task for the remainder of this section is to much more briefly argue that the remaining set of case-selection rules are far less useful.

To begin with, it should be clear that random sampling is never a powerful option for any of the goals considered in this analysis. The reason random sampling is a bad way to choose cases for case-study research is in fact the same as the reason it is a good way to draw survey samples: the law of large numbers. That law tells us that, on average, random sampling will select cases from a given category in proportion with that category's share of the overall population. But because the cases that constitute success for discovery-oriented case-study analysis are by definition the most unusual cases, it will be unusual for random sampling to produce successful case studies.

The main methodological justification for random sampling is that it prevents scholars from selecting cases, because those cases are likely to fit the substantive argument of interest (Fearon and Laitin 2008). Yet in fact any systematic case-selection algorithm has this same virtue, and thus there is really no viable justification for randomly selecting case studies.

4.2.4   Typical Cases

Choosing typical cases is also almost always a bad idea. The reasoning is simple: typical cases are by definition the exact opposite of deviant cases. Whatever deviant-case selection tends to maximize, typical-case selection tends to minimize. As a consequence, the pattern of strengths and weaknesses for typical cases is more or less a mirror image of those for deviant cases. Specifically, typical-case selection tends to *reduce* scholars' probability of making discoveries about sources of measurement error, omitted and confounding variables, pathway variables, and unknown sources of causal heterogeneity. However, it is helpful for the replication-oriented goals of studying a case in which the causal effect is as close to the population average as possible and reestimating a regression slope.

Case-study methodologists have long shared an intuition that typical-case selection should be a good idea. After all, these are the cases that best fit the overall relationships among variables. Yet this is exactly why typical-case selection is ineffective when the goal is to discover more about the relationship in question than what can be captured by regression. Simply put, it is hard to learn about problems with a regression by looking at the cases that fit well in that regression.

4.2.5   Influential Cases

Influential-cases strategies to date involve selecting cases based on their Cook's distance scores, which effectively combine the deviant-case criterion with attention to high-leverage cases. For a bivariate regression of Y on X, cases have high leverage if and only if they have unusually high or low values of X_i relative to the rest of the sample; hence, in this simple context, influential-case selection is a straightforward combination of deviant-case selection, discussed above, and selection of cases with extreme values on X_i. Such a combination may be helpful for discovering pathway variables, because it will tend to push the pathway variable toward extreme values from both directions – i.e., cases with high Cook's distance scores will tend to have unusual values of both X_i and Y_i, and therefore are likely to have unusual values of W_i.

The issue becomes more complex when the regression of interest is multivariate. In such situations, leverage scores reflect a complex weighted mixture of cases' degree of extremeness on X_i and on the various control variables included in the model. This feature waters down the focus and makes influential-case selection less appropriate for the various goals considered in this paper. Hence, for case selection in the context of multivariate models, the Cook's distance influential-cases strategy is likely to be suboptimal. The alternative influential-cases strategy of selecting for high values of DFBETA for the X coefficient recreates the relevant virtues of the bivariate Cook's distance statistic for models with control variables, and thus should be a fairly effective way of finding pathway variables.

4.2.6   Most Similar, Most Different, and Contrast Cases

The most similar cases-selection rule, using matching techniques to quantify similarity, is not an advisable approach to case selection for any of the case-study goals considered in this book. Matching chooses cases that are different on X_i but as similar as possible on a set of conditioning variables $\mathbb{Z}_j$. Yet that set of conditioning variables need not have a connection with the quantities of central interest for case-study goals.

Consider measurement error. By standard assumption, $\mathbb{Z}_i$ is independent of error in either X_i or Y_i. Hence, a most similar cases-selection rule for measurement error on X has traction only to the extent that the treatment and control cases selected by the rule reflect extreme scores on an underlying continuous variable X_i; the attention to $\mathbb{Z}_i$ is wasted. When there is measurement error on Y, both X and $\mathbb{Z}$ are by the usual assumptions irrelevant, so most similar cases are useless. For omitted variables, the problem is the same: $\mathbb{Z}$ is usually assumed to be independent of the omitted variable and therefore uninformative. Because causal pathways between X and Y are usually intended to be insulated from other causal factors, any unknown pathway variable should also be independent of $\mathbb{Z}$; once again, matching should be unhelpful. Most similar case selection may help reestimate the overall slope, given that it assures at least some difference between the selected cases on X_i, and may reduce the difference on error terms to the extent that the variables in $\mathbb{Z}$ are selected skillfully; however, in practice, maximizing the difference between cases on X_i can outperform the most similar case design. Finally, confounding variables are generally assumed to be unconnected with the magnitude of the causal effect for the case, so choosing most similar cases does nothing to help with the tasks of finding cases with causal effects close to the population average or discovering sources of causal heterogeneity.

This widely discussed case-selection strategy, like typical cases, is much less useful than its prevalence in the literature and in practice would suggest. For both case-selection techniques, the problem seems to be an insufficiently reflective imitation of regression-type causal inferential practices. In this case, the argument seems to be that control variables may solve some kinds of problems in regression, so for that reason they are used in case selection for qualitative research. Yet in fact case-study methods do not work by a logic of estimating conditional effects, and so control variables do not perform in the same way as in regression. It seems plausible that they do not in fact help at all; if they do, some new and careful argument to that end is needed.

Most case-study methodologists warn against most different case selection, and a simple argument suffices to all but rule them out. As with most similar cases, most different case selection depends almost entirely on the specification of the $\mathbb{Z}$ variables, which typically have little relationship with the quantities of interest in the scenarios considered here. Hence, there is little to be gained by selecting the least matched cases.

Finally, the contrast cases approach involves selecting cases that maximize a combination of the criteria used in two other sampling rules: extreme-cases-on-X and most similar cases. The properties of this approach are thus a mix of the two. For most goals, this makes the contrast-cases sampling rule a degraded version of the extreme-cases-on-X design, because the most similar cases-sampling rule rarely adds much to the process, and attention to matching therefore coarsens the quality of the selected cases. However, this may be a very good approach for reestimating the overall slope between X and Y, because it subtracts out confounders that may matter for such a task, and tends to maximize the variance in X.

4.2.7   Pathway Cases

One last case-selection rule deserves a brief discussion: the pathway-case selection rule discussed by Gerring (2007a), which, as a newer case-selection procedure, has not been widely discussed. Choosing pathway cases involves choosing the cases whose residuals are most reduced in magnitude by including X in the regression, in comparison with an otherwise identical model excluding X. In the special case that X has mean 0 and has no information about[10] the pathway variable, this case-selection rule simplifies to the extreme-cases-on-X strategy. When X is related to the pathway variable, this rule modifies extreme-cases-on-X selection by adding a kind of covariance adjustment based on the relationships among X, any included control variables, and Y. This covariance adjustment involves quantities that do not appear in any of the formulas connected with the goals of case-study research considered here, and thus may involve attention to an undesired quantity. On the other hand, the adjustment may sometimes reduce the variance of some irrelevant quantities in the selection formula. While the trade-off between these two considerations will depend on the parameters of the situation of interest, the pathway-case rule will usually perform about the same as extreme-case selection on X.

4.2.8   Conclusions

This section has argued that case selection should usually focus either on extreme cases on the independent variable or on deviant cases. These two case-selection procedures are sensitive to the kinds of discoveries that case-study researchers are most likely to pursue in multi-method contexts: discoveries about sources of measurement error, variables that constitute causal pathways from the independent to the dependent variable, sources of causal heterogeneity, and confounding variables. In particular, an extreme-cases selection rule on X is valuable for identifying omitted variables, identifying sources of measurement error on the X variable, discovering pathway variables or testing claims about such variables, and reestimating the overall slope. Deviant-case selection is useful for finding pathway variables, exploring sources of causal heterogeneity, and discovering reasons for measurement error on the Y variable.

In contrast, some popular case-selection rules are much less useful for these goals. Case-selection strategies that pay attention to control variables, such as most similar, most different, contrast, and pathway cases, are not usually optimal. Whereas control variables can be essential for some quantitative approaches to causal inference, they offer little help in dealing with measurement quality, discovering omitted variables, finding potential causal pathways, and achieving other central case-study goals.

Finally, the popular strategy of typical-case selection is not helpful as a way of discovering new things about cases, and indeed works well only for finding cases whose causal effects closely mirror the average for the population as a whole. Indeed, even this goal deserves further thought. Such cases will – by construction – be those where estimates from cross-case inferential techniques such as regression are most accurate. At the same time, they are cases that are least likely, for reasons discussed above, to produce new discoveries about causation or measurement. What, then, is the value of such case studies? The issue deserves clarification if a defense of the common practice of choosing typical cases is to be mounted.

4.3   The Fit Between Techniques and Goals: Simulations

Of course, the results above involve quite simple stylized scenarios for each potential research goal, and some analysis of the sensitivity of the results is worthwhile. For example, the relationship between Y and X is represented as bivariate, with no control variables entered into the analysis. In general, adding control variables changes some details of the results above but not the overall patterns; simulations demonstrating this claim are available from the author upon request. This section will focus on limiting conditions noted in the analysis above for techniques' value in finding omitted and pathway variables.

For each scenario, real data are randomly modified to capture the scenario of interest. Then case selection is carried out, and success or failure in terms of facilitating the designated goal for case-study research is recorded. This process is repeated a large number of times, generating Monte Carlo results regarding the propensity for success of each case-selection rule with respect to a given goal. Full details about the simulations, as well as replication code, are available from the author upon request.

The simulation study analyzes a data set focused on Latin American presidential elections, including every such election between 1980 and 2002, for a total of 84 elections, of which 19 are omitted from the analysis due to missing data. The dependent variable is the first difference in the vote share of the incumbent president's party in the election; independent variables are the largest opposition party's vote share in the prior election, a dummy variable indicating whether that largest opposition party has fielded a presidential candidate in the new election, the average inflation rate over the presidential term, the average growth rate over that term, and the country's per capita GDP during the year of the current election. All vote shares are transformed by the logit function, such that they range in theory from negative infinity to positive infinity; otherwise, the analysis is a standard OLS regression.[11]

First, in the discussion above of omitted variables, it emerged that the desirability of various techniques depends on the strength of the omitted variable's relationship to the main explanatory variable and to the outcome. Deviant-case selection may work when the confounder is relatively weakly related to X but strongly related to Y, while the value of extreme-case selection on either the cause or the outcome quite obviously depends on the strength of the relationship between the confounder and the variable used for selection. It remains unclear, however, how these techniques and others perform across the range of possible strengths of confounding.

To explore this issue, the first set of simulations below generates artificial confounders with varying degrees of statistical connection to the X and Y variables. Specifically, the confounder is generated by a linear combination of the observed value of X – assigned a weight strictly between zero and one – and a normal variable with mean and standard deviation equal to that of X – assigned a weight that is one minus the weight for the observed value of X. Thus, as the X weight approaches 1, the confounder and X become increasingly related.

A similar process is carried out to simulate new values of Y. Specifically, values are generated by, first, regressing Y on X and a set of control variables. The fitted value of Y from that regression is then added to a linear combination of the residual from that regression and the confounder – with a weight mixing the two quantities as above. As the Y weight approaches 1, the variance in Y that is unrelated to the observed variables becomes increasingly related to the confounder, and therefore the confounder becomes increasingly strong.

The results, shown in Figure 4.1, suggest that the undesirable regression adjustment involved in deviant cases – which removes any component of the confounding variable that is correlated with X or any other included variable – destroys the value of the technique in the vast majority of situations. In fact, the simulations find that deviant cases are only best for extremely weak confounders; for situations in which the X and Y weights are both below 0.1, which are not displayed here, deviant cases are best. However, discovering such weak confounders is of little practical inferential value.

Instead, important confounders are most likely to be discovered with extreme cases on Y and especially on X. There is an asymmetry between the two selection techniques because the simulation assumes that Y has multiple causes and that the confounder is not equally related to all of them. Under this assumption, extreme cases on X emerge as clearly superior for finding the strongest and most important confounders. This result will degrade if the confounder is the main or – at the limit – only true cause of Y, such that it necessarily has a confounding role for every control variable in the regression as well as X. In this scenario,

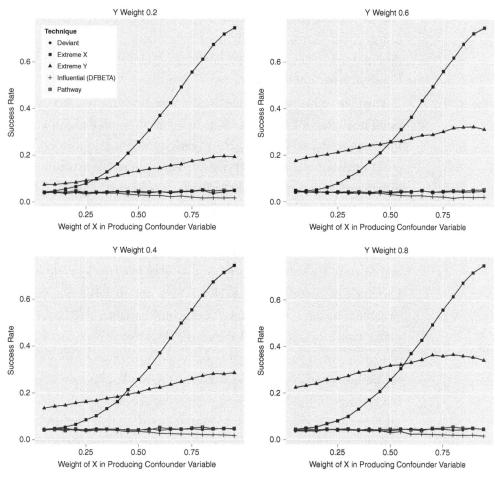

Figure 4.1   Confounder.

extreme cases on X and on Y will be equally valuable for finding the most important confounders, and extreme cases on Y will win out for confounders of moderate importance. More generally, both flavors of extreme-case selection have value here, but extreme cases on X are the most sensitive to particularly powerful confounders.

Second, the analysis of pathway variables reveals a similar scenario, in which the relative value of various techniques depends on the strength of the pathway variable's connections to both X and Y. To capture this situation, a pathway variable is simulated as a linear combination of a normal random variable with mean and standard deviation equal to that of X, and the observed value of X multiplied by a case-specific causal effect that is normally distributed with a mean and standard deviation of 1. Thus the stronger the X weight, the more the pathway variable consists of the effect of X.

Then an outcome variable is simulated by subtracting out the estimated effect of X and adding in a linear combination of X and the simulated pathway variable – each multiplied by the estimated effect times a random case-specific causal component that is normally distributed with a mean and standard deviation of 1. As the Y weight approaches one, the pathway variable comes closer to accounting for the whole effect of X on Y.

The results for pathway variables, shown in Figure 4.2, are simple and fit cleanly with the expectations developed in the analytic section. Extreme-case selection on X is the best option when the pathway variable is weakly connected to the outcome variable, Y. Of course, the performance of this case-selection rule does not depend at all on the outcome, and its success rate is not affected by the relationship between the pathway variable and Y. Extreme cases on the cause are best when the pathway only accounts for a portion of the effect of the treatment on Y because nothing else works especially well in that situation.

As the pathway variable captures a greater share of the overall effect of the treatment on the outcome, deviant- and extreme-on-Y approaches to case selection improve to the point that they beat extreme cases on X – ultimately by a substantial margin. As expected, deviant cases are consistently, if not substantially, better than extreme cases on Y. Indeed, for causal pathways that are powerfully connected to both X and Y, deviant-case selection meets the two-standard-deviation rule for success fully half the time. Thus, the simulations support the finding that deviant cases are best for major causal pathways, and that extreme cases on X are an acceptable fallback when the existing pathways are expected to be multiple and fragmentary.

It bears mention that the intended goal of selecting pathway cases is exactly to find pathway variables in the sense discussed here (Gerring (2007a): 238–39). Hence, it is striking that pathway case selection does

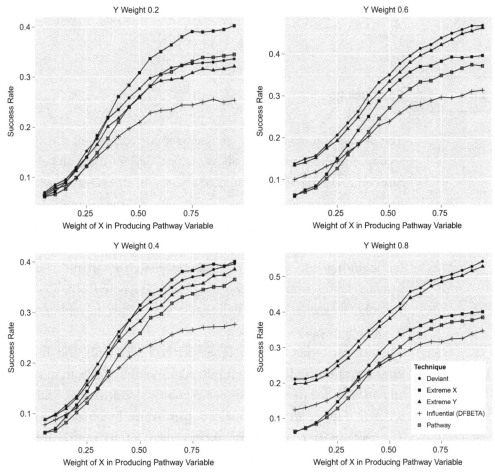

Figure 4.2   Pathway Variable.

not perform best at this goal in any of the simulations reported here. Instead, the success rate for pathway cases tracks, but is consistently lower than, the results for extreme cases on X.

These two simulations focus on the most intrinsically causal as well as the most parameter-dependent findings from this section's analysis, and the results emphasize the distinctive value of deviant and extreme-on-X case selection. One or the other of these techniques is the most efficient way to discover confounders or variables that form part of the causal pathway from the treatment to the outcome. When one considers as well the value of these variables in discovering sources of measurement error and causal heterogeneity, the pivotal role of these techniques becomes clear.

4.4   Conclusions

The overall argument of this chapter, supported by both the analytic section and the simulations above, is that deviant cases and extreme cases on X are the best ways to choose cases for close analysis when the goal is discovery. Deviant cases are an efficient means of discovering sources of measurement error, information about causal pathways, and sources of causal heterogeneity. Extreme cases on X are useful for inquiring into sources of measurement error on the treatment variable and discovering the most important and powerful confounding variables, as well as for the less justifiable objective of replicating the original slope estimate.

Other case-selection techniques perform less well, and in some cases are categorically unhelpful. Random sampling – both in relative and in absolute terms – performs poorly. Most similar and most different designs are substantially outperformed by other approaches. The pathway-cases design is outperformed for its central intended purpose of discovering causal pathways by extreme cases on X for pathway variables that explain only a fraction of the overall treatment effect and by deviant-cases selection for variables that are closer to a comprehensive account of the causal effect of interest. Similarly, the contrast cases design is dominated by selecting extreme cases on X. Finally, and perhaps somewhat surprisingly, deviant-case selection or extreme-case selection on X usually achieve the same goals more efficiently than the frequently discussed and applied approach of selecting extreme cases on the dependent variable. These techniques stand in need of a different kind of justification if they are to continue in use.

A concluding note of caution is in order. The analysis and simulation study above are both constructed around the assumption that the model for the relationships among the dependent, independent, and perhaps control variables is an OLS regression. While some of the conclusions reached here will no doubt generalize to nonlinear models, and perhaps also to semi- and nonparametric approaches such as matching, it is by no means certain that all of this section's findings will be general in this sense. Likewise, additional analysis will be needed to know how best to select cases when the goal is to interact with a quantitative natural experiment using more complex forms of statistical analysis (e.g. instrumental variables or contemporary approaches to the analysis of regression-discontinuity designs). These cautions notwithstanding, the arguments above do apply in an important context: case studies intended to interact with findings reached using the very common technique of OLS regression.

Notes

1 For example, Lieberman (2005) recommends typical cases for model-testing case-study research and deviant cases for model-building case-study research. Rogowski (2004) also argues in favor of some kinds of deviant cases. Collier and Mahoney (1996: 72–75) favorably discuss arguments in favor of selecting extreme cases on the dependent variable; see also Ragin (2004).

2 While the design of selecting extreme cases on the independent variable is not widely discussed or applied by qualitative methodologists, it is favorably considered by King *et al.* (1994: 140–41); these authors, however, miss the important roles of deviant cases.

3 Thus, for example, Lieberman's discovery of the role of regional as opposed to primarily class identities among elites as a possible cause of tax compliance was greatly facilitated by the selection of Brazil – characterized by unusually strong regional elite rivalries – and South Africa – in which elite attention to threats from poor black citizens was extreme in global perspective (Lieberman 2003).

4 This threshold is of course arbitrary, but also relatively inconsequential; the central arguments here hold for a range of thresholds in the neighborhood of the two-standard-deviation cut-off.

5 Bias can also sometimes propagate through to the inference about X from relationships between U and Z, among other possibilities.

6 In the discussion in this chapter, Y refers to the outcome in an analysis as a vector of random variables with one row per case. Y_i represents that random variable for case i. X and X_i are analogous for the main explanatory variable. $\mathbb{Z}$ is a matrix of random variables with one row per case and one column for each control variable that a scholar wishes to add to the analysis, while $\mathbb{Z}_{i\cdot}$ reflects the row in the matrix for case i.

7 In some instances, scholars have not reduced existing knowledge to a regression-like formulation. In such circumstances, much of the discussion in this chapter may only apply via analogy. However, even in such circumstances, added precision in terms of case selection may justify the extra work of producing a regression-type model for case-selection purposes.

8 For more discussion of the arguments in this section, including mathematical and statistical details, see Seawright (2015).

9 For the same reasons, scholars might consider searching for sources of measurement error in X by selecting deviant cases from a reverse regression using X as the outcome and Y and perhaps other variables as predictors. This possibility has not yet been considered in the case-selection literature, and so it is not pursued in further detail here.

10 This phrase refers specifically to orthogonality, the matrix-algebraic way of expressing that two vectors or matrices have no information about each other.

11 More details are available in Seawright (2012: 63–87).

5 Combining Case Studies and Matching

Case-study researchers have long used a certain interpretation of Mill's method of difference as a rationale for drawing causal conclusions from paired comparisons (e.g. Skocpol 1979: 36–39). The underlying argument can be translated into the potential-outcomes framework in a way that makes it more precise and simultaneously reveals why causal inferences based on paired comparisons are fundamentally unworkable in the social sciences.

Suppose a scholar is particularly interested in understanding the relationship between a treatment, D, and an outcome, Y, in case i. What must be true of a second case, j, in order for that case to allow causal inference via paired comparison with case i? Obviously, it must have the opposite score on D; for present purposes, let us assume that case i receives the treatment condition and case j the control.

More important and challenging requirements involve the counterfactuals. The second case in a paired comparison is intended to help reveal the unobserved potential outcome for the first case, and vice versa. That is to say, the observed value of $Y_{j,c}$ must reveal useful information about the unobserved quantity $Y_{i,c}$, while $Y_{i,t}$ must be informative about the counterfactual $Y_{j,t}$.

How can the value of $Y_{j,c}$ be inferentially connected to $Y_{i,c}$? The most common rationale for making such an inference is to claim that the two values have to be identical because the two cases are causally indistinguishable: they have *identical* values on *all* variables causally connected with the outcome other than the treatment, and are identical with respect to any background traits that relate to the causal efficacy of the treatment.

An example may help illustrate the strictness of this idea of causally indistinguishable cases. Consider a chemistry experiment in which a large bottle of a compound is split into two smaller beakers, both of which were thoroughly cleaned just before the start of the experiment. If no contamination has taken place, then the two new beakers should be causally indistinguishable: there is no reason to suppose that they will behave differently unless a treatment is applied to one but not the other (see Holland 1986: 948). In such a context, a causal inference might plausibly be drawn by subjecting one sample to the treatment of interest and comparing its behavior to that of the control sample, because there is reason to believe that the two samples share identical potential outcomes.

How often are interesting cases in the social sciences as indistinguishable as these hypothetical chemistry samples? It is hard to imagine that such scenarios could be at all common. A great deal of social science research involves either individuals or larger aggregates or organizations that are characterized by, even in part comprised by, relationships of various sorts with individuals. Individuals, of course, are wildly heterogeneous in a variety of ways that are socially and politically relevant. Even the most similar of individuals – identical twins raised in the same household – inevitably have at least somewhat contrasting information sets and social networks. Even at the most micro level of a shared social experience, it is impossible for distinct embodied humans to have identically the same experience, because they cannot occupy the same place and thus cannot have exactly the same perspective on the events in question.

So differences among cases at the individual level, and by aggregation at most other relevant levels, are endemic. In order to undermine causal inference via paired comparison, these differences need only cause cases' potential outcomes to be unequal: there must be at least a tiny causal effect on the outcome in at least one treatment condition. There is of course no good reason to believe that such effects would be rare in general, and also generally little reason to think that they would not exist for a given comparison. Since the evidentiary burden of demonstrating the absence of such distortions rightfully falls on the researcher advocating the comparison, the argument effectively ends here. The demonstrably widespread heterogeneity among cases, combined with the typical lack of compelling a priori evidence that existing heterogeneities do not affect the potential outcomes, renders paired comparison an implausible tool for causal inference.

Paired comparisons may of course be valuable for a variety of other goals; the point here is simply that they are a poor tool for making causal inferences. This conclusion notwithstanding, the intuition behind qualitative paired comparison remains compelling: it should be possible to work toward causal inference by comparing cases that are as similar as possible on a set of potential confounders but which differ in terms of the treatment. What is needed is a set of tools that facilitate such comparisons while allowing for the existence of heterogeneity among cases. Statistical matching methods are designed to fill this niche.

Recall that randomized experiments achieve causal inference because random assignment, combined with the law of large numbers, makes the treatment and the control group have the same average potential outcomes. That is to say, at the treatment group level – although obviously not at the individual level – experiments bring about the causal indistinguishability that is needed for the method of difference. This is because the causally relevant heterogeneity has the same distribution in the treatment and control groups, and so it effectively subtracts out when group averages are compared. In this way, we can reconcile a causally meaningful causally meaningful paired comparison with the existence of heterogeneity at the level of the individual case.

Suppose that, instead of an experiment, a researcher is dealing with a situation in which assignment to treatment is partly random but outside the researcher's control. To make things concrete, let us consider one specific story, with the understanding that the ideas involved are much more general. Suppose that there are two kinds of people included in the study: people who have $W = 1$ and people who have $W = 0$, with W representing (for example) completion of a college degree. Everyone in the study decides whether to expose herself to the treatment or the control condition by flipping a coin, although for some reason college grads use a different coin than people without a bachelor's degree. Those with $W = 1$ flip a fair coin, while those with $W = 0$ flip a coin that sends them to the treatment condition 30% of the time and the control condition 70% of the time. Furthermore, suppose that the average of both $Y_{i,t}$ and $Y_{i,c}$ is higher for cases with $W = 1$ than for cases with $W = 0$ (Y might represent a variable partly caused by education, perhaps including annual income or number of books read in a year).

Clearly, a simple comparison of the treatment group and the control group will fail: the treatment group is disproportionately made up of the college educated, who are just different in terms of the potential outcomes in question, so the comparison gives no causal insight. Yet a more structured comparison will work well. If we compare college-educated members of the treatment group with college-educated members of the control group, we remove the problem and have a research setup that works the same as an experiment; the same is true for a comparison strictly among those without a college diploma. These two comparisons can be averaged together in a variety of ways to recover overall average treatment effects of interest: for the sample (or perhaps even for the population) as a whole, for those who in fact receive the treatment, for those who receive the control condition, and so forth.

In practice, treatment assignment usually depends on more than one systematic variable, and there is often no way of knowing that treatment assignment is random within particular defined groups. Scholars have proposed a variety of methods for dealing with more complex sets of variables on which matches need to be found, and even for addressing the problem that exact matches may be impossible when the number of variables is too large or the relevant variables take on many values. These include techniques involving optimal full matching (Hansen 2004), propensity scores (Rosenbaum and Rubin 1983), post-matching regression adjustment (Rubin 1979), coarsened exact matching, and a range of others, the details of which are beyond the scope of this book.

The second issue, regarding the randomness of treatment assignment for groups of cases with identical scores on all of the matching variables, is more important here. If treatments are chosen through a process that is not analogous to random assignment, even within groups of cases that match well on the observed variables, then there is no reason to believe that the heterogeneity among cases will have the same distribution for the treatment and control groups even after matching has been carried out. Hence without this assumption, matching will not allow causal conclusions. For this reason, the claim that cases enter the treatment or control group through a process analogous to random assignment within groups defined by the matching variables is probably the most important assumption that stands in need of testing and evidentiary bolstering when matching is used for the purposes of causal inference.

It is also worth noting that this assumption is directly parallel to the key assumption needed to allow causal inference using regression in observational studies, as discussed in Chapter 3. Both assume that, conditional on some set of matching or control variables, cases join the treatment or control groups as if at random. For this reason, authors such as Morgan and Winship (2007: 87–165) treat regression and matching as two variants on the same strategy for causal inference. This underlying similarity in terms of key assumptions notwithstanding, there are obviously important procedural differences between the families of methods that are relevant for thinking about multi-method research design.

Regression analysis conditions on control variables through a covariance adjustment. In effect, regression estimates are constructed by looking at the covariance between the treatment and the outcome after discarding all the variance in either variable that is shared with any of the control variables (for a more elaborate presentation of the intuition behind regression, see Kennedy 2008, Chapter 3). Matching, by contrast, conditions on control variables by finding pairs (or sometimes larger sets) of cases that differ on the treatment of interest but are as close as possible to being identical on the set of control variables. Most of the quantitative work of matching is involved in selecting the pairs of cases that best meet the criterion of not differing on the conditioning variables. In a prototypical setup, the researcher begins with a set of cases that have been exposed to the treatment and a larger set of cases that have not been so exposed.[1] Then, in some way, the researcher chooses the set of control cases that best match the treatment cases on the variables for which conditioning is desired. If this matching is successful, then the mean difference between treatment and control cases, conditional on the specified set of control variables, can be estimated by simply calculating the average difference on the outcome variable between treatment and control cases across the selected matched pairs. Hence, rather than achieving conditioning by subtracting out undesired covariances, as is fundamentally the approach in regression, matching conditions by choosing cases such that undesired differences are removed from the sample.

In addition to these procedural differences, there are meaningful differences between regression analysis and matching regarding the results that the two families of techniques produce. Perhaps the most obvious difference is that matching techniques produce estimates for only one conditional difference at a time. Whereas regression generally produces a coefficient estimate for each conditioning variable as well as for the treatment of interest, matching estimates only the difference of central interest, facilitating a sharper analytic focus and a cleaner presentation of results. Under some circumstances, matching estimators may require less knowledge of functional forms for conditioning variables than do regression techniques, and matching estimators may sometimes have technical advantages compared to regression for purposes of causal inference. However, this book will not enter into these debates, other than to note that there is a fundamental relationship of similarity between regression and matching that casts doubt on claims of extreme advantage for either technique in comparison with the other (see summary of the literature in Morgan and Winship 2007: Chapters 4–5).

Matching estimators may be of particular interest to researchers interested in multi-method analysis, not because of modest possible gains in terms of causal inference in comparison with regression, but rather because matching methods allow for especially lucid and transparent combinations of qualitative evidence and quantitative analysis in the process of making a single inference. Like regression, matching fails for purposes of causal inference when there are omitted variables that affect the treatment assignment and change the distribution of potential outcomes. However, examining matched pairs of cases may sometimes facilitate the discovery of such variables. Matching, like regression and for similar reasons, may also be vulnerable to measurement error on the treatment variable or the outcome, and case-study investigation may help test for this possibility. Finally, just as with regression, matching methods offer relatively little help with the task of discovering possible causal pathways connecting treatment and outcome, and qualitative research may contribute here. These are obviously the same issues that provided a basis for several of the integrative multi-method designs involving regression discussed in previous chapters; however, some details of implementation change in moving to matching. These differences will be discussed below, followed by an analysis of the best way to select cases for each objective in the context of a matching analysis.

An early influential example of matching in the social sciences, economists Persson and Tabellini's (2003: 165–75) analysis of the effects of majoritarian versus proportional representation electoral rules on central government economic consumption, will provide a running example below. In this analysis, Persson and Tabellini use pairwise matching to find comparisons between countries that match as closely as possible on logged per capita GDP, share of elderly people in the population, degree of democracy, whether the state is federal or unitary, and whether the country in question is a former British colony. Then the average difference between these paired cases on the outcome of central government expenditure as a proportion of GDP provides an estimate of the economic effects of different electoral rules; the data suggest that, other things being equal, majoritarian electoral rules reduce central government consumption as a share of GDP by 6.6%. These results require a host of assumptions, especially that the matching variables have eliminated all confounding, and that measurement error does not distort the results. There is also the important question of whether the causal effect, if genuine, results from the kind of mechanism that Persson and Tabellini theorize earlier in the book. Matching methods cannot in themselves answer these questions, and thus there is an opportunity for multi-method work to refine and improve the causal inference.[2]

5.1   Finding Omitted Variables

Omitted relevant variables matter in matching because they can mean that the matched treatment and control cases have different average outcomes on the dependent variable because of the effects of the omitted variable, rather than because of the effects of the treatment. More formally, when there are omitted relevant variables, the average value of $Y_{i,t}$ among control cases will usually not equal the average value of $Y_{i,t}$ among control cases – and therefore causal inference breaks down. Hence, a key role for case-study evidence in evaluating matching results is to test for omitted variables.

An intuitive, but ultimately unhelpful, approach to this task is to ransack a pair of cases to find any and all differences between them. This approach seems appealing because it can often show that matched cases are, when taken as a whole, not altogether similar. Yet in fact this conclusion is at most a minor first step in demonstrating that there is a problem with a matching estimate. After all, statistical matching, as opposed to qualitative paired comparison, is an attractive idea in the first place exactly because cases are heterogeneous in a variety of causally and theoretically uninteresting ways. Finding a long list of differences between matched cases can be seen as simply confirming this prior belief, unless extra information can be brought to the table.

What more needs to be shown in order for evidence of difference between cases to imply problems of causal inference? First, the case studies or prior theoretical knowledge must imply a causal connection between the omitted variable and the treatment assignment. Second, there must also be reason to think that there is a causal link between the omitted variable and the outcome. If evidence supportive of these two links can be found, and if the two cases in a studied pair have substantially different scores on the omitted variable, then there is an important prima facia case that the omitted variable should be included in the set of matching variables.

This implies a useful three-step design for discovering possible omitted variables in matching studies. First, develop an inclusive inventory of omitted variables on which there is a large difference between the cases in a matched pair. This is a broadly inductive step; any difference may matter, so there is value in searching creatively and across both obviously important domains and less evidently relevant aspects of the cases in question.

After building a broad inventory of omitted differences between paired cases, the next two steps involve filtering for variables that have a plausible causal connection with the treatment and the outcome. Because scholars often think less intensively about the causes of their treatments than about the outcome, it may make sense to start the filtering process by searching for evidence of a causal tie between the omitted variable and the outcome. This will most likely involve intensive process tracing forward from the omitted variable to find any plausible signs of a path from it to the outcome of interest. While a number of variables will likely pass this test, at least some generally will not. Hence, it can save time and effort to carry out this check.

The second important filter test involves checking whether there is evidence consistent with a causal connection between the remaining omitted variables and the treatment assignment. Because scholars often start research with fewer insights into the causes of the treatment than the causes of the outcome, this stage of research will frequently be quite broadly exploratory. The goal is thus to check whether there is evidence making a causal link between the potential confounder and the treatment seem plausible. If so, then the potential confounder needs to be measured and added to the set of matching variables. Alternatively, if compelling within-case evidence can be found that the potential confounder could not have influenced the treatment, then the variable can safely be disregarded.

How can cases be selected for such close scrutiny? Because cases in matching setups are paired (or sometimes partitioned into larger matched groups), the most natural case-selection process involves choosing a matched pair or group for closer examination. Furthermore, the structure of the data and the analysis makes several of the case-selection techniques considered in conjunction with regression meaningless: there is no residual and thus no typical, deviant, or influential cases, the treatment is by definition dichotomous and therefore there are no extreme cases on X, and so forth.

Instead, a set of new possibilities must be considered. First, cases might be selected based on the size of the contrast between matched treatment and control cases on the outcome: either the matched pairs with the biggest or the smallest observed difference on Y might be analyzed. A variant of this approach would involve choosing the pair of cases whose contrast on Y is alternatively closest to, or farthest from, the estimated sample average treatment effect. Second, when matching is not exact, case-selection might focus the quality of matching: cases with the best (or the worst) overall similarity on the matching variables could be chosen. The operationalization of this would depend on the matching procedure; for propensity-score techniques, a sensible choice would be to choose the pairs of cases that are most similar and/or most different on the propensity score. Third, analysis may focus on the cases with the least likely treatment assignments, i.e., cases with very low propensity scores that end up in the treatment category, as well as cases with very high propensity scores that end up in the control category. These cases may be interesting because they represent the ones for which treatment assignment is least well understood – and therefore a great deal remains to be learned about the causes of treatment assignment for such cases. Finally, of course, if the outcome has multiple categories, it is reasonable to simply select cases with the most extreme values on the dependent variable.

Of these options, the best alternatives for finding omitted variables involve choosing cases that are extreme on the outcome variable in one way or another. Depending on the specific strengths of the causal relations among the treatment, the confounder, and the outcome, the best approach may be either to choose the pair of cases with the biggest contrast on the dependent variable, or to simply choose the case with the most extreme value on the dependent variable without paying attention to the matching process. The reasoning behind selecting extreme values on Y without regard to the matching setup is that, here as in regression scenarios, a confounder only matters to the extent that it causes Y – and if it does, then cases with extreme values on Y will be disproportionately likely to also have extreme values on the confounder. Of course, a confounder must also be correlated with the treatment, and if this correlation is relatively strong in comparison with the relationship between the confounder and Y, then matched cases with an extreme contrast on the outcome can outperform single cases with an extreme value on Y. For a wide range of possible relationships, however, the two selection rules perform better than their competitors.[3]

In application to Persson and Tabellini's analysis of electoral rules and government size, the two optimal rules suggest somewhat different case studies. The most extreme case on the dependent variable in the data is the Netherlands, whose government in 1985 consumed more than 51% of GDP. Alternatively, the matched pair with the largest contrast on the dependent variable involves a comparison between Uganda and Malta. While the mere mention of the Netherlands and Uganda no doubt sparks hypotheses about possible omitted variables – particularly involving ethnic political divisions and the strength of the left (two hypothesized causes of proportional representation electoral institutions) – a proper multi-method design involving the steps discussed above would clearly be needed to determine whether any of these variables was worth pursuing further, and more importantly whether there was evidence in these cases of influence from less obvious omitted variables.

5.2   Checking for Measurement Problems

Omitted variables are clearly an important potential obstacle to causal inference based on matching, just as for regression. Nonetheless, they are not the only important obstacle. Measurement error matters for matching-based inferences, just as for regression-based ones. As before, it is important to think about measurement error on the outcome as well as on the treatment variable. If the treatment variable is mismeasured, then some pairs of cases will be treating a comparison of two observations of Y_c (or two of Y_t) as if they were a comparison of Y_t and Y_c. This will often distort causal inference, and thus needs attention.

Measurement error on Y is less important as long as it is random, because it will just average out across a large sample. However, even so, it is worth identifying and eliminating if possible to enhance statistical power. For both forms of measurement error, the case-study research designs should be just the same as the corresponding designs discussed in Chapter 4. The single distinctive issue involves case selection.

If there is random measurement error on the treatment variable, and if the treatment and control groups have different distributions on the matching variables, then matched cases will overrepresent cases with measurement error. Furthermore, if the matching process involves a propensity score, then the cases most likely to have error can be narrowed down: control-group cases with high propensity scores and treatment-group cases with low propensity scores.

This is because there are now two ways for a case to get into the treatment group: via the actual causal patterns that assign cases to treatment, or via measurement error. By definition, cases with high propensity scores will have a lot of the causal factors that tend to produce assignment to treatment; hence when such cases are not in the treatment group, there is a good chance that they suffer from measurement error. Likewise, cases with low propensity scores tend to lack the causes of assignment to treatment, and therefore are rather likely to have measurement error when they in fact are in the treatment group.[4] Therefore cases with a comparatively high probability of measurement error can be selected by focusing on cases at the extremes of the propensity score distribution that have unlikely values on the main treatment variable.

For measurement error on the outcome variable, a different selection process is needed, focusing instead on the case or cases with the most extreme values on the outcome variable. This is the same technique, which is best for this purpose with respect to regression-type analysis, and it is also best here – for the same reasons discussed in Chapter 4. Specifically, when the dependent variable has measurement error, there are two paths by which a case can come to have an extreme score on that variable: either by having an unusual score on the underlying true value of the variable, or by having a great deal of measurement error. Cases with unusually extreme values on the error-laden variable will thus be drawn from the set of cases with atypical true values of the variable, high levels of error, or both; hence, selecting such cases can significantly facilitate the task of finding sources of measurement error.

In the real Persson-Tabellini data, application of these methods leads a researcher interested in looking for measurement error on the treatment variable to focus on four cases: France, Japan, Chile, and Malta. The first three are coded as majoritarian, yet for each the decision is complicated at best. France uses a runoff system for legislative elections, in which all candidates who receive at least 12.5% of the vote in the first round advance to a second election, the winner of which is ultimately elected. From one point of view, this might be seen as a variant of majoritarianism, yet it has important differences and has persistently sustained a substantially larger and more varied party system than is typically found in majoritarian contexts (Blais and Loewen 2009). Thus, it is ambiguous whether such rules adequately belong in the majoritarian category. Japan's elections included in this analysis operated under two electoral systems: the single non-transferable vote, a complex system that has elements of similarity to both proportional representation and majoritarianism although perhaps a preponderance of the latter (Grofman 1999); and a hybrid system in which 300 legislators are elected in single-member districts under majoritarian rules, while 180 are elected under proportional representation (Lin 2011). It is unclear how these elections should be coded, and there is a distinct possibility of error in Persson and Tabellini's data. In Chile, elections were under standard proportional representation rules prior to the Pinochet dictatorship of the 1970s and 1980s; subsequently, legislators have been elected using proportional representation with an unusually small district magnitude of two. This unusual system might plausibly be regarded as effectively a mix of proportional representation and majoritarian institutions (a point of view echoed by many sides in the debate over those institutions – see, for example, Rabkin 1996 and Siavelis 1997), but it seems a stretch to classify it purely as majoritarian. Malta, which is classified as an instance of proportional representation, also has an unusual system: the single transferable vote, in which voters rank-order candidates and through a complicated algorithm the top five choices in each district are elected. While this system has commonalities with both proportional representation and majoritarianism (Grofman 1999), in Malta it has produced a two-party system, making Malta at least an extremely unusual case of proportional representation and potentially misclassified.

Considering this set of countries as a whole, a generalization emerges: Persson and Tabellini's measurement of countries' electoral rules does not handle unusual systems well. Instead of adequately capturing the details of these systems – or perhaps even setting them aside – Persson and Tabellini group them as full members of the proportional representation or majoritarian categories alongside countries that are far better examples of those categories. Clearly, the analysis would be made more credible if a better decision rule were devised and adopted for such unusual systems, a conclusion that emerges from case analysis based on systematic case selection.

Similar analysis is, of course, needed for the outcome variable, central government consumption's share of GDP. The country with the most extreme score on that variable in Persson and Tabellini's data is the Netherlands, as noted earlier; case-study analysis of government record-keeping and the classification rules regarding how different kinds of consumption are put in the state or non-state categories in that country would provide useful insight as to whether this variable has measurement problems of its own.

5.3   Causal Pathways

Finally, scholars may wish to use case studies to test whether hypothesized causal pathways are actually present in real-world countries, or to attempt to discover unknown causal pathways. Here, again, research design considerations are mostly identical to those for case studies seeking causal pathways in conjunction with regression analysis. The one special issue involves case selection. For matching studies, given the very limited variation that exists on the treatment variable, it is difficult to get much purchase on causal pathways by focusing on anything other than the outcome variable. Fortunately, for non-dichotomous outcomes, focusing on the dependent variable is a sensible way to search for variables involved in causal pathways. After all, to be part of a causal pathway, a variable has to cause the outcome – and because this causal relationship exists, it follows that extreme cases on the dependent variable will have a relatively high chance of also experiencing unusual values on any existing pathway variables.[5]

Turning to this chapter's substantive example, it would be poor research practice to search for causal pathways in the context of an analysis for which there are open questions about omitted variables – an issue that was raised but not answered above – and for which the treatment variable seems to be dubiously measured for non-prototypical electoral systems. After all, the resolution of those two issues would very likely change the analysis in meaningful ways. In particular, it seems plausible that some cases would be dropped from the analysis because of membership in a poorly measured category or because adding new control variables would make them difficult to match. As such, the set of matched cases that have extreme scores on the dependent variable may not remain stable after problems in the analysis are corrected. If a scholar nonetheless wished to skip the process of refining the analysis and move directly to a search for causal pathway variables, however, the most useful cases would be those with the most extreme scores on the dependent variable: the Netherlands, Hungary, and Belgium.

5.4   Conclusions

Matching methods are an exciting addition to the social science toolkit, although they are in many ways less novel than they initially appear. Matching's fundamental approach to causal inference is the same as that of regression, i.e., it attempts to reach causal clarity by controlling for confounders until the remaining conditional relationship between the treatment and outcome variables works like an experiment. This concept is no less challenging or problematic in a matching context than it is in regression-based studies. Furthermore, regression can often execute this strategy with greater statistical efficiency. Nonetheless, matching can be a highly defensible choice in multi-method contexts because of the way that matching methods clarify the connection between specific cases and overall causal inferences.

This chapter has offered a set of research designs that help case-study methods contribute to matching analysis by interrogating cases for problems of omitted variables, measurement error, and evidence related to causal pathways. These are the same central issues that are relevant for multi-method designs involving regression, for the central reason that regression and matching are vulnerable to the same fundamental challenges to causal inference. Nonetheless, details are important, and the discussion has highlighted differences between regression-oriented and matching-oriented multi-method designs with respect to case selection, as well as with respect to other considerations of research design. The following chapters take us further away from regression, into multi-method designs that face somewhat different obstacles to causal inference.

Notes

1 If the set of cases in the treatment condition is in fact larger than the set of control cases, the researcher can simply reverse the labeling of treatment and control without any real sacrifice of meaning.

2 This discussion is inspired in part by Hidalgo and Richardson (2008).

3 Simulation results support this analysis. A simulation based on the Persson and Tabellini analysis, and adding confounding, shows that the highest probability of finding cases in which a confounding variable is unusually far from its mean comes from choosing the cases with the most extreme scores on the dependent variable; the second-best choice involves matched pairs with the biggest contrast on the dependent variable. Of those pairs, the most useful case may be alternately the treatment or the control depending on the polarity of the relationship between the confounder and the treatment variable. Full details and replication code are available from the author upon request; since the process of simulation is similar to that used for regression and due to considerations of space, results are omitted here.

4 As before, simulation results based on the Persson and Tabellini analysis confirm this argument; details are available upon request.

5 As before, simulation results supporting this claim are available upon request.

6 Combining Case Studies and Natural Experiments

Continuing the movement away from observational regression studies, this chapter considers designs that combine qualitative research with natural experiments. Natural experiments have become an important research design in the social sciences because they can – when all goes well – extend the powerful leverage for causal inference generated by randomization into domains of the social sciences where scholars lack the knowledge, the resources, or the capacity to intervene in a true experimental manner (Dunning 2012: 1–15). In such non-experimental situations, it is sometimes the case that some actor intervenes to assign a treatment of interest randomly: using a lottery to distribute vouchers for reduced-cost private schooling (Angrist *et al.* 2002), for example, or assigning new voting procedures to districts in what is argued to be an effectively random sequence over time (Hidalgo 2010). If such randomized interventions are strictly implemented, and if some collateral assumptions – to be discussed later – are met, then causal inference works the same as if the research design were a true experiment. After all, the law of large numbers (which justifies treating the control group in an experiment as revealing the average potential outcome of the treatment group under the control condition) does not care whether the person implementing a randomization has a PhD in the social sciences. Whether a randomization is part of an academic research project, is part of a policy for distributive justice, or arises for other reasons has no real bearing on causal inference: randomized intervention, with a few additional assumptions, justifies causal inference even if that was not the original intent of the intervention.

Recall the potential-outcomes framework: for each case i, the potential outcomes are $Y_{i,t}$ under treatment and $Y_{i,c}$ under control. The treatment variable, D_i, determines which of these is observed. If that treatment is randomly assigned – by the researcher or anyone else – then the law of large numbers applies, and the mean of $Y_{i,t}$ among treatment cases becomes equal to the mean of $Y_{i,t}$ among control cases as the sample size increases. This means that, as in a laboratory experiment, the treatment group and the control group can serve as each others' counterfactuals, and causal inference at the group level is justified.

As always with the potential-outcomes framework, causal inference using natural experiments requires the SUTVA assumption; research design considerations involving this assumption will be discussed in the chapter on experiments. More distinctive assumptions are needed that focus on the treatment assignment. In the first place, it must be genuinely random: individuals (regions, organizations, etc.) must not be able to opt out of randomization, appeal unfavorable results, or otherwise act to strategically alter their treatment assignment. If such strategic responses to randomization are possible, then the treatment assignment is not altogether random, and the argument sketched above does not apply. Hence even when treatment assignment is putatively random, an assumption must be made that the assignment is in fact random and not modified by strategic behavior.

Furthermore, to achieve valid causal inference the scholar must assume that the randomization and treatment administration process has no effect on the outcome other than through the value of the treatment itself. If people respond differently to a treatment because they know it was randomized, for example, then the natural experiment cannot succeed.[1] Hence, assumptions for causal inference with natural experiments involve not only the process leading up to treatment assignment but also the assignment process through to the outcome.

In all of these assumptions, attention focuses heavily on the cause. This is in contrast with the assumptions behind causal inference with regression or matching, which involve a great deal of attention to the causes of the dependent variable other than the treatment of interest. These variables matter because they may be confounders for the relationship between the treatment and the outcome. Yet with natural experiments, confounders are less of an issue. If the treatment really is randomly assigned, that addresses the issue of confounding. Alternatively, if the randomization is flawed or illusory, then the study fails as a natural experiment, confounders or no. Hence, causes of the outcome other than the treatment are less central for natural experiments; instead, distinctive attention is focused on the causes of the cause.

The discussion up to this point has assumed a rather generic and direct randomization of the treatment. In practice, scholars face situations that depart from this ideal in large and small ways while still retaining something of the natural experiment's signature element of randomization. With this diversity in mind, it is natural to expect that different assumptions about the precise nature of the causes of the cause generate divergent subspecies of natural experiments. The remainder of this chapter will work through three such subspecies: the true natural experiment, the regression-discontinuity design, and the instrumental variables natural experiment.[2] For each type of natural experiment, we will first review the specific assumptions needed for causal inference. Next, attention will turn to qualitative research designs that can provide targeted evidence regarding those assumptions, including case selection. Each section concludes by considering whether and how to incorporate qualitative findings into the next cycle of quantitative analysis.

In talking about multi-method designs where the quantitative component involves a natural experiment, there are relatively few compelling examples to draw on. Quantitative analyses of natural experiments often report some qualitative evidence to justify their research designs, but these discussions are typically informal. Qualitative scholars, for their part, have produced few important pieces of research interacting in detail with natural experiments. This lack may be due in part to the relative novelty of natural experiments in the social sciences and to their comparative technical complexity. In any case, the result is that few important examples of natural experimental multi-method research are available. This section thus necessarily discusses research designs that should work – based on the logic of causal inference and general principles regarding the contribution of case studies – rather than research designs that have in practice been successful. Furthermore, the illustrative examples will primarily be purely quantitative studies, in which multi-method designs are offered as suggestions rather than as summaries of actual research.

6.1   True Natural Experiments

The first, and simplest, kind of natural experiment is the true natural experiment, in which some social or political actor randomly assigns the treatment of interest (Dunning 2012: 48–52). While such direct, real-world randomizations may seem atypical and therefore rare, creative and attentive scholars have found natural experiments relevant to a wide range of substantive issues.

Does attending a better school improve a child's life prospects? It seems impossible to randomize such an outcome, and it would probably be unethical for researchers to intervene directly in a way that sends some students to lower-quality schools. Yet several schools in the Chicago Public Schools system admit students by lottery among the set of applicants. Cullen *et al.* (2006) compare students who won admissions lotteries at 19 highly desirable Chicago schools to students who applied to the same schools but lost the lottery; winners are randomly selected to attend a school with a high reputation, while losers are assigned to make do with some kind of second-best alternative. The researchers find few meaningful differences in terms of educational or other life outcomes between lottery winners and losers – providing evidence that the causal effect of school quality is smaller than expected.

Of perhaps more personal interest to readers, it is reasonable to ask how gender affects scholars' prospects for academic promotion. Gender is a classic example of a variable that is hard to manipulate experimentally, to the point that some scholars argue that gender cannot even be discussed intelligibly as a potential cause (Holland 1986: 954–55). Yet Zinovyeva and Bagues (2010) analyze a natural experiment in which the gender of key actors in the promotion process – evaluators who examine Spanish academics to determine their qualifications for promotion – *is* randomly assigned. This is possible because the evaluators are randomly selected; hence, whether a woman faces a female or a male evaluator is a randomized treatment. This is genuine randomization, but of a complex nature: the assigned treatment is an entire evaluator, not just a gender role. To the extent that female academics in Spain have different traits, networks, or prominence on average than male academics, those differences will also be part of the treatment. Zinovyeva and Bagues consider some such differences, concluding that there is a complex causal interaction between gender dynamics and academic networks in promotion decisions.

These two examples, as well as the many others discussed in Dunning (2012), show that in-depth case knowledge, combined with a creative methodological eye, can uncover randomizations in the real world connected with a variety of important but hard-to-study treatments. For this reason, it is worthwhile for even pure case-study researchers to know something about natural experiments: if they have the specialized knowledge needed to uncover such randomizations, that can be a significant contribution to social scientific knowledge.

Yet these illustrations – if considered further – suggest some of the important complexities that routinely arise in natural experiments. In the case of the Chicago Public Schools study, it is clear upon reflection that the lottery results do not determine children's actual school attendance. Some students may win admission to more than one desirable school, requiring a choice post-randomization. Still others may win admission to a selective school but choose to attend a neighborhood school, effectively crossing over from the treatment to the control group. Finally, some students who lose the lottery may move to a different school district or turn to private school to obtain a better schooling outcome. These sorts of strategic responses to randomized treatment assignment represent an additional (and in this instance undesirable) potential causal path from the randomized intervention to the outcome of interest, and as such require either assumptions or additional evidence. The same issues are relevant to the study of academic promotion, in which traits other than gender are randomized together with the treatment of interest; those other traits become potential additional paths from treatment assignment to the outcome other than via gender, and therefore require attention.

While researchers using natural experiments need to be attentive to the possibility that the randomized treatment has effects other than those of theoretical interest, they also must consider the possibility that the randomized administration of the treatment in itself changes individuals' behavior in ways that are relevant to the causal process of interest. Social interactions that are known to be randomly assigned, for example, may not be evaluated and reacted to in the same way as intentional interactions; would a randomly assigned insult carry the same weight as one that was personal? Similar issues are likely to arise in a range of other contexts; this and related concerns will be discussed in more detail in the chapter on experiments.

For the moment, it suffices to discuss a qualitative research design that can test the assumption that the randomization has not altered the causal effect of the treatment. It is unreasonable to expect case-study work to validate or reject this assumption with quantitative precision, but some progress can nonetheless be made. After all, the assumption that the causal effect of treatment is the same under randomization as when the treatment takes on its value via a less artificial assignment process has implications not only for the overall treatment effect but also for the qualitative character of the causal process connecting the treatment to the outcome. In particular, if some decision-making considerations or causal influences are part of that process under randomization but not when the treatment takes on its value through normal social processes, then the nature of the causal link between the treatment and the outcome has demonstrably been changed by randomization. If the overall causal picture is thus affected by randomization, the assumption that the causal effect of treatment is unaffected by randomization becomes untenable. By contrast, if the same considerations and influences are involved in the causal narrative for cases that are randomized as for cases that are not, then the assumption remains viable – and indeed the qualitative evidence provides some degree of support for the assumption. The same argument works when there are considerations or influences that are present only under naturalistic treatment assignment and not under randomization; either way, finding steps in the causal path that are not parallel across these two categories undermines the assumption.

Thus, a useful qualitative component to add to a natural experiment is as follows. The researcher selects a case in which the treatment is randomly assigned, as well as a similar case in which the treatment is not randomized. In both, the case study focuses on constructing evidence regarding the causal pathway connecting treatment and outcome. That is, documents, interviews, and other qualitative data should be used to assemble a step-by-step account of how the treatment connects to the outcome. Because the real opportunity for discovery here involves finding factors that matter in one kind of case but not in the other, this causal-pathway account should be as inclusive and fine-grained as possible, giving the scholar the best possible chance of discovering important differences between the cases.

A best-case result for the natural experiment would be finding that the same kinds of considerations and influences are involved in both kinds of cases. Yet there are good reasons to expect that such a pattern will be rare. After all, as has been emphasized throughout this book, cases are often causally diverse. Treatments usually interact with the preexisting traits of cases to produce a range of causal effects, and indeed a variety of related but distinct causal pathways. For this reason, even if it is true that randomization does not change the nature of the causal link between the treatment and the outcome, it is still likely that a diligent scholar will find evidence of differences in the causal path connecting those variables when comparing a given case with randomized treatment to another case with naturally assigned treatment. Hence, while finding an identical set of causal steps in the process of interest for randomized and nonrandomized cases is the strongest favorable evidence, some kinds of differences are generally to be expected and cannot count strongly against the assumption.

A useful way to distinguish between steps in the causal pathway that pose a problem and those that likely do not is to look for connections between those steps and the fact of randomization. That is to say, when such differences arise, the scholar should process-trace backwards from the components of the causal pathway that differ to see if there is a connection between those components and the randomization process (or the nonrandom assignment process, depending on the case). If the process tracing provides evidence that these causal steps differ because of a self-aware reaction to randomization, then the assumption under discussion is almost certainly violated; if no such evidence emerges, that tends to support the viability of the assumption.

The set of assumptions needed for causal inference becomes even more complex if the treatment is not actually randomly assigned, but is instead assigned via a process that is "as-if" random (Dunning 2012: 53–59). As-if random assignment is a way of describing a situation in which there is no actual randomization, but in which the treatment variable takes on its score because of a causal chain that is arguably unrelated to the actors or processes of interest. Perhaps the prototypical example of as-if randomization is one component of Snow's classic study of the connection between contaminated water and the spread of cholera (Snow 1855; Cameron and Jones 1983; Freedman 1991; Dunning 2012: 12–15). Snow discovered an area of London in which different water companies competed to provide supplies at the time houses were constructed. In the subsequent years, the water supplier for each residence was unchanged and often even forgotten. However, the Lambeth company moved the location of its water intake from a location on the Thames in the middle of London to a cleaner location upstream of the city in advance of an 1853–54 cholera outbreak, while the competing Southwark and Vauxhall company did not. While residences were not in fact randomly assigned to one water company or the other, Snow argues persuasively that the water supplier was generally unaffected by any choice of the current residents and uncorrelated with any obvious traits of those residents. Thus, the water supply is as-if randomly assigned: even though no randomization is involved, it is plausible that the treatment has the same properties it would have had under actual randomization.

Whether the scholar believes the treatment to be assigned randomly or only as-if randomly, the facts about how the treatment is assigned will determine the credibility of the causal inference that can be drawn from a natural experiment. In both cases, the key condition to be met in order for causal inference to succeed is that: (a) the average value of $Y_{i,t}$ among treatment cases is the same as the average value of $Y_{i,t}$ among control cases, and (b) the average value of $Y_{i,c}$ among treatment cases is the same as the average value of $Y_{i,c}$ among control cases. Substantively, this means that the treatment group as a group must be the true causal counterfactual for the control group as a group.

This condition can of course be met in true natural experiments: if the randomization process for the treatment is genuinely random and it is the only path to treatment assignment, it follows that for large samples the only differences between the treatment and control groups will be the effects of the treatment itself. To test that the randomization is genuine, a close examination of that process is in order. How plausible are the kinds of theories that would be needed to support the claim that the randomization is in fact rigged? How verifiable was the randomization process – was randomization done in public using standard equipment, or in secret using ad hoc procedures, for example? Whatever evidence is available on these points will be helpful. Often, however, hypotheses that a putative randomization was in fact nonrandom will have the form and character of conspiracy theories and may thus be somewhat difficult to deal with in a serious social scientific manner.

Two process-tracing designs make sense to test the second assumption (that the randomization is the only causal path to treatment assignment). The first, and most general, involves carrying out inductive process tracing backwards from the treatment assignment for one or more cases. Was treatment assignment a simple one-step result of randomization, or was there a more involved process? If there was more than simply a one-step assignment process, what was involved? Any evidence of strategic behavior in response to randomization is a warning sign that randomization may be compromised, and any evidence of cases opting out after the fact is a serious problem for the assumption.

Yakusheva *et al.* (2011) analyze a fascinating natural experiment related to the effects of social networks on weight gain or loss. They take advantage of a Midwestern university's policy of randomly pairing incoming freshmen who do not name a preferred roommate. Due to this policy, most freshmen are randomly assigned a friendship by the computer system that manages the university's on-campus residences. Yakusheva *et al.* then administered two surveys – one in the fall of the freshman year, and one in the following fall – that asked about diet, exercise, height, and weight. They found evidence of a surprising negative causal effect of the roommates' weight: students randomly assigned to live with someone who weighs more, gained fewer pounds over the course of their freshman year and adopted more diet and exercise behaviors than those with lighter roommates.

The pivotal assumption for this causal inference is that roommates are in fact randomly selected. The university in the Yakusheva *et al.* analysis is unnamed; however, it is possible to find similar universities with the same housing policy. In an in-depth interview, an administrator at this university's Office of Residence Life confirmed the existence of the program.[3] The randomization process is carried out in a strictly automated way, using the random-number generator in the office's database software. Furthermore, the administrator confirmed that most students in fact comply with their randomized roommate assignment. Over the course of the 2014–15 academic year, only 2% of randomly assigned roommate pairs ended up reassigned. Indeed, the residential housing office has a roommate dispute policy that requires extensive attempts at compromise and reconciliation before reassigning a roommate – with the result that most room reassignments came at the beginning of January, rather than in the first weeks of school. Thus, for the vast majority of randomly assigned students, the treatment assignment mechanism described by Yakusheva *et al.* works as intended. Students can appeal and be reassigned, but few students take this option, and those that do are mostly still exposed to the randomly assigned relationship for months. This qualitative evidence about the assignment and reassignment processes thus strongly supports the assumption of random assignment in this natural experiment.

For some natural experiments, one treatment category is more advantageous to research subjects than the other. For example, counties may receive a grant, households may get a monthly stipend, or students may get access to a better school. In such scenarios, the most important problems arise when subjects who receive the less advantageous treatment assignment are able to deploy power or influence to get transferred into the more advantageous treatment group. If such behavior is possible, then the cases that ultimately comprise the less advantageous treatment group will overrepresent the powerless, the deferential, and those lacking in strategic foresight, while the more advantageous group will disproportionately include cases with the opposite traits. In general, such patterns should be regarded as evidence that the condition required for causal inference is not met in the natural experiment. Hence, when some treatment categories are more advantageous than others, an important research design is to select potentially powerful cases that have been randomized to the less desirable treatment group and examine the kinds of responses those cases made to the randomization. If power plays are attempted – or, even worse, successful – then that is evidence of trouble with the natural experiment; if there is no evidence of strategic response to treatment assignment, that serves as an important form of evidence in favor of the assumption that randomization in fact worked.

When a natural experiment instead involves as-if randomization, the research designs just discussed are still a good idea. However, they are no longer sufficient. Because the treatment assignment process is not in fact random, the analyst needs to add an additional assumption to those required in true natural experiments: whatever the treatment assignment process, it is statistically uncorrelated with all causes of the outcome other than the treatment. When there is a true randomization, this assumption is implied by the design. For as-if random natural experiments, it remains a brute assumption and needs direct evidence of some sort. Because this is a very inclusive assumption, it is useful to test it both by process tracing backwards from the treatment and by using similar techniques to explore the process leading up to the outcome. Any factors that are involved in both of these processes are evidence that the assumption fails and the natural experiment does not work. Thus, casting a broad exploratory net in searching for factors allows for a strong test: if a careful and open-ended search of the causes of the treatment and of the causes of the outcome shows no overlap, then there is meaningful reason to believe the as-if random assumption, while any meaningful overlap effectively rules the assumption out. Qualitative evidence is thus if anything even more helpful with as-if random natural experiments than with true natural experiments.

For example, in John Snow's study of the causes of cholera, the assumption of as-if randomization requires that a household's exposure to water from one or another supplier be entirely arbitrary and unrelated to any social, economic, or other relevant traits. To test this assumption, Snow engaged in classic qualitative fieldwork: he went door-to-door, asking residents about their water supplies. He famously observed no relevant differences among treatment groups:

The pipes of each Company go down all the streets, and into nearly all the courts and alleys. A few houses are supplied by one Company and a few by the other, according to the decision of the owner or occupier at that time when the Water Companies were in active competition. In many cases a single house has a supply different from that on either side. Each company supplies both rich and poor, both large houses and small; there is no difference either in the condition or occupation of the persons receiving the water of the different Companies (Snow 1855: 75).

However, more importantly, he also collected key causal-process observations about the causal pathway leading to households' treatment assignment. For the large number of renters in the areas Snow studied, "the rates are invariably paid by the landlord or his agent, who often lives at a distance, and the residents know nothing about the matter" (Snow 1855: 77). Even for residents, Snow found that they rarely knew the name of the water company that serviced them before checking a recent bill. These facts show that few individuals are consciously aware of the treatment group they are in – and therefore strongly imply that the treatment assignment has mostly arbitrary causes and should meet the assumption of as-if random assignment (Snow 1855: 77)

Good case selection for the qualitative designs discussed above involves careful thought about the causes of treatment assignment when that assignment process is not random. For the design in which cases with randomly assigned treatment are compared to cases with naturally assigned treatment, the key issue is to choose cases that are as similar to each other as possible in terms of all factors that influence the treatment assignment; hence, cases may be selected by carrying out a statistical matching procedure using randomized versus natural treatment assignment as the "treatment" variable and a list of hypothesized causes of treatment assignment when not randomized as the matching variables. Any well-matched pair can serve for this design, because it is not altogether obvious that the factors which make naturally assigned cases different from randomized cases would be related to any observed variable in particular.

For designs focused on testing assumptions of randomization or as-if randomization, somewhat more can be said. For the most part, scenarios in which treatment assignment is in fact nonrandom, even though there is a random-seeming assignment mechanism, involve a distinctive subset of cases: cases that are randomly assigned to a treatment that they would have been highly unlikely to receive under natural treatment assignment. These are the cases in which some actor is especially likely to intervene in a way that undermines the randomization, especially if one treatment is more desirable than the rest. Hence, case selection will require a model of the process by which cases acquire their scores on the treatment variable when there is no randomization:

$$P(D_i = T|\mathbb{X}) = f(\mathbb{X}\beta)$$

This may be a linear probability model, a logit, or whatever other specification is best. Furthermore, given that this model is intended as an auxiliary tool in a test rather than as a direct source of statistical or causal inferences, the stakes regarding assumptions of complete and correct specification are somewhat reduced.[4] Let the estimated probability from this model that case i receives the treatment be labeled as $\hat{P}_i$. Furthermore, suppose that the scholar has no access to an intent-to-treat type variable that shows the treatment group to which each case was randomly assigned before any process of strategic interaction took place;[5] instead, the scholar can only see the treatments that were in fact assigned. Then the cases that are most likely to in fact have altered their treatment assignment are cases that turn out to receive the treatment and have very high scores of $\hat{P}_i$, and cases that turn out to receive the control and have very low scores of $\hat{P}_i$. If violations of randomization are widespread, then a significant proportion of cases in one or the other of these two categories should be those that strategically opted out of their randomized assignment. Thus, if a collection of case studies drawn from these two categories show no evidence of strategic response, then there is some reason to suppose that the assumptions discussed here are workable for the cases in question.

Suppose that multi-method work turns up problems with one or more of the assumptions discussed above. How should the analyst react? Put simply, it depends on the assumption that was violated. If there is evidence that the randomization was not really random or that the as-if random assumptions do not hold, then the study really is not a natural experiment and should probably be analyzed like the observational studies discussed in previous chapters. If the problem instead involves the assumption that the effect of randomized treatment is the same as the effect of naturally assigned treatment, then the natural experiment can be analyzed and will produce a valid causal inference – except that the results will only apply to the context of the natural experiment. In either case, additional information and assumptions (about the set of possible confounding variables that need to be controlled, or about the magnitude and direction of difference between the causal effect in the natural experiment and in the broader population of interest) will have to play a central part in securing the causal inference.

6.2   Regression-Discontinuity Designs

Causal inferences involving as-if randomization are not inferentially equal – for some, the key assumptions are highly credible, while for others, they are dubious. Given this variation, research designs that identify relatively credible sets of as-if random natural experiments are obviously of significant value. One such design stands out as being of particular importance in the literature: the regression-discontinuity design (Thistlethwaite and Campbell 1960; Imbens and Lemieux 2008; Dunning 2012: 63–102). This design identifies and formalizes a set of circumstances that seems particularly likely to yield natural experiments in which the as-if randomization assumption is credible.

The setup is as follows. The treatment of interest is assigned on the basis of a well-established rule based on an assignment variable, Z_i. Specifically, regression-discontinuity designs require some kind of institution that establishes a threshold, t, such that cases are assigned to the treatment if and only if $Z_i > t$.[6] If this institution holds firmly true, and if a few technical conditions are met regarding the Z variable, then it should be that the set of cases just above the threshold, t, and the set just below that threshold are similar other than that one group gets the treatment and the other does not. For this reason, any substantial difference between the two sets of cases in terms of the outcome variable is probably due to the treatment and not to preexisting differences between the cases, because the research design makes it unlikely that any such differences are large.

For example, scholars and policymakers have long been interested in learning whether and how class size is causally connected with academic performance among elementary school students. An obvious problem is that students in large elementary classes are often different in other ways from students in smaller classes; furthermore, it is difficult to come up with a comprehensive list of such differences in order to pursue causal inference via regression-type analysis. To make matters worse, it is unusual (although, as discussed in the previous section, not unheard of) for students to be randomly assigned to schools with very different traits. Clearly, a natural experiment would be useful.

Angrist and Lavy (1999) use a regression-discontinuity design to address this challenge. Their design relies on the interesting fact that the state of Israel, for reasons related to the views of the philosopher Maimonides, imposes an absolute cap on the number of students in a class and allocates funds to hire another teacher whenever a school district's number of pupils in an age cohort exceeds that cap. This policy creates a sharp discontinuity in the relationship between cohort size and class size. A child in an age cohort of 40 will typically have a class of 40 students, while a child in a cohort of 41 students will have a class about half as large. Thus, comparisons of verbal and math test performance just above and just below the threshold provide a tantalizing possibility of valid causal inference.

There are two key assumptions that help establish that the treatment and control groups in a regression-discontinuity design are similar, and therefore that causal inference is plausible. The first is that the cases (or people and organizations connected with them) are unable to respond strategically to the assignment threshold. Suppose there are traits that allow some cases to deliberately adjust their score of Z_i to get into the treatment group when they expect the outcome to be close to the threshold but perhaps below, or alternatively to opt out of the assignment process or remeasure Z_i when the outcome is unfavorable. Then those traits will be disproportionately represented among cases that just barely exceed the threshold and underrepresented among cases that fall just below the threshold. If those traits are correlated with the potential outcomes, $Y_{i,t}$ and $Y_{i,c}$, then the treatment and the control group will differ on average on those key causal quantities – and therefore causal inference will fail.

In the context of the Maimonides' Law study discussed above, this assumption entails – plausibly enough – that parents in an area do not strategically coordinate their fertility decisions with a goal of bringing about smaller class sizes. It also requires more difficult assumptions, such as that parents do not move to school districts on the basis of the class sizes that this rule would provide for their children, that parents are not able to get permission to send their children to different school districts in order to find smaller classes, and that parents cannot exert pressure to get an additional teacher before the Maimonides' Law cutoff is reached. Deciding whether these assumptions are plausible would obviously require detailed knowledge of the official as well as the real-world workings of the Israeli educational system – and qualitative work could help a great deal in this.

The same assumption (that cases cannot react strategically to the existence of the threshold) has become a centerpiece of debate in studies of US politics. Scholars in that domain have made creative efforts to apply regression-discontinuity designs to study the effects of one party (Democrats, as opposed to Republicans, for example) beating the other in congressional elections. For example, Butler and Butler (2006) look at whether a party's victory in a senate election has a contagion effect on the next senate election in that state. In this analysis, the Z_i variable is the Republican candidate's share of the two-party vote, and the treatment assignment threshold is 50%. Thus, comparing senate elections following close Republican victories (for example, by a margin of less than 1%) to those following close Republican defeats might generate a useful natural experiment because these sets of elections may well be quite similar when taken as groups.

In fact, this design may be problematic. Caughey and Sekhon (2011) find that politicians who just barely win elections in the United States are far more likely to be incumbents, while those who lose are more likely to be non-incumbent challengers. Since incumbents are likely to be different from challengers in a number of different ways, this finding casts significant doubt on the validity of causal inferences using electoral victory as the treatment in a regression-discontinuity design.

In this example, quantitative evidence about incumbency rates plays a key role in testing – and casting doubt on – the assumption under consideration here. Yet often qualitative evidence can be helpful as well. Case studies may help identify variables that may be imbalanced between treatment and control, an important contribution because such variables are not always obvious. This can happen through close attention to the causal process involved in connecting the Z_i variable with treatment assignment. This kind of research design can also provide positive evidence in favor of a regression-discontinuity design: if the analyst carries out a thorough inductive search for variables that contaminate the link between the assignment variable and the treatment, and no such variables are found, that process generates meaningful support for the viability of the design.

The second essential assumption for regression-discontinuity designs is that the Z_i variable is distributed in such a way that there are a good number of cases close to the threshold. Obviously, if all cases are clustered at scores far away from the threshold (because that is how the data are distributed, or perhaps measured), then the entire argument collapses. Of course, there is some complexity here, in that an adequate definition of "far away from the threshold" depends a great deal on the causal situation in question. A very small distance from the threshold can be a huge problem – if that distance is caused by a confounding variable with a powerful effect on Y; by contrast, a much larger distance caused by measurement error would obviously be unproblematic. Nevertheless, there are sensible quantitative approaches to this problem, and hence this second assumption is not especially in need of multi-method attention.

It is difficult to design a case-selection rule that is powerful for testing the key assumption that treatment assignment involves no strategic reaction to the value of the Z_i variable vis-à-vis the treatment assignment threshold. Researchers cannot select extreme values on the treatment variable, because that variable is dichotomous in such designs. It is also impossible to select extreme values on Z_i, because only a narrow range of such values enter into the design. Furthermore, other variables are useless: either those variables are unrelated to treatment assignment and therefore unhelpful in case selection, or they are already quantitative evidence that the design is flawed and thus that case-study evidence is not particularly needed. Hence, in the absence of any evidently superior case-selection strategy, random sampling is acceptable.

6.3   Instrumental Variables Natural Experiments

The designs considered to this point in the chapter are comparatively simple. They involve direct randomization or as-if random assignment of the treatment of interest. In these designs, the validity of the causal inference revolves around a set of claims about the treatment assignment process – and little else.

Yet there is a wide range of social, economic, and political outcomes for which direct randomization or as-if random assignment of potentially relevant treatments is hard or even impossible to find. For example, potential college students, education policymakers, and a range of other actors would benefit greatly from accurate information about the causal effects of getting a college degree on lifetime earnings. Yet it is hard to imagine a situation in which a democratic society randomly assigns some people to be compelled to receive a college education while others are coerced not to receive a degree. Instead, it is most plausible to conceive of situations in which individuals are randomly assigned to receive encouragement (i.e., scholarships or other incentives) or discouragement (i.e., no scholarships, admission to a less desirable university, or alternative life opportunities) to complete a college degree. That is to say, at best analysts may find a cause of the treatment that is randomly assigned, rather than finding random assignment of the treatment itself. Such a setup can be called an instrumental variables natural experiment (Dunning 2012: 87–101).

In fact, scholars have proposed a number of solutions of this sort to the problem of estimating the causal effect of education on lifetime earnings. One fascinating example (Angrist and Krueger 1992) uses the Vietnam draft lottery as a source of randomization. Among individuals who were not exempted from the lottery, and assuming that no conspiracies existed to manipulate the process, assignment to be drafted to serve in Vietnam was random. Furthermore, people who fought in Vietnam received college subsidies from the US government after completing their tours of duty. Thus the draft lottery represents – among other things – a randomized encouragement to seek a college diploma.

Can such randomizations of a cause of the treatment provide insight into the effect of the treatment on the outcome? In some special circumstances, they can. If the randomization or as-if randomization of the cause of the treatment is a genuine natural experiment, and if that natural experiment only causes the outcome via the treatment, then a reasonable estimate of the effect of the treatment on the outcome is the ratio of the effect of the randomization on the outcome to the effect of the randomization on the treatment.

To see how this proposal works, let us formalize it in potential-outcomes notation. The randomized cause of the treatment is Z_i; to simplify things, we will consider the case in which Z_i is dichotomous and takes on only the values 0 or 1.[7] Because Z_i is believed to cause the treatment, we need to introduce potential outcomes of the treatment depending on the value that Z_i in fact takes on: $D_{i,1}$ if Z_i is randomized to 1, and $D_{i,0}$ if Z_i is randomized to 0. Obviously, the effect of Z_i on the treatment D_i for case i is just the difference between these two quantities, and appropriate sample average treatment effects can be defined in the usual ways.

If Z_i is less than a necessary and sufficient cause of D_i, then there will be cases in which $D_{i,1} = D_{i,0}$. Furthermore, cases may have opposite reactions to the randomization. For example, it may be the case that for most cases $D_{i,1} = t$ and $D_{i,0} = c$, but for a few cases $D_{i,1} = c$ and $D_{i,0} = t$. This latter kind of heterogeneity, in which some cases react oppositely to the randomization, creates special problems and will be assumed away for the moment for the sake of simplicity.

The ultimate outcome, Y, is hypothesized to depend on D and may also depend on Z. Thus, we must consider four possible potential outcomes for Y: $Y_{i,t,1}$ when $D_i = t$ and $Z_i = 1$, $Y_{i,t,0}$ when $D_i = t$ and $Z_i = 0$, $Y_{i,c,1}$ when $D_i = c$ and $Z_i = 1$, and $Y_{i,c,0}$ when $D_i = c$ and $Z_i = 0$. One of the key assumptions for instrumental variables natural experiments is that Z only affects Y through D. This assumption allows us to collapse back to the standard two potential outcomes, $Y_{i,t}$ and $Y_{i,c}$.

This notation allows us to look carefully at the causal structures involved in instrumental variables natural experiments. To see how such natural experiments can work, consider first the causal meaning of the average observed value of Y among cases with $Z_i = 1$. This average is a constant times the sum of observed values of Y for the relevant cases. That sum, in turn, has two components:

$$\sum_{Z_i=1} Y_i = \sum_{Z_i=1, D_{i,1}=t} Y_{i,t} + \sum_{Z_i=1, D_{i,1}=c} Y_{i,c}$$

The first summation includes cases where D_i is positively affected by Z_i, as well as cases where $D_i = t$ no matter what value Z_i takes on. Because of the simplifying assumption above (that there are no cases with opposite causal relations between D and Z), the second summation is made up only of cases where $D_i = c$ no matter what value Z_i takes on. Thus, the equation can be rewritten as follows:

$$\sum_{Z_i=1} Y_i = \sum_{Z_i=1, D_{i,1}=t, D_{i,0}=c} Y_{i,t} + \sum_{Z_i=1, D_{i,1}=t, D_{i,0}=t} Y_{i,t} + \sum_{Z_i=1, D_{i,1}=c, D_{i,0}=c} Y_{i,c}$$

By a similar argument, the average value of Y for cases with $Z_i = 0$ can be written as constant times:

$$\sum_{Z_i=0} Y_i = \sum_{Z_i=0, D_{i,1}=t, D_{i,0}=t} Y_{i,t} + \sum_{Z_i=0, D_{i,1}=t, D_{i,0}=c} Y_{i,c} + \sum_{Z_i=0, D_{i,1}=c, D_{i,0}=c} Y_{i,c}$$

In instrumental variables analysis, the causal inference involves the difference between these two sums, each divided by the number of cases randomized to the relevant score on D. With a large enough sample, these weighted sums will converge to constants. Furthermore, because Z is random and only affects Y through D, summations in the first and second expression that differ only in terms of the value of Z for included cases converge to the same constant. Thus, $\sum_{Z_i=1,D_{i,1}=c,D_{i,0}=c} Y_{i,c}$ and $\sum_{Z_i=0,D_{i,1}=c,D_{i,0}=c} Y_{i,c}$ converge to the same value, as do $\sum_{Z_i=1,D_{i,1}=t,D_{i,0}=t} Y_{i,t}$ and $\sum_{Z_i=0,D_{i,1}=t,D_{i,0}=t} Y_{i,t}$. This means that these quantities simply subtract out and do not affect the causal inference at all.

Instead, the instrumental variables estimator for large samples is just the ratio of $\sum_{Z_i=1,D_{i,1}=t,D_{i,0}=c} Y_{i,t}$ to the total number of cases with $Z_i = 1$ minus the ratio of $\sum_{Z_i=0,D_{i,1}=t,D_{i,0}=c} Y_{i,c}$ to the total number of cases with $Z_i = c$. This difference of ratios in turn simplifies to the average treatment effect of D on Y for cases where Z causally affects D multiplied by the ratio of such cases to the total size of the sample – this second ratio simply being the average treatment effect of Z on D. Thus, dividing the effect of Z on Y by the effect of Z on D gives a meaningful estimate of at least part of the overall causal effect of interest: the effect of D on Y, at least for cases where D is affected by Z.

This setup is clearly complex, and in practice it can get even messier. Sometimes Z, D, or both are continuous rather than dichotomous, making everything more difficult to describe and requiring stronger assumptions. In other situations, the assumptions described above are credible only if some set of variables $\mathbb{W}$ is controlled for within the analysis. A variety of other additional complications has been discussed in the literature. However, for the purposes of this chapter, the simplest instrumental variables setup, described above, is already complex enough.

As a schematic summary, the discussion suggests that useful causal inferences can sometimes be made using instrumental variables natural experiments if certain key assumptions are met. First, the Z variable must be genuinely randomized, or legitimately as-if random in its relationship to the treatment variable. That is to say, the Z to D relationship must be a true natural experiment and should be tested via the techniques described earlier in the chapter.

Second, the causal effect of Z on D must be nonzero. If this causal effect is in fact zero, then the instrumental variables estimator described earlier will contain a division by zero and thus will be undefined. Conceptually, this problem arises because a randomization that does not cause the treatment of interest gives no random shock to that treatment with which to justify an inference about the relationship between D and Y. If the first assumption is met, then this second assumption can be checked quantitatively by regressing Z on D.

Third, there must be no causal effect of Z on Y, conditioning on D and any included control variables. This assumption can be at most partially tested via quantitative analysis. Thus, there is an important opportunity for an integrative research design component here. Two alternative process-tracing approaches fit the problem. Analysts may inductively process trace backwards from Y, looking for any evidence of causal influences that can be connected back to Z without involving D as an intervening step. Alternatively, scholars may begin with a broadly inclusive sense of the possible effects of Z and search for any evidence of a causal pathway from any of those possible effects forward to Y that does not pass through the main treatment along the way.

For an example of what such qualitative design components would look like in a concrete setting, consider the draft lottery, education, and lifetime earnings example introduced above. For the approach starting from the dependent variable and working backwards, the analyst would look at an individual's income history, searching for moments of unusual change or turning points that set the lifetime earnings path on a particular trajectory; for example, debilitating injuries or chronic illnesses, acquisition of technical skills or higher education, or professional breakthroughs. Each of these would be closely examined for evidence of a connection with the individual's draft status during the Vietnam War. If the researcher found, for example, that the individual's income took a permanent upward step upon getting an entry-level job in a highly skilled and high-paying industry – and that the job was attained in significant part through connections with a close associate during military service – this would indicate a potentially troubling causal channel.

Starting from the Z variable, the researcher would instead start by assembling a list of possible effects of service in the Vietnam War other than educational attainment. If this list includes any variables that have potential causal effects on lifetime earnings, the next step would be to select one or a few cases and deductively search for causal-process observations that support or undermine the existence of the causal link in question. Thus, a researcher may find case evidence suggesting that a veteran acquired economically valuable technical or leadership skills from military service itself, and not from subsequent education. Alternatively, case evidence might show that military service caused some individuals lasting physical or psychological harm that limited their lifetime earnings. Any such finding would constitute evidence against the third assumption for causal inference from instrumental variables natural experiments.

Regarding case selection, two designs specific to instrumental variables setups have been discussed: tracing backwards from the dependent variable to find causal paths that connect with Z independent of the treatment, and searching for evidence of causal paths moving forward from the Z variable to the treatment. However, because both designs are trying to find the same problems, only one case-selection design is needed.

For the design that starts from the dependent variable, the relevant design is perhaps easier to see. The idea is to find cases in which there is a large component to Y's score that cannot be accounted for on the basis of D and any included control variables. The idea is to pick cases that are highly likely to show a significant causal effect from Z to Y, excluding effects of the treatment and control variables – so cases that are hard to fully predict on the basis of those variables are likely to be the most useful ones. Thus scholars should carry out an ordinary regression, predicting Y on the basis of D and any desired control variables. Then from that regression, deviant cases should be selected as the most likely to reveal information about problematic causal pathways from the randomization. When starting from the randomization, the same cases are useful for the same reason.

6.4   Conclusions

Natural experiments can be powerful research designs, sometimes permitting more credible causal inference than can be achieved via regression-type or matching methods. Yet they do not allow assumption-free causal inference. Additional information is needed to justify causal claims even in the best of cases, in which a classic natural experiment exploits a true randomization. In more elaborate and assumption-driven situations, such as instrumental variables natural experiments using as-if randomization, the causal inference depends heavily, perhaps even primarily, on a series of complex assumptions.

Because such assumptions are crucial and have implications that can be at least partly tested via qualitative methods, integrative multi-method designs promise more powerful causal inferences than can be achieved via purely quantitative natural experiments. In fact, as the next chapter will show, integrative multi-method designs have a great deal to add even in the context of the prototypical strong design for causal inference: randomized experiments.

Notes

1 This may seem an obscure assumption, but in practice it is easy to think of situations where the fact of randomization changes the effect of a treatment. Consider, for example, the treatment of being told "I love you." Surely this treatment has a different effect when it is known to be randomly assigned rather than freely chosen. Parallel examples abound in all domains of the social sciences.
2 This typology of natural experiments draws on Dunning (2012).
3 This personal interview, conducted on August 20, 2015, was carried out on the condition of anonymity for the administrator and the university.
4 That is to say, this model is only used as a means of generating fitted probabilities – usually the most robust output of models of this sort in the face of omitted variables and similar problems.

5 If the analyst has access to both the randomized assignment and the actual list of treatments received, then the assumptions of interest here can be tested directly.

6 Obviously, there is no important difference if the rule is that cases enter treatment if and only if $Z_i < t$; in this case, the scholar can simply swap treatment and control groups.

7 This is a close fit for the Vietnam draft lottery example, because individuals are either drafted or not. Many other studies would not fit this setup as neatly, but the core ideas remain the same as presented in this simpler setting.

7 Embedding Case Studies within Experiments

Experimental research has received major new attention in the social sciences recently. This phenomenon has crossed disciplinary lines; economics has seen a surge of field experiments, particularly in the development subfield (Duflo *et al.* 2008), as well as laboratory experiments related to studies of decision-making with roots in game theory and behavioral economics (Camerer 2003). In political science, experiments have gone from a marginalized method to a major source of insight in studies of political communication (Druckman and Leeper 2012), ethnic politics (Wong 2005; Dunning and Nilekani 2013), conflict studies (McDermott *et al.* 2002), political mobilization (Green *et al.* 2013), clientelistic politics (Vicente and Wantchekon 2009; Gonzalez-Ocantos *et al.* 2012; De La O 2013), and more. This growth stands alongside well-established experimental traditions in psychology as well as related subfields in sociology. Furthermore, institutional developments such as the Time-Sharing Experiments in the Social Sciences program have made experimental research more accessible to political science and sociology researchers without the resources to run their own laboratories.

This emergence of experiments as a major tool for social science research raises issues for multi-method research design. Experimental designs strive to reduce the number of assumptions needed to justify causal inference. Do experiments still benefit from multi-method designs incorporating case-study research? If so, how? This chapter argues that multi-method designs combining qualitative and experimental methods are unusually strong. While experiments depend on a different and narrower set of assumptions in comparison with regression-type designs, they still require assumptions about measurement, causal interconnections among cases, and experimental realism. Furthermore, while evidence regarding causal pathways between the treatment and the outcome is not required to make a causal inference using an experiment, it can vastly increase the social scientific value of experimental results, and qualitative research can contribute substantially to this objective.

7.1   Experiments and the Potential-Outcomes Framework

Experiments are important because they are a particularly strong tool for causal inference. Indeed, experiments are the paradigm of causal inference under the potential-outcomes framework. As explained in more detail in Chapter 2, the reason is that random assignment in combination with the law of large numbers makes the treatment and control group (or, in some experiments, the various treatment groups) credible counterfactuals for each other. That is to say, the treatment group taken as a collective has just about the same traits as the control group, aside from any causal effects of the treatment itself. Thus, any difference between the treatment and control groups in terms of the distribution of the outcome variable can be credibly attributed to the treatment assignment, because everything else will approximately balance due to randomization.

A key point to emphasize is that, in contrast to every other design discussed in this book so far, omitted variables are not a central challenge to causal inference in a properly randomized experiment. Instead, other issues – relevant in any study – become the focus of debate in dealing with experiments. Key among these generally important assumptions are issues of measurement, the existence of causal pathways, the separateness of treatment in each case (SUTVA), and experimental realism (a concept that captures the most significant component of the larger and messier idea of external validity). The chapter will address each of these themes, in turn, considering relevant multi-method designs along the way.

7.2   Case Studies and Experiments: Basic Considerations

Are case studies logically compatible enough with experiments to contribute in addressing these key issues of causal inference? One important argument to the contrary would focus on the contrast between experiments' standard emphasis on the sample average treatment effect with case studies' much greater attention to causation at the level of the individual case (Goertz and Mahoney 2012: Part 1). This is a compelling argument against any simple or direct comparison between the findings from an experimental and a case-study analysis of the same topic. Because of this fundamental difference, the two methods might produce seemingly opposite results without contradicting each other. For instance, an experiment might find no causal effect of a particular treatment on the outcome of interest, while a case study finds substantial evidence of a major effect. Both findings could be completely correct; the case study might simply focus on a case that is causally unusual in comparison with those studied by the experiment. To echo a recurring theme of this book, there is little to be gained from a triangulation-style comparison of overall causal effects between experiments and case studies.

Even so, integrative multi-method designs have already proven useful in a range of experiments, and there is substantial scope for further, as yet mostly unrealized combinations. Scholars previously discussed "experimental ethnography" (Sherman and Strang 2004; Levy Paluck 2010b) as a set of research designs that use qualitative methods to strengthen one or more aspects of a standard experimental research design. In experimental ethnographies, analysts do not carry out qualitative and experimental designs in parallel, but instead use qualitative techniques to fill one or more roles within a true randomized experiment.

In particular, work in experimental ethnography has highlighted the possibility of using qualitative research design components to measure one or many outcomes of an experiment (Sherman and Strang 2004: 210–15). The idea here is to go beyond the most common measurement strategies for the outcome in social science experiments – survey questions or behavioral responses to situations – by using in-depth interviews and other qualitative approaches to provide insights into emotions, thought processes, and models of understanding, as well as to allow for surprising inductive discoveries of possible effects in these domains and others. Because such qualitative measurement involves a great deal of effort, both Sherman and Strang, and Levy Paluck discuss experimental ethnography with small treatment group sizes: 10 total subjects in Sherman and Strang's (2004: 211–12) discussion, for example. Such small samples would render experimentation less powerful for causal inference; smaller samples make random assignment less able to balance out potential confounders. Nonetheless, the idea of experimental ethnography highlights the potential for multi-method designs involving experiments and qualitative methods.

Levy Paluck's (2010a) work on talk radio and inter-group conflict in the Democratic Republic of Congo (DRC) provides a fascinating example of the additional information that can result from using qualitative research practices to measure an outcome variable in an experiment. In this study, conflict-laden regions of Eastern DRC were randomly assigned to a control condition in which a local radio station broadcast a soap opera or a treatment condition in which the soap opera was followed by a 15-minute talk show encouraging listeners to adopt an empathetic perspective toward members of their out-group. After a year of these broadcasts, the research team interviewed a large sample of citizens in both treatment groups.

These interviews included survey questions, allowing for a set of standard quantitative outcomes to be analyzed (Levy Paluck 2010a: 1176–79). However, the research protocol also included an open-ended interaction, in which participants are gifted a 2-kilogram bag of salt and then invited to gift part of that salt to a group with which they are uncomfortable. Two outcomes result from this interaction. First, researchers weigh and record the amount of salt, if any, that the respondents ultimately choose to donate. Second, they capture a much more qualitative, open-ended record of anything the respondents say to justify their decision about donation.

While participants' degree of generosity in donating to a group with which they are uncomfortable is a valuable objective indicator with clear connections to the state of inter-group politics, the social meaning of this indicator is inevitably ambiguous. An individual might choose not to donate for clearly negative reasons, such as outright hostility to their out-group. Yet it is also possible to imagine alternative, less explicitly negative motivations: valuing self-help over charity, concern that giving to a (possibly lower-status) out-group might seem patronizing, or fear of retaliation from extremist members of the in-group. Qualitative analysis of the remarks made by participants while deciding about their contribution goes a long way to resolve this ambiguity. For example, Levy Paluck cites a participant who remarked that, "They have killed family members, made us poor – I would rather die than help them" (Levy Paluck 2010a: 63). It is difficult to imagine a person primarily concerned about promoting self-help, for example, making a comment of this nature. Furthermore, the degree of personal emotion expressed in this remark tends to support an interpretation based on hostility rather than on fear of reprisals from the in-group; someone avoiding retaliation by extremists could simply refuse to help without expressing such visceral rejection toward the out-group. In this way, a qualitative reading of open-ended, unsolicited rationales helped Levy Paluck reduce the ambiguity involved in her more quantitative outcome measure.

Of course, the qualitative component in such designs is by no means limited to the task of measuring outcomes in the experiment. The remainder of this chapter will extend the idea of experimental ethnography to encompass multi-method designs in which experiments are complemented by qualitative components targeted at other assumptions, beginning with measurement issues connected to compliance.

7.3   Old Issues: Measurement and Causal Pathways

For every design discussed in this book, the validity and precision of measurement is an essential issue for causal inference. It is therefore appropriate that the theme has been discussed at various points in the book. Experiments raise a few new issues, so measurement receives a fresh consideration here.

The same is true for causal pathways: there probably has to be some series of causal steps connecting a treatment and an outcome if there is in fact a treatment effect, and this issue is a concern in every research design. Experiments are often criticized for not providing evidence about how a causal effect comes about (Deaton 2010). This is a fair criticism in one sense, because inferences about causal pathways are weaker and more assumption-laden than inferences about overall causal effects in experimental studies (Robins and Greenland 1992). Yet the criticism is ultimately unfair, in that experiments certainly provide no less leverage for inference about causal pathways than any other quantitative design. Nonetheless, the existence of a causal pathway consistent with the overall causal effect is an important issue in experiments, even if it is not in any sense a distinctive challenge for such designs. Furthermore, some issues specific to experiments arise; thus a renewed discussion is in order.

Turning first to issues of measurement, there is little new to say about the outcome variable. Measurement problems for the outcome are the same as in any other research design and should be addressed using the same strategies. Issues regarding the treatment variable are more interesting, however. Because the treatment variable is deliberately assigned by the researcher, it may seem as if there should be nothing whatsoever to discuss. Unless the research endeavor is hopelessly disorganized, records of treatment assignment should be perfect and unambiguous. Several sources of measurement error simply do not arise.

Even so, there are measurement-related problems to consider with respect to the treatment variable in an experiment. The issue involves experimental noncompliance (Imbens and Rubin 1997): to what extent do subjects in the experiment in fact receive the treatment to which they are assigned? Or do cases instead routinely cross over to an unassigned treatment category? For example, consider experiments on the effects of emotion on social and political behavior (e.g. Brader 2005). If a scholar wishes to randomly assign individuals to feel anger, prior research suggests that showing certain selected clips from films is a generally effective treatment (Gross and Levenson 1995). Yet it would be ridiculous to expect each subject in an experiment to become angry on seeing such a film clip. Some would surely fail to pay attention and thus have no emotional response at all. Still others might reach atypical conclusions regarding predictability, culpability, and other themes causally implicated in emotion – with the consequence that these individuals have an unexpected emotional response (fear or guilt, for example) to the film clip. Similar problems in which some cases respond differently than intended to their treatment assignment are quite common across experimental designs.

These issues, discussed in terms of compliance or treatment crossover, are obviously strongly causal. Yet they are also an issue of measurement: problems of crossover mean that there is a measurement discrepancy between the treatment assignment variable and the actual treatment received by the case in question. Treatment crossover forces scholars to make decisions about analysis. Should attention focus on the treatment effect of the assigned treatment or of the actually received treatment? If treatment crossover is nonrandom and the analyst estimates the effect of the actually received treatment, then omitted-variable bias is possible. Because this undermines the central strengths of experiments, the most common advice is for analysts to instead estimate the effect of treatment assignment, often called the ITT ("intent-to-treat") estimator (Lachin 2000).

The ITT estimator has the attractive property of generally being conservative relative to the true average treatment effect. To see why this is the case, it will be useful to briefly think about the ITT estimator in terms of potential outcomes. The ITT estimator is, of course, just the difference between average scores on the dependent variable for the group assigned to treatment and the group assigned to control. Each of these groups is a mix of four kinds of cases (Angrist *et al.* 1996). First are "compliers," i.e., people who will receive the treatment in fact if assigned to the treatment group, and will receive the control in fact if assigned to the control group. Second are "always-takers," who receive the treatment regardless of the group to which they are assigned. Third are "never-takers," who are likewise unaffected by treatment assignment but receive the control. The last group are the most problematic: "defiers," who receive the treatment when assigned to the control group and the control when assigned to the treatment group.

Because treatment is randomly assigned in an experiment, these four groups will usually have about equal representation in the treatment and control groups. This is good news. Always-takers will contribute $Y_{i,t}$ to the treatment group average and to the control group average – and because such cases are evenly split between the two groups, these contributions will subtract out. The same holds true for never-takers. Thus the presence of these two kinds of cases tends to shrink the ITT estimator toward zero.

Compliers, of course, will contribute a nonzero average to the ITT estimate (whenever the actual effect for such cases is nonzero!) because they respond as expected to treatment. If there are no defiers, the ITT estimate is a weighted average of zero and the true causal effect of interest, and is thus conservative.

Things become more complicated if there are defiers in the data. Because defiers contribute $Y_{i,c}$ to the treatment group average and $Y_{i,t}$ to the control group, their scores will not generally cancel out as do those of always- and never-takers. If defiers on average have the same treatment effect as compliers, then the groups will pull in opposite directions. If defiers are rare relative to compliers, then the existence of defiers will bias the ITT estimate toward zero; if, unusually, defiers are more common than compliers, then the ITT estimate can even have the wrong sign. Furthermore, if defiers are differently affected by treatment than are compliers, then the distortion they cause in the ITT estimate can have almost any direction and magnitude, especially if the number of defiers is not small.

For these reasons, if qualitative analysis can provide some evidence about the number of defiers and about the extent to which they are causally affected by treatment along the same mechanisms as compliers, which can significantly strengthen causal inferences drawn from experiments. Both of these inferences are difficult, depending inherently on counterfactuals. To find a defier, for example, a scholar must identify a case that not only receives the treatment while in reality assigned to the control group, but also *would* receive the control if assigned to the treatment group.

The task can be made somewhat easier by recognizing that defiers can by definition only be found among cases that do not receive their assigned treatment condition. Thus for purposes of testing for the presence and proportion of defiers, all treatment-group cases that in fact receive the treatment and all control-group cases that in fact receive the control can be safely set aside.

Furthermore, because of random assignment, defiers will be about equally split between the treatment and control groups. Thus, it is possible to improve the odds of finding defiers, if they actually exist, by selecting cases from the group in which the lowest proportion of cases fail to receive their assigned treatment. For example, suppose that 80% of treatment group cases in fact receive the treatment while 90% of control group cases in fact receive the control. Then at least 10% of cases must be never-takers – such cases accounting for the discrepancy in compliance between the treatment and control groups. Choosing a treatment-group case that receives the control thus gives at most a 50% chance of finding a defier. No such constraint exists for the control group, where the chance of finding a defier may be as high as 100%.[1] For this reason, it is a good idea to choose noncompliant cases from the group with the highest compliance rate when searching for potential defiers.

Once such cases are selected, what should scholars look for in qualitative evidence to identify possible defiers? Attention must be paid to the character of the causal link between treatment assignment and actual treatment received among selected, noncompliant cases. Always-takers and never-takers should have causal processes characterized by immutability: the treatment assignment simply does not play into the causal chain at all. For example, if the experimental treatment involves the manipulation of information presented to subjects, then individuals who are simply inattentive may well end up as always-takers or never-takers. By contrast, an individual who demonstrates suspicion toward the information even before examining it is more likely to be a defier. More generally, causal-process evidence pointing toward the inefficacy or irrelevance of the treatment assignment for a case implies an always- or never-taker, while causal-process evidence that the treatment assignment mattered in atypical ways suggests a defier. If several cases appear to be defiers, then there is reason to worry that the experimental results may not accurately reflect the causal effect of theoretical interest.

Having identified potential defiers, the next step is to process-trace forward from the actual treatment received to the outcome. Are the kinds of variables and influences that seem relevant to this pathway for potential defiers similar to those that matter for cases that appear to be compliers? If so, then there is some reason to think that the defiers simply make the ITT estimate conservative, as discussed above. However, if there is reason to think that the defiers are affected differently by treatment than are the compliers, then it will simply be hard to know how the ITT relates to the quantities of real theoretical interest.

In addition to these issues of measurement, in the guise of treatment compliance, experiments also revive the recurrent question of causal pathways. Experimental research designs shed no special light on the causal steps that stand between the treatment and the outcome.

Sometimes, sharp theory or clever research design can help illuminate such steps – but the same is true in any kind of research design. This limitation of experimental research designs – the fact that they often contribute little to working out causal pathways – is a standard critique of experimental research. Yet it is a substantially unfair critique: the same limitation applies in essentially the same ways to quantitative work in general, as has been discussed in previous chapters.

While the limitations are the same, experiments do pose some issues for multi-method designs in which case studies are used to work through inferences about causal pathways. First, the strategy of selecting extreme cases on the treatment variable is usually unworkable: experimental treatments are almost always categorical and often not even ordered, so it is unclear what an extreme case could even be.

The dependent variable may have any level of measurement, of course, raising the prospect of selecting extreme cases on the outcome. Yet this is problematic for practical reasons. The dependent variable is measured after the experiment begins, so case selection on the dependent variable would need to take place after the experiment. For a variety of reasons, this is only sometimes feasible. How, then, can case-study work address causal pathways if the most plausible case-selection technique is not feasible?

In fact, it may sometimes be possible to set up an experiment such that researchers always collect the data that would be needed to do qualitative analysis for all experimental subjects. Then, relevant cases can be selected (according to the extreme cases on the outcome criterion, if possible, or otherwise perhaps at random) and given an in-depth analysis. This may seem an unreasonable idea. After all, one of the reasons that case-study designs usually focus on few cases is the difficulty of data collection. Yet certain kinds of data can be collected within experiments at low cost that allow for rich and interesting after-the-fact case-study analysis.

For example, consider experimental process-tracing designs in psychology.[2] Here, scholars use video recording, computer track- ing, eye-movement recorders, or other such technology to track the sequence in which participants in the experiment consider each available piece of information, as well as the amount of time they spend considering that information.[3]

These data permit subsequent inferences about the kind of information that played a role in the subject's decision-making, and sometimes even about the relative importance of different pieces of information in the decision that was made. An interesting example involves Mintz *et al.*'s (2006) comparison of the decision-making processes of political science undergraduates and military officers. In this study, parallel samples of subjects were recruited from each of these two populations and were asked to choose among various alternative strategies for US counterterrorism policy. Experimental treatments involved the probability that each strategy would be funded and the communicated certainty that it would work. In this study, process tracing was used to determine the number of pieces of information that each subject consulted during the process of making a decision. Students used significantly more information to decide than did military officers – students considered an average of about 11 separate pieces of information, while officers on average considered 9. More careful analysis of the actual content of the information search showed that students were drastically more likely than officers to engage in maximizing (as opposed to satisficing) decision-making processes.

While such analysis is often quantitative, there is no reason whatsoever that it could not be qualitative. Indeed, qualitative analysis of such process-tracing evidence could explore interactions between subjects' pre-experimental traits and experiences and their decision-making path, and otherwise provide a richer if less inclusive analysis than could a quantitative study of the data. The central point, of course, is that such process-tracing data are routinely collected for all cases, allowing analysts to conduct case selection after the fact and thereby to potentially select extreme cases on the outcome.

Several other techniques for collecting qualitatively analyzable evidence may also be feasible to use on all cases in experiments. For example, measurement within the experiment – both at the time the outcome is measured and, potentially, during the course of the experiment itself – can include open-ended survey questions.[4] Such questions produce text responses that can be analyzed in just the same qualitative ways as can answer in open-ended interviews or in focus groups. Furthermore, because they involve the qualitative repurposing of fairly standard survey techniques, it is obviously feasible to collect such data from a significant subsample of participants in an experiment – or even from all of them.

The alternative of implementing full-scale experimental ethnography, along the lines discussed above, will be more challenging if applied to all participants in a large experiment, and indeed may only sometimes be feasible. It is simply hard to ask a scholar to conduct one thousand or more in-depth, ethnographic interviews within the course of a single research project; all the more so if only a fraction of those interviews will ultimately be subjected to serious analysis. Nonetheless, a variety of alternatives remains.

First, a scholar may choose to conduct ethnographic interviews with a moderately sized, randomly selected subset of experimental subjects. This approach obviously gives up altogether on any agenda of deliberate case selection. Even so, it has the significant virtue of allowing serious qualitative research, controlled and conducted personally by the head researcher, to be embedded in the experiment while the study is taking place. Such a hybrid allows for experimental ethnography to take place just as proposed by Sherman and Strang (2004), while maintaining the quantitative leverage for causal inference that comes from the combination of randomization and the law of large numbers.

Second, in some circumstances it can be feasible to train and employ a team of research assistants to carry out ethnographic interviews alongside or instead of the primary researcher (LeCompte and Goetz 1982: 41–42). If this is workable for the project in question, and if sufficient resources are available, it may again be possible to carry out in-depth interviews for all subjects (or a relatively large random subsample of subjects), from which some can be selected for in-depth qualitative analysis after the fact.

Third, if the above alternatives are unacceptable, it remains possible to select cases after the fact and carry out interviews later on. Obviously, this is easiest if the research subjects agree to be reinterviewed after the experiment. Even when this is not feasible, however, it is often possible to search for and locate substitute cases that are equivalent as far as the experimental analysis is concerned. This may seem implausible, because people are multifaceted and never serve as perfect (and rarely as even close) substitutes for each other. Yet people's full complexity – or that of other kinds of research subjects – does not enter into experimental causal inferences. Instead, in an ITT analysis, only two aspects of a person in fact contribute to the causal inference: their assigned treatment and their score on the outcome variable. Hence, any individual with the same scores on those two variables is – for the limited purposes of evaluating causal pathways relative to the ITT estimate of the treatment effect – interchangeable with the original research subject. Analysts could locate such replacement individuals by recruiting a small pool of potential replacements, giving each of them the treatment condition received by the case of interest, and selecting whichever one comes closest to matching the case of interest on the outcome for in-depth interviewing and subsequent qualitative analysis. Thus, a range of research design strategies is available for testing hypotheses about causal pathways in experimental settings.

7.4   Testing SUTVA

Like issues of measurement and dealing with causal pathways, SUTVA is an important or even essential issue for causal inferences in general. As discussed in Chapter 2, the potential-outcomes framework simply requires SUTVA to hold in order for a causal effect to even be defined.[5] When SUTVA does not hold, it can sometimes be recovered by moving to a higher level of analysis, thus grouping together the cases that causally interact, or by altering the definition of the treatment to include the treatments assigned to other cases. However, either of these remedies requires knowing both *that* SUTVA has in fact failed for a causal inference, and also *how* it has failed, i.e., which cases' treatment assignments are relevant for each case's potential outcomes.

Laboratory experiments have the distinct advantage that they can often be designed to guarantee that SUTVA holds. If participants in the experiment can be segregated from each other such that they have no contact between the moments of receiving the treatment and measuring the outcome, then SUTVA holds by design. For some experiments, interaction among small groups of subjects is essential to the research; here, SUTVA will generally hold at the level of the small group but not at the level of the individual. Hence, if analysis focuses on the group's treatment rather than on that of individuals within it, the design again guarantees the assumption. For these reasons, laboratory experiments have fewer issues regarding SUTVA than does virtually any other research design.

Field experiments have advantages in some other regards (Harrison and List 2004), but they are more vulnerable to problems of interdependence among cases. Because field experiments occur as interventions in the normal world of social and political life, they can rarely be designed to strictly separate experimental subjects in the way that laboratory experiments can. For example, consider the field experiment discussed by Braga *et al.* (1999), in which the Jersey City, NJ, police department varies policing tactics in a set of different locations by random assignment: one location is given "problem-oriented" policing, while the other is given traditional policing tactics. In this study, if selected locations are near each other, then crimes deterred by successful police tactics at one location may be displaced to another location in the experiment (Reppetto 1976); alternatively, successful policing may have positive spillover effects, making nearby locations less crime-prone (Clarke and Weisburd 1994). If either of these is the case, then the crime level at a given location depends not only on that location's treatment assignment but also on those of other nearby locations. Such dependency would violate SUTVA and makes causation difficult to define or assess.[6]

Because field experiments often raise such possible interactions among cases, some research design component intended to test SUTVA is essential. How can case studies contribute in this regard? SUTVA is in essence a claim of no causal influence: treatment assignments have no effect on other cases. This claim – like any other causal claim – is in principle subject to testing via process tracing. The relevant design involves selecting cases that are particularly likely to influence each other and then examining the causal process by which the dependent variable comes about for evidence of influence from other cases.

For some kinds of experiments, this design is easy and natural to carry out. If the treatment of interest involves providing one group with distinctive information, for example, the researcher must merely search for evidence that a selected control-group case had the information – and ideally also evidence about how the control-group subject found out. This sort of tracking of information flows is one of the classic paradigms of process-tracing research in both experiments and case studies, and thus presents no special challenges.

For other kinds of treatments, however, it can be more difficult to know what to look for in testing SUTVA. Consider the Jersey City policing example. What is needed here is evidence about whether crimes that occur (or, worse, fail to occur) in location A are caused by policing practices at location B. While this kind of evidence may be hard to find, it is certainly possible to imagine what it would look like. For instance, a researcher might find that a range of individuals who have in the past often been arrested for a certain crime at location B are now being arrested for that crime at location A. Obviously, a range of other kinds of evidence may be useful, as well. Thus, even when the possible kinds of causal interactions among cases are complex and hard to directly observe, close case-study work can contribute at least partial tests of SUTVA.

Obviously, since SUTVA is important in causal inferences of all sorts, this idea about using case studies to test the assumption can be usefully applied to the various research designs discussed earlier in the book. SUTVA is considered in this chapter instead of earlier ones not because it is more of a problem for experiments, but because experiments have fewer other problems.

7.5   Experimental Realism and External Validity

A problem that is more distinctive to experiments, however, is the issue of experimental realism (Aronson and Carlsmith 1968). This issue is often discussed in terms of external validity (Campbell and Stanley 1963): do the findings from an experiment apply outside that experimental context? This framing unfortunately conflates two quite different issues (Berkowitz and Donnerstein 1982). The first involves simple generalization. Do the results at hand apply to different times, places, and kinds of people? This is of course an important issue, one that has recently received prominent attention in psychology (Henrich, Heine, and Norenzayan 2010).

While generalization of findings is an important intellectual issue, it is not in fact a distinctive weakness of experiments. The same issues apply for *any other* kind of research. Does a case study capture the way things work in other cases (Geddes 1990)? Do survey results apply in a different culture (Harkness *et al.* 2003), or to a different generation of respondents, or to people who refused to be interviewed (Berinsky 2008)? Simply put, there is no research design that evades or completely resolves issues of generalization. Furthermore, for all of these methods the best response to such concerns is clear: replicate the original research design in a new context of interest and check whether the results hold true. This is, after all, the practice that has led to the important discoveries about cross-cultural differences in psychology discussed by Henrich *et al.* (2010). While it may not always be feasible, replication in new contexts is in principle simply the answer to the issue of generalization.

A distinct issue connected with the relationship between the experiment and the outside world, the issue of experimental realism, is trickier: for the people (or other kinds of cases) who in fact participate in the experiment, is the environment they experience sufficiently vivid and engaging such that behaviors and decision-making processes in the experiment involve the same kinds of causal considerations – and the same decision rules – as corresponding processes of interest in the non-experimental world? That is to say, does the context presented by the experiment motivate participants to act as they would in a non-experimental setting?

It is helpful to see that experimental realism can be restated as the assumption that the same causal pathways operate within the experiment as in the relevant non-experimental context. If the same pathways operate – even if with somewhat different quantitative weightings – in the real world as in the experiment, then the experimental results are generally informative and useful for theoretical development; it is hard to see how this could be true if the causal pathways were substantially divergent.

This understanding suggests a straightforward research design to test for experimental realism. First, choose a set of participants in the experiment, perhaps even at random. For those participants, carry out careful process tracing to build up as much evidence as possible regarding causal pathways between the treatment and the outcome. Then, find non-experimental cases making the decision or exhibiting the behavior of interest that are as similar as possible to the selected experimental cases. The criteria of similarity should be all background variables that might serve as experimental moderators, i.e., variables that might alter the causal effect of the treatment. These selected experimental cases should then also be studied using careful process tracing to build up a picture of the probable causal pathways leading them to their outcome. If this evidence suggests similar causal pathways inside and outside the experiment, then that is the key evidence in favor of experimental realism. Patterns of important divergence, by contrast, indicate that there is a problem and that the experiment should be redesigned to be more compelling and easier for participants to take seriously.

Such supplemental qualitative research focused on testing the assumption of experimental realism is not, to date, standard practice in experimental research. Hence, an example of a study that builds in a serious focus on these issues may help clarify how the proposed research design would work. Grossman and Baldassarri (2012) use an experiment to test the hypothesis that, in the context of a public goods problem, the legitimacy of a centralized sanctioning authority affects the degree to which individuals contribute to collective goods. Their experiment involves multiple rounds in which people receive a certain amount of cash and have to split the money between a private fund (which they keep for themselves) and a public fund (which is doubled and then split equally among all participants). The treatment involves random assignment of groups to have (a) no sanctioning authority who can punish people for failing to cooperate, (b) a randomly selected sanctioning authority, or (c) an elected sanctioning authority. The experiment shows that sanctioning works; both sets of groups with sanctioning authorities contributed more than the baseline groups. However, it also shows that the elected authority produces more cooperation than does the randomly selected one.

The question of experimental realism here involves whether the schematic and highly measurable action of splitting a pile of coins between a public and private fund is psychologically and socially similar to the far more heterogeneous and difficult-to-measure behaviors involved in everyday community cooperation or defection. Grossman and Baldassarri address this question through a quantitative comparison of behavior in the experiment with pro-community economic behavior in the real world, measured via survey questions. This allows them to show that people who cooperate when facing an elected sanctioning authority also tend to cooperate in the real world, while those who defect in this treatment group also usually defect in the everyday decision they analyze. Showing that behavior in the experiment goes along with behavior in non-experimental settings helps support the assumption of experimental realism.

Yet a more powerful case could still be made. The theoretical argument developed by Grossman and Baldassarri proposes a series of ways in which individuals may think about elected leaders differently from appointed or randomly selected ones (966–67). A researcher might draw on this inventory of psychological and ideational mechanisms to create a qualitative coding scheme, categorizing legitimacy-related ideas of various sorts, as well as marking a boundary to identify themes that do not connect with legitimacy. This scheme could then be used to code data from two sets of semi-structured interviews. The first set of interviews would be with experimental subjects, asking these individuals to discuss their thought process during the experiment and (for the treatment groups with sanctioners) their thoughts about the individual acting as leader within the group. The second set would involve demographically and socially similar individuals who had not participated in the experiment, and would instead focus on their decision process regarding a real-world choice about cooperation or defection – as well as thoughts about real-world community leaders. If themes of legitimacy come up at similar rates, and are deployed rhetorically in similar ways, between these two groups, that would count as substantial evidence in favor of experimental realism, while failures of correspondence between the two sets of interviews would weaken the case.

7.6   Conclusions

Even though experiments provide an unusually powerful basis for causal inference, qualitative evidence can strengthen them in a number of ways. This chapter has discussed integrative multi-method designs in which qualitative evidence improves experiments by speaking to issues of compliance, causal pathways, SUTVA, and experimental realism. This discussion, in conjunction with those of the preceding chapters, makes a case that integrative multi-method work can always improve on single-method quantitative analysis by bringing evidence to issues that would often otherwise stand as pure assumptions. The next chapter looks from the other point of view, asking how quantitative design elements can contribute to research that uses qualitative analysis to generate its main causal inferences.

Notes

1 Of course, both of these probabilities depend on defiers' actual share of the population; the argument in the text provides a limit condition for the example.
2 The term "process tracing" has a longer history, and a somewhat different meaning, in experimental research than it does in case-study research. For a relatively early programmatic discussion, see Payne *et al.* (1978).
3 For examples and methodological discussion, see Patrick and James (2004).
4 Such questions can be tricky in written form, because respondents will vary substantially in their degree of comfort with free-form writing. This complication can be partly addressed either by using face-to-face interviewing, or by using computer-based survey measurement and allowing respondents to answer open-ended questions verbally.
5 The reader will recall that SUTVA is the assumption that the potential outcomes for a given case are not affected by the treatment assignments of any other cases. This assumption can break down when cases interfere with each other – through network ties or equilibrium effects, for example.
6 The study design required locations that were not "spatially adjacent" (Clarke and Weisburd 1994: 550–51), apparently requiring locations to be at least four blocks apart to allow testing for displacement effects (Clarke and Weisburd 1994: 560–61). This separation could conceivably be sufficient to allow SUTVA to hold, although the analysis of spillover effects in the two-block areas around treatment locations does show some evidence of such effects (Clarke and Weisburd 1994: 567–69). It would be easier to know what to make of these patterns if targeted evidence regarding SUTVA were available.

8   Multi-Method Case Studies

For much of this book, the focus has been on designs in which quantitative methods of one sort or another are used to make the main causal inference of interest, with qualitative components added to test assumptions and make new discoveries. These designs should not be seen as privileging one method over the other. Assumptions about confounding, measurement, the existence of causal pathways, random or as-if random assignment, SUTVA, experimental realism, and so forth are the heart of quantitative causal inference. When the qualitative component of a multi-method design is the element responsible for connecting evidence to these assumptions, that component is contributing directly to clarifying the core issues of causal inference.

However, while it is spurious to read these designs as privileging quantitative over qualitative methods, there is nothing special or logically privileged about the framework in which quantitative methods make the final causal inference and qualitative methods speak to assumptions. This chapter turns the tables to consider integrative multi-method research designs in which qualitative research structures the overall study and produces the final causal inference, and in which quantitative research design components are used to test and refine critical assumptions. The relative length of the discussion of these two frameworks in this book reflects the relatively greater degree to which the assumptions necessary for causal inference using quantitative and experimental methods have been analyzed and formalized, not the relative value of the two paradigms.

In exploring ways that quantitative methods can contribute to primarily qualitative causal inferences, this chapter considers several options. First, it discusses the option of using a quantitative analysis to test the generalizability of findings from one or more case studies – a framework widely regarded as the major way in which to construct multi-method research, but one for which deep difficulties emerge. More viable options are then analyzed. The chapter discusses how quantitative analysis can sometimes add information by estimating the size of causal effects that are pivotal to case-study arguments. Alternatively, scholars can sometimes benefit from using quantitative (ideally experimental) methods as a step in a process-tracing design. Another useful integrative design involves taking an initial set of similarities and differences among quantitative causal effect findings for different research contexts as the outcome to be explained in a comparative-case-study analysis. While these are major options, they clearly do not exhaust the range of possibilities, and a brief section raises the possibility of combining quantitative methods with other sorts of qualitative research practices.

8.1   Testing Generalizability

One common integrative use of multi-method design at present involves carrying out one or more case studies and using a regression-type model to test for the "generalizability" of the results – a design discussed by, among others, Lieberman (2005). The logic is perhaps evident: while qualitative methods can provide deep insights regarding specific cases, they cannot usually provide much information about whether the causal patterns found in one or a few cases are typical or unusual. Hence, a regression analysis across a broader set of cases can check whether the initial case-study results were distinctive or general.

While this is a common design in which quantitative research plays a supporting role vis-à-vis qualitative analysis, it faces serious complications. One central issue is that it is perfectly possible for a case study to produce a causal inference that is entirely correct and perfectly general, and yet regression fails to replicate that result – because of omitted variable bias or other distortions in the regression analysis. That is to say, for regression analysis to work as a test of generalizability, the regression itself must be credible. This in turn requires that the range of issues for regression analysis considered earlier in the book be addressed; a separate, full-blown multi-method design may be needed in order to get much leverage out of a regression test of generalization.

A second issue, which has been extensively discussed in the multi-method literature, is that the regression-type study must be carried out on a set of cases from the same population as the case study, relative to the causal effect of interest. This criterion is not necessarily clear in practice. For example, in debating the possibility that selection bias leads to incorrect conclusions in a range of high-profile qualitative literatures, Geddes (1990) and Collier and Mahoney (1996) reach quite different conclusions about the boundaries of the causally relevant populations for the literatures in question. Collier and Mahoney are quite attentive to the suggestions of the original authors, while Geddes argues that a broader population is nonetheless relevant. When such divergent views are plausible to scholars, it is clear that deciding on the pertinent population for a test of generalizability is a nontrivial issue.

These debates about the correct set of cases to use in testing a proposition are complicated because their resolution is in fact a matter of causal inference. The central idea of testing the generalizability of case-study findings is to determine the largest set of cases for which: (a) the distribution of case-specific causal effects of treatment for the larger set of cases is similar to the distribution for the original case studies, and (b) the same basic causal pathway is in operation as in the original cases.[1] Determining a population of cases that meets these two criteria – and perhaps also inferring causal or theoretical reasons for the boundaries of that population – clearly entails a complex set of causal inferences.

Furthermore, a real test of the generalizability of a case study cannot merely check the overall relationship between a main causal variable and the outcome of interest. Showing that one key overall relationship generalizes to the population of interest is obviously a useful first step – but only a first step. A truly meaningful test will also include a consideration of whether the rest of the causal story from the case study is also general. In particular, most case studies offer theories and evidence about a series of steps along a causal pathway from the treatment to the outcome. Do these steps also generalize, or is the match between the overall causal effect in the case study and the wider population the result of a fortuitous alignment of fundamentally quite different causal processes?

At a minimum, attention to mediation analysis is essential in any attempt to quantitatively establish the generalizability of case-study results. As discussed in the Appendix, mediation is a statistical framework for testing claims that a cause brings about its effect by first causing one or more intermediate variables along a pathway. Such analysis involves complex statistical assumptions, with different kinds of additional knowledge needed for each step tested along the causal pathway (Green *et al.* 2010; Imai *et al.* 2011). Thus, if a scholar intends to seriously test the generalizability of a case-study causal finding, attention is needed to the full range of assumptions treated in the chapters above on regression for each step in the case study's causal pathway. This is a daunting task, and one that will inevitably provoke difficult-to-resolve disputes. Nonetheless, a regression-type study that does not take up this challenge simply does not suffice as a genuine generalizability test of a case-study causal finding.

A final note of caution regarding the use of regression to test the generalizability of case-study findings is that situations where regression results conflict with case-study findings are difficult to interpret. The results may differ, among other reasons, because the larger set of cases has a different distribution of causal effects than does the narrower set, because the regression is affected by omitted-variable bias, or because of inconsistencies in measurement. None of these reasons implies any problem with the causal inference drawn from the case studies. Alternatively, the results may differ because the regression got the causal inference right and the case-study research was flawed. Thus, using a regression on a larger set of cases to discredit a causal inference drawn in case-study research requires a complex, multipart argument, in which the regression itself answers only a few of the relevant questions.

8.2   Quantifying Effect Sizes

Although generalization tests of case-study findings are complex and assumption-laden, it obviously does not follow that quantitative research has nothing to add to case studies. Scholars should consider the use of quantitative analysis of a set of cases drawn from the same population as the original case studies for a quite different purpose: quantifying the effects discovered in the case studies. There is, after all, a great deal more information in the inference that the average treatment effect of a certain kind of social pressure on citizens' turnout decision is approximately 8% (Gerber *et al.* 2008: 38–40) than there is in the more qualitatively flavored conclusion that social pressure is an important contributing cause of turnout. Generating such additional information via quantitative analysis informed and shaped by a prior, highly credible qualitative research endeavor is an excellent example of integrative multi-method research, combining the strengths of case-study research (regarding in-depth causal inference in one or a few contexts and detailed attention to measurement and causal process) with the precision that can only come from quantification.

When credible, a regression-type analysis can serve as the quantitative component in such a design. Unfortunately, it is quite challenging to design a credible regression-type analysis of observational data to quantify effect sizes in this way. Once again, the whole range of assumptions discussed in the last section and throughout much of this book has to be addressed in some meaningful way. Furthermore, the issue discussed in the last section of the proper domain of generalization must also be resolved. If not, then the effect size could be misquantified because causally distinctive cases are mixed into the analysis.

Because of the vast range of assumptions needed to use statistical analysis with an observational research design to quantify the effect size from a set of case studies, it may often be more reasonable to use other research designs. On occasion, a plausible and relevant natural experiment may be available as a tool for effect-size quantification. Even fewer assumptions are needed to quantify effect sizes with a field or laboratory experiment. Beyond the issues of measurement validity, experimental realism, and SUTVA discussed in the last chapter, the most important remaining concern involves finding cases that are causally equivalent with the case-study cases. If that admittedly difficult challenge can be overcome, and if the cause of interest can be at least partially manipulated, then experiments can quantify the size of case-study causal effects with credibility and, when large samples are possible, to a high precision.

Of course, as emphasized throughout this book, scholars should not simply assume something as pivotal as the causal comparability of a case study and a broader set of cases used to estimate the magnitude of a causal effect. Instead, new components need to be added to the research design to test this additional assumption.

The best approach to testing whether a new set of cases is causally similar to an initial case study is to carry out additional case studies using the new cases. If the new case studies produce findings similar to the original – in terms not only of overall causal inferences but also of causal pathways – that provides grounds for trusting the cases to be causally comparable in the way required for quantifying causal effects. Cases might be selected for this purpose at random, although a more meaningful test will result if cases are chosen for maximum dissimilarity from the original case study.

Provided that evidence of this sort confirms the suitability of the cases for analysis, and that other issues of causal inference are satisfactorily resolved, quantitative analysis can enrich the causal findings of case study work by giving a sharp numerical range to the causal effect in question, rather than a broad verbal claim. This additional precision in itself constitutes new knowledge.

8.3   Quantitative Analysis as a Step in Process Tracing

To this point in the chapter, the focus has been on quantitative analysis that occurs chronologically after a case study and is designed to test or refine the already-complete findings of that study. However, such designs do not exhaust the ways in which statistical analysis can play a supporting role vis-à-vis case studies. Sometimes quantitative work can serve as a component in an overall case-study design. The next sections consider two such designs.

One version of process tracing involves assembling the best possible evidence regarding each step along the causal pathway connecting a treatment and an outcome (George and Bennett 2004). Such a procedure may be partially inductive if the scholar does not fully know all such steps in advance, but it is largely a deductive and theory-testing mode. That is to say, it falls within the category of pattern-matching (Campbell 1975) designs in which support for a theory is assembled by finding joint evidence of each of a number of separate implications that fall somewhere along the causal path described by that theory.

In such a design, the step in the theoretical causal path for which the empirical evidence is weakest plays a disproportionately large role in determining the credibility of the overall causal inference. This is because causal effects along a pathway are more or less multiplicative: the effect of an arbitrary treatment we will call D on an outcome Y through a mediating variable Z that stands at the middle of the causal pathway is roughly the effect of D on Z times the effect of Z on Y.[2] Suppose that the effect of Z on Y is known, with a great deal of certainty, to be large and positive. However, the effect of D on Z is highly uncertain and might equally well be positive or negative. What can we say about the overall effect? If the first step involves a negative causal effect, then the second step will magnify that into a large, negative overall causal effect. Yet if the first step has a positive effect, the second step will once again magnify that into a large, positive overall effect.

Thus, the overall effect is highly uncertain – because the first step in the causal pathway involves an effect that is itself highly uncertain.

For this reason, not all steps in a process-tracing argument are equally important. More inferential weight attaches to those which involve causal effects that – because of problems of evidence, limitations of prior theoretical knowledge, or issues of causal inference – are particularly uncertain. Improving the inference about the most uncertain steps will offer disproportionately large payoffs in terms of the quality of the overall causal inference. Hence, it can sometimes be worthwhile to invest in quantitative research design components, especially experimental components when feasible, to strengthen the argument about such causal linkages.

The design, in brief, is to use a quantitative analysis to increase the plausibility of the key link in the case study's causal pathway. Of course, for some kinds of causal linkages, quantitative design components may not contribute as much as qualitative components. The task, then, is to identify traits of causal steps for which quantitative evidence would strengthen the overall process-tracing argument.

Relevant steps in a causal pathway share two traits. First, they pose difficult challenges for purely qualitative causal inference. Second, they are open to well-established quantitative (and, with luck, experimental) designs. Very often, the steps in case-study arguments that share these traits involve mass social or political behavior and decision-making. While there are productive strategies for studying mass phenomena qualitatively (e.g. Chong 1993), such approaches are rarely combined with more general process-tracing arguments. Far more common is the approach in which marginal distribution estimates from a survey stand in for careful analysis of causation and decision-making in mass publics (see, for one very prominent example, Linz and Stepan 1996: 108–9, 135–36, 171–77, 214–15, 283–87). In these process-tracing designs, a very simple quantitative analysis has already taken the place of more qualitative evidence. A strengthened design can result from swapping out the simple marginal distributions in favor of quantitative design elements that make a greater contribution to causal inference.

Quantitative evidence may also be useful in other sorts of process-tracing arguments, beyond steps that require the analysis of mass behavior or decision-making. A useful marker for process-tracing steps that might productively be made quantitative is the temptation to use rough or simplistic quantitative analysis (i.e., survey marginals or simple numerical comparisons over time) in setting up the case-study argument.

Once the scholar has identified a relevant step in the process-tracing argument, an appropriate quantitative design element must be selected. If the argument pivots around descriptive issues (how popular was the president, did most people hear about the court case, etc.), then a survey or other random-sample design is valuable. After all, random sampling in conjunction with large numbers of cases provides the best available assurance that a descriptive claim is fully representative of the population – thus resolving a key issue in making claims about mass decision-making or behavior, for example. The quality of description using a survey will also be affected by question and questionnaire design, but these issues have been thoroughly studied (Schuman and Presser 1996; Tourangeau *et al.* 2000). For these reasons, it is hard to beat a well-designed survey for making descriptive claims about a large group of people.

Often, the key issue in the process-tracing argument will be causal rather than purely descriptive: did some event or situation *lead* people to think or behave in a certain way? For reasons explored at length in earlier chapters of the book, the strongest quantitative inferences about causation will come from experiments, so it is always worth pausing to think through the question of whether there is a way of nesting an experiment within the case study to clarify the causal relationship of interest.

For example, in my (Seawright 2012) study of party-system change in South America, I argue that emotion plays a critical mediating role in connecting specific kinds of societal crisis with voters' decision to abandon existing political parties en masse in favor of new alternatives. The study as a whole uses a comparative case-study design, focusing on three countries (Argentina, Peru, and Venezuela) and arguing that macro-level variables related to governance and party-system structure account for party-system collapse in two cases, as opposed to flexible reconfiguration in the other.

Within this overall case-study design, several key causal linkages along the process-tracing path are analyzed quantitatively. For present purposes, the most interesting step involves the claim that societal crises which produce anger, rather than anxiety or fear, play an especially important role in accounting for party-system change. While fragmentary qualitative evidence could be found in support of this proposition (Seawright 2012: 144–49), it at best demonstrates that anger at the existing parties was widespread and provides minimal support for the causal linkage between anger and the decision to vote outside the established party system.

Hence, an experiment provides evidence in support of that step in the process-tracing argument. Peruvian voters are randomly assigned to watch a nonpolitical film clip that provokes either anger or no emotion, and then are asked to vote in a simulated election between a candidate from an established party and one from a made-up party. The results support the existence of a causal effect by which anger increases the probability of voting for an outsider candidate (Seawright 2012: 149–59). In this example, the experiment cannot confirm that emotion was causally pivotal in the Peruvian and Venezuelan elections that brought about party-system collapse, because those elections are past and because the simulated election necessarily involves a different choice set. However, it contributes to the process-tracing argument by providing evidence that voters from the same culture and political system as those who participated in the elections of interest at least sometimes exhibit the hypothesized causal effect. Thus, the experiment provides a kind of evidence in support of the case-study argument that would be far more difficult to replicate through purely qualitative efforts.

More generally, it is worthwhile to consider which steps in a process-tracing argument are least credible, or more pragmatically the steps for which scholars are most skeptical. Random-sampling designs such as surveys can substantially increase the credibility of descriptive process-tracing claims about large populations, while experiments and related designs can similarly bolster process-tracing claims about causal inference. Improving the credibility of the weakest step in a process-tracing argument generally does a great deal to increase the credibility of the causal inference as a whole, and thus such design components within case studies can be exceptionally productive.

8.4   Quantitative Causal Effect Estimates as the Outcomes to be Explained

The potential-outcomes framework reminds us that we should not expect causal effects to be uniform or constant across all cases. This is of course a point that applies equally to qualitative and quantitative analysis, and indeed important qualitative research traditions have long emphasized that the causal effect of a given treatment may depend entirely on case-specific or more generalizable elements of context (Skocpol and Sommers 1980: 178–81). Scholars often deal with causal heterogeneity as if it were a pure methodological problem (e.g. King *et al.* 1994: 91–94), but it can of course also become a substantive research agenda. Once credible case-specific causal effect estimates have been found for a set of cases, the pattern of similarities and differences across those cases naturally becomes a theoretical puzzle. If causal effects are positive in some cases and negative in others, what brings about this difference? Even if all causal effects are in the same direction, similar puzzles arise if causal effects for some cases are much larger than others.

That is to say, evidence of heterogeneity in causal effects poses a second-order problem of causal inference: what causes the contexts in question to differ in terms of their causal effects? This kind of question can sometimes be addressed quantitatively through multilevel models (Gelman and Hill 2007), although the assumptions involved for causal inference in such an analysis are rather daunting, and the number of different contexts available for study is not always large. A multi-method alternative is to use case-study analysis to build an explanation for the origins of the causal heterogeneity.

An interesting example involves the decision-making of members of different small-scale societies worldwide (Henrich *et al.* 2001). The researchers asked individuals in each society to play an ultimatum game. In this game, one participant is given a comparatively large sum of money and required to make an offer about how to split the money to a second participant. The second individual responds by either accepting the offer – in which case both receive the amount of money offered – or rejecting the offer – in which case nobody gets any money at all. Because respondents are randomly assigned to one of these two roles, the observed average offers and rejection rates provide evidence about the causal effect of roles on behavior across societies.

Standard economic theory predicts a uniform solution to the ultimatum game. The first participant should propose an offer in which the second participant is given the smallest possible share; the second participant should accept that offer, because even a minuscule reward is better than nothing. Experiments carried out in societies across the world never confirm this prediction, but otherwise provide extremely varied results. Most notably, the average proportion of the money offered to the second participant by the first participant varies from 26% (Peru's Machiguenga) to 58% (Indonesia's Lamelara), a large and statistically robust range (Henrich *et al.* 2001: 74). What accounts for these large differences in how people trade off between norms of self-interest and the equitable treatment of others?

Asking this question immediately turns the findings of an initial set of studies into the outcome variable for a new research agenda. That new agenda of explaining patterns of differences in causal effects across contexts can of course be pursued using various methods, and indeed the original authors report simple quantitative and qualitative analyses. Quantitatively, they report that regression analysis using these causal effects as the outcome variable shows significant effects for a variable measuring a society's payoffs to cooperation outside the context of the experiment, as well as for another measuring that society's degree of market integration. Qualitatively, they discuss several societies' norms of sharing in everyday life and illustrate a convergence between such norms and the outcomes of the experiment (Henrich *et al.* 2001: 75–76).

How might a more qualitatively focused scholar build a more rigorous qualitative design for such a study? A natural move would be to go beyond simple regression analysis and illustrative qualitative facts, in the direction of a full-scale comparative historical analysis. As in the example above, the outcome to be explained in such an analysis would be the pattern of observed causal effects inferred in the contemporary statistical or experimental research. Scholars might plausibly group cases into those with similar effects: positive- and negative-effect cases, if the variability is so extensive, or large- and small-effect cases, if the heterogeneity mostly involves the size, rather than the direction, of the causal effect. The agenda would then be to develop parallel process-tracing analyses, building a credible causal argument about each case and systematically comparing those arguments across cases to find uniformities and particularities.

A good comparative historical analysis of this sort will avoid the theoretical pitfall of developing a causally plausible but shallow explanation (Kitschelt 2003). To continue with the current example, Henrich *et al.* point toward an explanatory framework in which the strength of norms of everyday sharing determines the effects of the economic game situation. This is plausible enough. However, even if this is exactly true, a good comparative historical design would take this finding as the basis for another, deeper causal question. Why do some small-scale societies have strong sharing norms in everyday life, while others do not? A standard analytic strategy is to process trace backwards from this finding until a causal moment is found in which it seems plausible for each society to develop stronger or weaker sharing norms (Mahoney 2000; Collier and Collier 2002: 27–39); whatever events or processes are involved in the resolution of this critical juncture would then serve as the ultimate explanation for the pattern of causal effects found in the initial experimental economic games.

Such a research design does more than answer a question left pending by the initial quantitative analysis. It also resolves one of the major assumptions driving comparative historical analysis. Because such comparative analysis centrally relies on a comparison of causal processes among cases measured as having similar and contrasting scores on the outcome of interest, comparable measurement of the dependent variable is pivotal to the entire enterprise (Przeworski and Teune 1970; Adcock and Collier 2001). Using quantitative causal inferences as the outcome to be explained can, when done well, help satisfy this key assumption.

It is of course possible for quantitative causal inferences to fail in terms of measurement equivalence. If data sources with divergent measurement quality are used across contexts (Lieberman 2010), if survey questions or experimental instructions are translated poorly (Behling and Law 2000; Jowell *et al.* 2007), or if other pertinent research procedures vary substantially from one context to the next, then quantitative causal inferences may suffer from problems of measurement equivalence. On the other hand, if researchers attend to these issues and ensure that the practical details of the quantitative causal inference are equivalent, then this issue can be set aside. In effect, this design turns the major issues of measurement equivalence into a checklist of well-studied technical considerations. In particular, well-designed experiments should produce causal inferences that are highly comparable across contexts.

More subtle concerns regarding interpretation, culture, institutional environment, and other aspects of context can of course change the meaning of a causal inference across cases. Yet this is not a problem: these contextual factors should become a part of the causal narrative uncovered and analyzed during the comparative historical analysis. Thus using a quantitative causal inference – or, ideally, an inference drawn from an experiment – as the dependent variable in a comparative case-study design is a prime example of an integrative multi-method approach: the quantitative component, if executed well, helps safeguard a key assumption for the qualitative method.

8.5   Multi-Method Research with Other Modes of Qualitative Research

In the research designs discussed so far in this chapter – and indeed through much of the book – discussion has focused on qualitative tools related to process tracing. Primarily this set of tools has been the focus because process tracing is intended explicitly as a technique for causal inference (Bennett and Checkel 2015: 10–13), while many other qualitative techniques have a debated or ambiguous relationship with that task (Schwartz-Shea and Yanow 2012: 49–53). Even so, qualitative research obviously involves a vast range of tools beyond process tracing. Scholars have developed and used methodologies related to semi-structured and unstructured interviews (Brinkmann and Kvale 2014), focus groups (Morgan 1996; Stewart and Pramdasani 2014), participant observation (DeWalt and DeWalt 2011), the critical reading of discourse (Schiffrin *et al.* 2001), and more. There is no reason these diverse techniques could not make major contributions as qualitative components of a multi-method research design.

How could the integrative approach to multi-method research design extend to these other techniques? The question is especially important when it is recognized that these methods often have a central focus other than causal inference: description, interpretation, representing a marginalized population or perspective, and so forth. While this book has said a good deal about multi-method designs focused on description, the other goals go well beyond the framework employed here and necessarily raise novel considerations, and may thus require distinctive research design tools.

Even so, the integrative multi-method framework may have something to say in these domains. As always, the approach is to ask what is being assumed in order to generate the knowledge claims of interest in a given study. Some kinds of assumptions create openings for important multi-method contributions from quantitative work, while others do not. Quantitative tools – when used well, tested carefully, and tuned to the relevant context – can contribute to testing assumptions about the representativeness of an individual, an idea, a behavior, and so forth in comparison to a broader defined group (Thompson 2012); about the prevalence or novelty of a particular frame, concept, or ideological stance vis-à-vis a large collection of texts (Grimmer and Stewart 2013); about changes over time (Baltagi 2013) or contrasts among groups (Good 2005: 51–63); about the existence and causal relevance of implicit attitudes and ideologies (Cunningham *et al.* 2001; Chong and Druckman 2007); and more. These strengths may offer value to a wide range of different research objectives and, as such, creative use of integrative multi-method designs deserves consideration across the spectrum of qualitative research practices.

8.6   Conclusions

Integrative multi-method designs in which qualitative causal inferences are bolstered or refined by quantitative research design components are varied and intriguing, and deserve broader and more careful application. Such designs can, in the right circumstances, produce stronger and more informative causal inferences than can a single-method qualitative analysis.

Of course, the same is true more generally of the integrative multi-method designs discussed in this book. When carefully designed and executed – with key assumptions tested and with each research component carried out in ways that correspond with best practices – integrative multi-method designs provide unified causal inferences for which there is more and better evidence than in an otherwise similar single-method design.

Table 8.1 Integrative Multi-Method Designs: Questions, Strategies, and Case Selection.

Question	Strategy	Tools	Case Selection
Are treatment and outcome variables measured well enough to justify causal inference?	Compare in-depth information with quantitative score, and process trace to discover systematic sources of error.	Regression Matching Natural experiment Experiment	Deviant, extreme X Extreme p-scores Deviant, extreme X Deviant
Is the outcome measured comparably across a set of cases under study?	Explain patterns of difference and similarity in quantitative causal inferences in each of several macro-level cases.	Comparative Case studies	Samples within Cases
Does a causal pathway exist that fits with the estimated causal effect?	Process trace to assemble step-by-step evidence linking treatment and outcome; seek isolated and exhaustive path.	Regression Matching Natural experiment Experiment	Deviant, extreme X Deviant Deviant, extreme X Deviant
Does the causal inference suffer from post-treatment bias?	In studying causal pathways search for evidence that control variables are part of the causal path.	Regression Matching	Deviant, extreme X Deviant
Does the causal inference suffer from confounding?	Process trace causes of the treatment and omitted causes of the outcome, searching for commonalities.	Regression Matching	Extreme X Extreme p-scores

(continued)

Table 8.1 (*cont.*)

Question	Strategy	Tools	Case Selection
Do colliders create the risk of avoidable bias in the causal inference?	In studying the causes of the treatment, search for control variables that play no role and consider omitting them.	Regression Matching	Extreme X Extreme p-scores
Is the treatment really randomly or as-if randomly assigned?	Process trace the causal history of the treatment, looking for exceptions or evidence of strategic behavior.	Natural experiment	Extreme p-scores
Does the randomized treatment have the same effect as nonrandomized versions of the treatment?	Process trace to compare causal pathways in a randomized and a matched nonrandomized case.	Natural experiment	Similar cases
Does the instrument affect the outcome other than through the treatment?	In studying causal pathways, search for evidence that instrument plays a direct causal role.	Instrumental variables	Unclear
Does SUTVA hold, or do cases' treatments causally interfere with each other?	In studying causal pathways, search for evidence that cases influence each other.	Experiment Regression Matching Natural experiment	Strongly connected pairs of cases

Does experimental realism hold, or do participants take an unusual approach to decision-making within the experiment?	Process trace to compare causal pathways in an experimental and matched non-experimental case.	Experiment	Similar cases
Do case-study findings generalize, or is the studied case causally distinctive?	Use a regression-type analysis and mediation analysis, with attention to replicating concepts and measurement from the case study.	Case study	Relevant universe
Are the causal effects discovered by the case study the expected size?	Use a regression-type analysis with attention to replicating concepts and measurement from the case study.	Case study	Relevant universe
Is the weakest link in a process-tracing argument nonetheless viable, or in need of revision?	Use an experiment or other strong quantitative method of causal inference to test, and if necessary, revise that step in the argument.	Case study	Sample within case

The chapters above have provided over a dozen integrative multi-method designs, focused on different assumptions for causal inference. Table 8.1 provides a schematic review of the key designs. Following the integrative model, each design answers a question motivated by a key assumption for causal inference, and these are listed in the first column of the table. The second column proposes multi-method analytic strategies appropriate to each question. Of course, not all assumptions apply to every method for causal inference, and the third column identifies the tools for which a given question – and therefore a given research design – is relevant. The fourth column lists efficient case-selection approaches for each causal-inferential tool within the context of a given research design. As Table 8.1 makes clear, the integrative approach to multi-method research design is very flexible. It can generate designs focused on issues of measurement, appropriate sets of control variables for observational studies, specialized assumptions in natural experiments, and foundational assumptions for either experimental or case-study causal inference.

Indeed, the integrative approach to multi-method research can serve as a general-purpose template for constructing productive research designs that combine various kinds of research activities, practices, and tools. Because this approach pushes scholars to convert assumptions made into claims empirically tested, it helps ground our inferences more solidly in evidence. It can thus be part of a push toward a more resilient and inferentially justified social science.

Notes

1 The issues here are quite similar to those involved in tests of poolability for panel data (e.g. Baltagi and Hidalgo 1996). Mistaken assumptions about poolability can have major consequences in substantive literatures – for example, Haber and Menaldo (2011) argue that statistical findings supporting the existence of a political "resource curse" in which oil causes authoritarianism only arise because of incorrect assumptions about poolability. Case-study scholars should perhaps be given pause by the scope and weight of such debates in quantitative fields for which there are significance tests of the hypothesis of poolability: if consequential debates about the boundaries of relevant sets of cases continue in methodological areas where relevant

formal tests have been devised, the prospects of resolving such debates in qualitative inquiry must be remote.

2 The multiplicative nature of causal pathways is exactly true if causal effects are linear and constant across cases, as in the famous analysis of mediation by Baron and Kenny (1986). When effects vary across cases, and especially when they contain nonlinearities, the size of the pathway need not correspond to the products of the effects along the pathway. However, in the more general case uncertainties accumulate in a similar although not identical way, and hence the linear intuition remains a useful reference point.

Appendix: Qualitative Causal Models and the Potential-Outcomes Framework

The argument in Chapter 2, that a suitably broad reading of the potential-outcomes framework captures most of the ideas and intuitions about causation that have been important in both qualitative and quantitative methodological work in the social sciences, loses all traction if in practice adopting the potential-outcomes framework as a shared causal language would serve to rule out important qualitative causal hypotheses and models. Hence, it is important to demonstrate that at least many such models fit well with the potential outcomes setup. The discussion below argues not only that the potential-outcomes framework can successfully represent a set of key qualitative causal ideas, but also that the process of translation illuminates key aspects of those causal ideas that may otherwise be more difficult to spot. This argument will be developed through a discussion of necessary and/or sufficient causes, INUS and SUIN causes, path-dependent and critical-juncture causal models, and ideas about causal mechanisms and pathways. Brief concluding reflections will be offered regarding some other causal categories sometimes seen as related to a qualitative-quantitative divide in causal conceptualization.

1.1   Necessary and/or Sufficient Causes

Qualitative methodologists have drawn a great deal of attention to causal models involving necessary and/or sufficient causes (Dion 1998; Braumoeller and Goertz 2000; Ragin 2000; Goertz and Starr 2002; Seawright 2002; Goertz and Levy 2007). Applied qualitative researchers have of course made heavy use of such concepts for many years, as has the occasional piece of quantitative research. In brief and in deterministic form, necessary causes are those causal factors whose absence makes an outcome impossible; however, their presence need provide no special information about the likely score of the dependent variable. Sufficient causes are those factors whose presence makes the outcome inevitable, although their absence may tell us little about the probable outcome.

Some scholars extend the concept of necessary and/or sufficient causes from this deterministic starting point toward a probabilistic formulation that allows for some exceptions (see especially Ragin 2000). In probabilistic necessary/sufficient causal formulations, some predefined proportion of exceptions to the defining rule is allowed. For example, a cause may be 85% necessary if at least 85% of cases without the cause also fail to have the outcome. As a causal model, these probabilistic proposals are ambiguous. For example, should claims about an 85% necessary cause be taken to mean that the cause is deterministically necessary for at least 85% of cases, or that all cases have a shared, fundamentally probabilistic causal pattern in which the absence of the cause sets the probability of the outcome at a level of 0.15 or lower? In the discussion below, I will adopt the first interpretation, in which probabilistic necessary/sufficient causes are causes that are deterministically necessary/sufficient for most cases, but the data include a priori unidentifiable exceptions.

The central task for this section is to show how the key ideas of necessary and/or sufficient causation can be persuasively represented in terms of the potential-outcomes framework. In fact, necessary causation is simply a specification of one of the two potential outcomes for each case. A treatment is a necessary condition for some outcome if and only if, for all i, $Y_{i,c} = 0$. One key empirical implication of this definition is that all observed cases in the control group will have $Y_i = 0$; this condition has been the centerpiece for most empirical tests of necessary causation hypotheses, and is sometimes mistaken for a definition of the causal model. However, calling a treatment a necessary cause implies more: it also tells us that, for cases that are in fact in the treatment group, those cases would have also had $Y_i = 0$ if they had instead not been exposed to the treatment. In other words, a potential-outcomes definition of necessary causation reveals that many discussions of testing for necessary causes have confused a hoop test for a smoking gun test (Van Evera 1997; Bennett 2010): finding the specified pattern among observed cases is necessary for inferring necessary causation, but is not sufficient. Evidence about some counterfactual conditions – drawn, perhaps, from case-study research, or from experiments – is also needed.

Probabilistic necessary causes are also easy to represent within the potential-outcomes setup. Adopting the interpretation that such probabilistic models imply an unmeasurable mixture of cases for which the treatment is deterministically necessary and other cases for which it is not, we may define a treatment as being p% necessary if and only if, for at least p% of possible values of i, $Y_{i,c} = 0$.

Some analysts of necessary causes discuss a special subtype of trivial necessary causes, i.e., causes that are causally necessary but are always present among the cases relevant to a given research agenda (Braumoeller and Goertz 2000; Ragin 2000: 98). Given that a particular independent variable is in fact a necessary cause, it can be classified as trivial if and only if all cases are in the treatment condition; the requirement that all cases be in the treatment condition is of course completely observable, even though determining that the variable is a necessary cause still requires counterfactual information. The potential-outcomes formulation also makes clear a second kind of triviality: all treatments are always necessary causes of any impossible outcome.[1] To avoid this second class of triviality for a deterministic necessary cause, it must be the case that there is at least one case j (and preferably several cases) for which $Y_{j,t} > 0$. For a probabilistic necessary cause, a parallel form of triviality arises if the proportion of cases for which $Y_{j,t} > 0$ is less than or equal to $(1 - p)\%$.

Another important extension of thought about necessary conditions involves ordered, multicategory treatments and outcomes, often represented as fuzzy sets. That is to say, the hypothesized cause and the outcome are represented as taking on one of a fixed set of values between zero and one, inclusive. A score of zero represents the complete absence of the variable, while a score of one represents its complete presence; intermediate values represent different degrees of partial presence (for complete discussion, see Ragin 2000, 2008). For fuzzy sets, necessity is taken to mean that the outcome is never more present than the cause. Can this causal model also be represented within the potential-outcomes setup?

In fact, it can, although some additional notation will be needed. Instead of working with two treatments, t and c, we will need to introduce K treatments, one for each possible value that the hypothesized cause is allowed to take on. For ease of notation, each of these treatments will be labeled with the numerical value it is given in fuzzy-set representation; thus complete absence is the treatment 0, while partial absence might refer to treatments 0.5 or 0.7. Because K different treatment levels are defined, we will also need K potential outcomes of the dependent variable. Just as with the two-treatment setup, each potential outcome represents what would have happened to case i if the independent variable had been hypothetically manipulated to a given treatment level.

With this notation in hand, defining a deterministic fuzzy-set necessary cause in the potential-outcomes language is possible, although still complex. A fuzzy-set treatment is a necessary cause of an outcome if and only if, for all i and for any treatment k, $Y_{i,k} \leq k$. Likewise, a fuzzy-set treatment is a probabilistic necessary cause of Y whenever, for at least p% of possible values of i and for any treatment k, $Y_{i,k} \leq k$. These definitions are essentially exact parallels to the two-treatment cases, but they also reveal that the fuzzy-set version of causation is far more inferentially challenging. Instead of requiring counterfactual information about one unobservable state of the world for each case, a fuzzy-set causal claim requires supplementary counterfactual information about $K - 1$ such states per case.

Sufficient causation is intimately interrelated with necessary causation; if X is a necessary cause of Y, then the absence of X is a sufficient cause of the absence of Y, and vice versa. Hence, it is unsurprising that sufficient causation is as easy to represent in the potential-outcomes framework as necessary causation. It therefore makes sense to simply spell out the potential-outcomes conditions for sufficient causation, without much of the kind of discussion offered above for necessary causes. A treatment is a deterministic sufficient cause if, for all i, $Y_{i,t} > 0$. It is p% necessary if, for at least p% of possible values of i, $Y_{i,t} > 0$. To avoid triviality, it must be the case that there is at least one case j (and preferably several cases) for which $Y_{i,c} = 0$; similar modifications of the necessary-cause conditions hold for trivial and fuzzy-set sufficient causes.

This section has shown that necessary and/or sufficient causes fit neatly within the potential-outcomes framework, and also that representing such cases in this framework offers added clarity in terms of the identification of counterfactuals that need justification to support a causal inference. The discussion thus far has not addressed the issue of whether necessary and/or sufficient causes would always count as causes given the definitions offered by the potential-outcomes framework. For example, suppose that an outcome has two necessary causes, both of which are absent for the cases of interest. Furthermore, let the first of those causes be regarded as the treatment. Then for all i, it is true that $Y_{i,t} = Y_{i,c} = 0$, because both causes would need to be simultaneously manipulated to bring about a change in the outcome. It may be the case that the potential-outcomes framework would regard each of these variables as having no causal effect, but that a qualitatively oriented scholar would insist that both are necessary causes. In my view, this difference in terminology should be regarded as benign, because scholars working within both traditions have a shared model of the counterfactual and causal dependencies at work in this example and thus differ only in terms of labeling.

1.2   INUS and SUIN Causes

Relatively complex causal situations such as the two-necessary-conditions scenario of the last paragraph have received extensive attention in both the philosophical and social science qualitative methods literatures on causation and causal inference. In particular, Mackie (1974) has argued that the independent variable in a causal relationship is generally what he characterizes as an INUS condition, an acronym standing for an insufficient but necessary part of an unnecessary but jointly sufficient condition. In causal terms, an INUS condition arises when there are multiple causal paths by which the outcome may be brought into existence, and when each of those paths works only when several different factors are brought together. Such conditions are, perhaps, an interesting causal model in their own right, but they take on added importance due to Mackie's proposal that most causal relationships, including evidently stochastic ones, might at some level of detail involve INUS conditions.

INUS conditions are complex enough that rendering their causal logic in terms of the potential-outcomes framework may help make them more intuitive. To systematically represent the setup of an INUS condition, we need to envision a scenario in which there are at least three separate independent variables or treatments that may have a causal effect on the outcome of interest. The first takes on values A when set to the treatment condition or a when set to the control condition; the second is either B or b, and the third is either C or c.[2] Furthermore, there is now one version of Y_i per combination of treatment conditions across the three specified sets. Thus, $Y_{i,a,b,c}$ is distinct from $Y_{i,A,b,c}$, and so forth.

The first treatment, which takes on scores of a and A, is an INUS cause of Y for case i when $Y_{i,a,B,c} = Y_{i,a,b,c} = Y_{i,A,b,c} = 0$, $Y_{i,A,B,c} > 0$, $Y_{i,A,B,C} > 0$, $Y_{i,A,b,C} > 0$, $Y_{i,a,B,C} > 0$, and $Y_{i,a,b,C} > 0$. Complexity obviously arises in interpreting this pattern. Having the first treatment set to A as opposed to a may or may not cause a difference in Y_i – depending on the values of the second and third treatments. Hence, the pattern of differences in the outcome to be anticipated across cases depends in complicated ways on the values of all three treatments. Furthermore, obstacles to inference abound, given that counterfactual information is needed about seven scenarios per case. Nonetheless, the essential structure of an INUS cause is replicated here. In particular, for some configurations of the second and third treatment, the presence of the first treatment is both necessary and sufficient for the outcome; for other configurations, the first treatment has no effect on the outcome.

More recently, Mahoney *et al.* (2009) have called attention to the possibility of SUIN conditions, which are sufficient but unnecessary components of a jointly insufficient but necessary condition. If the outcome of interest were the occurrence of a house fire, for example, lighting a match might be a SUIN cause. A lighted match provides ignition, which is obviously necessary for a house fire. However, it is equally clear that a lighted match is not sufficient – for example, there must also be oxygen, flammable materials, and so forth. Furthermore, a match is self-evidently not the only possible source of ignition, which could also be provided by an electrical short, a lightning strike, etc.

Once again, the logical structure of a SUIN condition as a causal hypothesis can be made precise by rendering it in terms of the potential-outcomes framework. Again, suppose that there are three sets of treatments, as with INUS conditions. The first of these independent variables or sets of treatment conditions, i.e., the one that takes on values a and A, is a SUIN cause of Y for case i whenever $Y_{i,a,b,c} = Y_{i,A,b,c} = Y_{i,a,B,c} = Y_{i,A,B,c} = Y_{i,a,b,C} = 0$, $Y_{i,A,b,C} > 0$, $Y_{i,a,B,C} > 0$, and $Y_{i,A,B,C} > 0$. Here, the outcome is above zero whenever the third treatment is set to C and either the first treatment is set to A or the second is set to B.

This discussion of necessary, sufficient, INUS, and SUIN causes does differ from some treatments in the qualitative literature, in particular in its increased emphasis on counterfactual patterns related to hypothetical manipulations of the treatment variables; qualitative methodologists have more heavily focused on the cross-case empirical implications of these causal models for observational studies. Yet this difference in treatment is not intended as a change in content, but rather as a clarification of the relationship between these models of causation and other philosophical and statistical discussions. Thus, I hope these changes will be regarded more as friendly amendments than as contradictions of previous work about such patterns of causation.

As a concluding point, it perhaps bears mention that INUS and SUIN causes are just two of a potentially limitless range of complex models of causation often labeled as multiple and/or conjunctural causation (Ragin 1987, 2000). In general, such causal models can be translated into the language of the potential-outcomes framework along the lines of this section's treatment of INUS and SUIN causes.

1.3   Path-Dependent and Critical-Juncture Causal Models

Scholars in the social sciences, often writing from a qualitative methodological orientation, have developed a fascinating family of causal models grouped under the labels of path dependence and critical junctures (Collier and Collier 1991: Chapter 1; Arthur 1994; Goldstone 1998; Mahoney 2000; Pierson 2000; Bennett and Elman 2006a; David 2007). A central feature of these models is the idea that time is causally relevant, that similar treatments administered at different moments in history or development (however conceptualized) may be causally quite distinctive indeed.

Let us consider how this core commitment to time as relevant property of causal treatments can be expressed within the potential-outcomes framework. Consider a relatively simple hypothesis in which three causally relevant time periods have been identified (periods 1, 2, and 3) and in which there are only two values of the treatment of interest (t and c). Because time periods are causally relevant, a complete description of a case's treatment condition is a sequential listing of its treatment value in each of the three periods. Thus, (t_1, t_2, c_3) represents the overall history of the independent variable for those cases that were in the treatment group in periods 1 and 2 but in the control group in period 3. There are eight such possibilities, and we must define a potential value of the outcome for each of them: Y_{i,t_1,t_2,c_3} may be different from Y_{i,c_1,t_2,c_3}, and so forth.

One kind of path-dependent causal model imposes the restriction that the group of potential outcomes Y_{i,t_1,c_2,c_3}, Y_{i,t_1,t_2,c_3}, Y_{i,t_1,c_2,t_3}, and Y_{i,t_1,t_2,t_3} are relatively similar. Furthermore, that first group of potential outcomes is required to be strikingly different from the four remaining potential outcomes, for which the case is in the control group in the first time period. It is not usually necessary that these two groups be absolutely homogeneous; later treatments may make a difference, even in a path-dependent model. However, it is of the essence that the first treatment matters most. This corresponds to the general notion, often discussed in broad terms as path dependence, that "history matters."

Some path-dependent models build in more elaborate causal structure, in which treatments after the first period are influenced by the case's received treatment in the first period. For such models, we would need to explicitly represent the causal structure behind treatments at times 2 and 3, introducing potential outcomes to represent the treatments received at each of those times for a given hypothetical manipulation of the case's earlier treatment history. Let $X_{i,2,t_1}$ represent the treatment that case i takes on if the case is in the treatment group in the first period, and $X_{i,2,c_1}$ is that same case's value of the treatment at time 2 if the case is assigned to the control group at time 1. Potential treatment assignments $X_{i,3,t_1,t_2}$, $X_{i,3,c_1,t_2}$, and so forth have parallel interpretations. Path dependence is often taken to mean that, for most cases, $X_{i,2,t_1} = X_{i,3,t_1,t_2} = t$ and $X_{i,2,c_1} = X_{i,3,c_1,c_2} = c$. That is, because of institutional inertia, increasing returns to scale, or some other similar causal mechanism, cases rarely change their treatment assignment after the first period (e.g. Arthur 1994; Mahoney 2000; Pierson 2000).

In such a model, potential outcomes like Y_{i,t_1,c_2,c_3} and Y_{i,t_1,c_2,t_3} may be of theoretical interest but have limited practical relevance because such treatment assignments are rare and, indeed, causally implausible for most cases. Instead of focusing on such conceptually messy potential states of the outcome variable, qualitative scholars' interest in this kind of path dependence often revolves around causal hypotheses linking t_1 to t_2, and so forth (Mahoney and Thelen 2009). It is certainly possible to use the potential-outcomes framework to represent causal dependencies among treatment conditions over time, as well as between the treatment and the outcome; doing so would turn the model discussed here into a version of the mediation models discussed in the next section.

Critical-juncture models expand on path-dependent models by stipulating that treatment assignment before a specified period is less relevant for outcomes than is treatment assignment during that critical period. Furthermore, they often provide a causal account of the reasons why a particular time period is causally important, effectively adding a second set of treatment assignments that account for the causal relevance of time in more substantive, social scientific terms (Collier and Collier 1991; Mahoney 2001). Because such models require a second set of treatment assignments regarding the causal character of periods, the potential-outcomes notation becomes burdensome and is not reproduced here; however, no new conceptual issues arise in comparison with path-dependent models. In summary, the attention these models pay to differences in treatment effects over time is entirely consistent with the emphasis on possible causal heterogeneity in the potential-outcomes framework; it seems worthwhile to connect these two causal traditions.

1.4   Causal Mechanisms and Pathways

Although not all qualitative research focuses closely on causal mechanisms and pathways,[3] distinctive attention to the sequence of steps connecting causes and effects is close to being a defining trait of contemporary qualitative research (Collier *et al.* 2003; Gerring 2004). Some quantitative methods have, of course, long attended to such sequences of causal steps (Lazarsfeld 1958; Blalock 1961; Duncan 1966; Baron and Kenny 1986; Joreskog 2006); however, it is probably true that in practice such attention is relatively much less common in quantitative research than it is in qualitative analysis.

As discussed above, standard presentations of the potential-outcomes framework largely ignore the question of the steps by which the treatment affects the outcome. However, Imai and collaborators have extended the framework to capture such causal hypotheses (Imai *et al.* 2010, Imai *et al.* 2011). This section briefly recapitulates their setup, adjusting the notation somewhat to fit more closely with the present book's usage, making the case that the potential-outcomes framework is entirely capable of representing hypotheses regarding causal mechanisms and pathways.

For simplicity of presentation, we will consider a causal hypothesis in which a dichotomous treatment is believed to cause an outcome, Y, at least in part through its effects on an intervening or mediating variable, M. Because the treatment may affect M, two potential outcomes of that intervening variable need to be defined: $M_{i,t}$, which is the value it takes on if case i is (perhaps hypothetically) manipulated to be in the treatment group, and $M_{i,c}$, or the value the mediating variable takes on for case i when that case is assigned to the control group. These two quantities are, of course, sufficient to define the effect of treatment on M, which is given by $M_{i,t} - M_{i,c}$, but that is not a quantity of central interest.

Instead, our central attention is on the effect of treatment on Y, partly via M. Because both the treatment and M may affect Y, four potential outcomes of the dependent variable need to be introduced. $Y_{i,t,M_{i,t}}$ is the value that the outcome takes on if the case is assigned to the treatment group and M takes on the value that it normally would in light of that treatment; $Y_{i,c,M_{i,c}}$ is the parallel quantity for assignment to the control group. The total causal effect of treatment on Y for case i is, of course, the difference between these two numbers: $Y_{i,t,M_{i,t}} - Y_{i,c,M_{i,c}}$.

Thinking carefully about causal paths also requires us to consider two other, less intuitive, potential outcomes: $Y_{i,t,M_{i,c}}$, or the outcome that would take place if the case were assigned to treatment but some special intervention were made to set M to the value it would normally take on in the control group; and $Y_{i,c,M_{i,t}}$, or the outcome that would take place if the case were assigned to the control group but some special intervention were made to set M to the value it would normally take on in the treatment group.[4] These quantities are never observed in the normal course of events, so inferences about them must either depend on very strong assumptions or rely on information drawn from sources such as carefully designed experiments (Imai *et al.* 2011: 780–81) or case studies (Weller and Barnes 2014). With this notation in hand, we can now define a set of different causal effects that highlight various aspects of the overall set of relationships among treatment, M, and Y.

There are two different possible versions of the direct effect of treatment on Y net of M: $Y_{i,t,M_{i,t}} - Y_{i,c,M_{i,t}}$ and $Y_{i,t,M_{i,c}} - Y_{i,c,M_{i,c}}$. Each of these expressions represents the causal effect of manipulating the case to be in the treatment as opposed to the control group, while holding M constant; they differ in the value at which M is held constant. Both versions of the direct effect may be of interest, and there is no general reason to suppose that they must necessarily be equal.

Likewise, there are two possible versions of the indirect or mediation effect, i.e., the effect of M on Y holding treatment constant: $Y_{i,t,M_{i,t}} - Y_{i,t,M_{i,c}}$ and $Y_{i,c,M_{i,t}} - Y_{i,c,M_{i,c}}$. These are the effects of manipulating M so that it takes on the values it would take if the case were assigned to treatment or to control, while simultaneously holding the main independent variable constant. In other words, these quantities represent the causal effect of treatment on the outcome only through M. The total effect of treatment on Y is the sum of one of the direct effects and one of the indirect effects just defined, so it is reasonable to discuss the proportion of the overall effect that is captured by the path through M, which quantitatively is just the ratio of an indirect to the total effect.

Qualitative discussions of causal mechanisms and pathways can be roughly divided between those that emphasize the potential cross-case heterogeneity of patterns of causal sequence and linkage (Hedström and Swedberg 1998; McAdam *et al.* 2001) and those that are more interested in discovering patterns that are general or at least repeated in relatively similar ways across multiple cases (Kiser and Hechter 1998; Gross 2009). The potential-outcomes treatment of causal mechanisms and pathways just presented is agnostic on this point. It allows for diversity and heterogeneity in the strength and even kind of causal linkage across cases – and a more complicated potential-outcomes model that represented multiple paths and perhaps several steps per path could come quite close to fully representing the more extreme kinds of diversity regarding causal mechanisms that have been discussed in the qualitative methodological literature. Yet the potential-outcomes model of intervening causal steps does not insist on or require heterogeneity; there is no reason why the different versions of direct and indirect effects need be unequal, and there is not even a requirement in the model above that these effects vary across cases. Instead, the potential-outcomes treatment of causal mechanisms and pathways is flexible enough to incorporate a wide range of qualitative views about such issues.

1.5   Other Causal Categories

A range of other causal categories sometimes debated in the literature on qualitative methods can effectively be treated with benign neglect once this potential-outcomes account is adopted. For example, the causal framework considered here is indifferent between proximate and distant causes.[5] As long as an appropriate pattern of counterfactual dependence between the outcome and the treatment hold under (hypothetical or real) manipulations, the treatment is a cause. Whether the treatment happens five seconds, five years, or five millennia before the outcome is in principle irrelevant, although for practical purposes extremely long timescales may obviously complicate inference.

Likewise, the potential-outcomes framework can accept causation involving either events or constant causes.[6] For this framework, events and constant causes are just two different kinds of treatments, and as long as the treatment of interest and relevant hypothetical manipulations are defined carefully and unambiguously, either variety is entirely acceptable.

Obviously, this appendix has not discussed all models of causation and causal concepts that are important to qualitative methodologists and applied researchers in the social sciences. However, the goal has not been to produce an encyclopedia of causal hypotheses, but rather to demonstrate that a broad range of key qualitative ideas about causation can be translated into the potential-outcomes framework without major distortions or loss of important content; an added benefit is that the process of translation has sometimes provided new insights into the kinds of claims entailed in and evidence relevant for these causal hypotheses. Many other qualitative causal setups could probably be rendered in the language of potential outcomes with equal success. The fact that, in practice, this kind of translation seems to do little violence to qualitative causal ideas strongly suggests that there is in fact no deep conceptual or ontological divide between qualitative and quantitative definitions of or ideas about causation. Hence, multi-method research designs need not be ruled out a priori due to ontological considerations; no philosophical contradictions need arise in using interview or archival evidence to design an experiment or refine a regression model, nor in using quantitative results to shape a case-study narrative.

1.6   The Effects-of-Causes versus Causes-of-Effects Distinction

As a side note to this appendix's central argument that quantitative and qualitative concepts of causation are comparable, it may be worth paying some brief attention to a frequently discussed distinction regarding the process by which causal hypotheses are formulated and interpreted: that between research focused on the causes of effects and inquiry that attends instead to the effects of causes (Mill 1891/2002; Bennett and Elman 2006b; Goertz and Mahoney 2012). This distinction highlights an interesting apparent divergence in research styles among scholars: some enter into the process of causal inference motivated by fascination with or intellectual curiosity about some striking treatment or independent variable, and seek to discover the effects of that factor on one or more outcomes, whereas others are more centrally motivated by the goal of explaining an event, a contrast among cases, or some other outcome, and then seek to inferentially work backwards toward causes of that outcome.

This distinction will not be taken up again in this book, for the simple reason that it seems to be more an interesting claim for sociologists of knowledge than a point about methodology per se. Some authors treat this distinction as parallel with, or perhaps even redundant to, the quantitative-qualitative distinction in methodology. Yet there are large numbers of quantitative scholars whose research trajectories are motivated by causes-of-effects goals such as understanding class or gender inequality in political participation (Verba *et al.* 1995; Burns *et al.* 2001), learning about the causes of civil wars (Fearon and Laitin 2003), or figuring out why some countries are persistently more democratic than others (Acemoglu *et al.* 2008). Likewise, there are qualitative scholars interested in the effects of causes: what does democratization (Jaquette and Wolchik 1998) or revolution (Kampwirth 2004) change for women, for example, or how have institutions of participatory governance altered local political and economic dynamics (Goldfrank 2012)?

In any case, whether the analyst begins the process of theory building with special interest in a cause, a family of causes, an effect, or all of the above is essentially irrelevant for the issues of causal inference that are central to this book. The starting point of causal inference per se – as opposed to theory building, description, exploratory research, and other related scholarly endeavors – is a causal hypothesis involving some hypothesized cause or set of causes, an outcome, and potentially other moving parts. The intellectual route by which this starting point is reached is important, and merits methodological attention in its own right. However, for present purposes, it is purely preliminary.

Notes

1 This version of triviality is equivalent to extremely low coverage in Ragin's (2006, 2008) usage.
2 The second and third sets of treatment conditions may in practice represent complex combinations of multiple different treatments. In that case, the discussion

here would have to be revised to allow multiple different levels on those variables. However, the thrust of the argument would not change substantially.

3 Studies designed around the method of structured, focused comparison (George 1979), in particular, pay more attention to systematic cross-case comparison of scores on key independent and dependent variables, rather than to exploration of the steps linking causes and effects.

4 There may well be causal situations for which these two quantities are simply unworkable, i.e., situations in which M cannot be manipulated other than by the treatment. For such contexts, a different approach to causation would probably be needed.

5 For methodological reflection on this distinction, see Kitschelt 2003, and Schneider and Wagemann 2006.

6 For discussions advancing one or both of these kinds of causal models, see Stinchcombe 1968, Elster 1989, Abbott 1992, Pierson 2004, and Gerring 2005.

References

Abbott, Andrew. 1992. "From Causes to Events: Notes on Narrative Positivism." *Sociological Methods and Research* 20:428–55.

Acemoglu, Daron, Simon Johnson, James A. Robinson and Pierre Yared. 2008. "Income and Democracy." *American Economic Review* 98(3):808–42.

Adcock, Robert and David Collier. 2001. "Measurement Validity: A Shared Standard for Qualitative and Quantitative Research." *American Political Science Review* 95(3):529–46.

Ahmed, Amel and Rudra Sil. 2009. "Is Multi-Method Research Really 'Better'?" *Qualitative and Multi-Method Research* 7(2):2–6.

Ahram, Ariel I. 2013. "Concepts and Measurement in Multimethod Research." *Political Research Quarterly* 66(2):280–91.

Alvarez, Michael, Jose Antonio Cheibub, Fernando Limongi and Adam Przeworski. 1996. "Classifying Political Regimes." *Studies in Comparative International Development* 31(2):1–37.

Angrist, Joshua D. and Alan B. Krueger. 1992. "Estimating the Payoff to Schooling Using the Vietnam-Era Draft Lottery." *NBER Working Paper* 4067.

Angrist, Joshua D., Guido W. Imbens and Donald B. Rubin. 1996. "Identification of Causal Effects Using Instrumental Variables." *Journal of the American Statistical Association* 91:444–55.

Angrist, Joshua D. and Victor Lavy. 1999. "Using Maimonides' Rule to Estimate the Effect of Class Size on Scholastic Achievement." *Quarterly Journal of Economics* 114:533–75.

Angrist, Joshua D., Eric Bettinger, Erik Bloom, Elizabeth King and Michael Kremer. 2002. "Vouchers for Private Schooling in Colombia: Evidence from a Randomized Natural Experiment." *American Economic Review* 92:1535–58.

Angrist, Joshua D. and Jorn-Steffen Pischke. 2009. *Mostly Harmless Econometrics: An Empiricist's Companion.* Princeton University Press.

Arenas, Jacobo. 1972. *Diario de la Resistencia de Marquetalia.* FARC-EP.

Aronson, Elliot and J. M. Carlsmith. 1968. Experimentation in Social Psychology. In *The Handbook of Social Psychology*, vol. 2, 3rd edn., eds. G. Lindzey and E. Aronson. Reading: Addison-Wesley, 1–79.

Arthur, W. Brian. 1994. *Increasing Returns and Path Dependence in the Economy.* University of Michigan Press.

Axinn, William G. and Lisa D. Pearce. 2006. *Mixed Method Data Collection Strategies.* Cambridge University Press.

Baltagi, Badi H. 2013. *Econometric Analysis of Panel Data.* New York: Wiley.

Baltagi, Badi H. and Javier Hidalgo. 1996. "A Nonparametric Test for Poolability Using Panel Data." *Journal of Econometrics* 75:345–67.

Baron, Reuben M. and David A. Kenny. 1986. "The Moderator-Mediator Variable Distinction in Social Psychological Research: Conceptual, Strategic, and Statistical Considerations." *Journal of Personality and Social Psychology* 51(6):1173–82.

Baumgartner, Michael. 2008. "Regularity Theories Reassessed." *Philosophia* 36:327–54.

Beck, Nathaniel. 2006. "Is Causal-Process Observation an Oxymoron?" *Political Analysis* 14:347–52.

Beck, Nathaniel. 2010. "Causal Process 'Observation': Oxymoron or (Fine) Old Wine." *Political Analysis* 18(4):499–505.

Behling, Orlando and Kenneth S. Law. 2000. *Translating Questionnaires and Other Research Instruments: Problems and Solutions.* Thousand Oaks, Calif.: Sage.

Belsley, D. A., E. Kuh and R. E. Welsch. 1980. *Regression Diagnostics: Identifying Influential Data and Sources of Collinearity.* New York: Wiley.

Bennett, Andrew. 2008. Process Tracing: A Bayesian Perspective. In *The Oxford Handbook of Political Methodology*, eds. Janet M. Box-Steffensmeier, Henry E. Brady and David Collier. Oxford University Press.

Bennett, Andrew. 2010. Process Tracing and Causal Inference. In *Rethinking Social Inquiry: Diverse Tools, Shared Standards*, eds. Henry E. Brady and David Collier. Lanham, Md.: Rowman and Littlefield.

Bennett, Andrew and Jeffrey T. Checkel. 2015. Process Tracing: From Philosophical Roots to Best Practices. In *Process Tracing: From Metaphor to Analytic Tool*, eds. Andrew Bennett and Jeffrey T. Checkel. Cambridge University Press.

Bennett, Andrew and Colin Elman. 2006a. "Complex Causal Relations and Case Study Methods: The Example of Path Dependence." *Political Analysis* 14:250–67.

Bennett, Andrew and Colin Elman. 2006b. "Qualitative Research: Recent Development in Case Study Methods." *Annual Review of Political Science* 9:455–76.

Berinsky, Adam J. 2008. Survey Non-Response. In *The SAGE Handbook of Public Opinion Research*, eds. Wolfgang Donsbach and Michael W. Traugott. Thousand Oaks, Calif.: Sage.

Berk, Richard A. 2004. *Regression Analysis: A Constructive Critique.* Thousand Oaks, Calif.: Sage.

Berkowitz, Leonard and Edward Donnerstein. 1982. "External Validity Is More Than Skin Deep: Some Answers to Criticisms of Laboratory Experiments." *American Psychologist* 37:245–57.

Blais, Andre and Peter John Loewen. 2009. "The French Electoral System and Its Effects." *West European Politics* 32:345–59.

Blalock, Hubert M., Jr. 1961. *Causal Inference in Nonexperimental Research.* Chapel Hill, NC: University of North Carolina Press.

Boix, Carles. 1999. "Setting the Rules of the Game: The Choice of Electoral Systems in Advanced Democracies." *American Political Science Review* 93(3):609–24.

Bollen, Kenneth A. 1989. *Structural Equations with Latent Variables.* New York: Wiley Interscience.

Bollen, Kenneth A. 1993. "Liberal Democracy: Validity and Method Factors in Cross-National Measures." *American Journal of Political Science* 37(4):1207–30.

Bollen, Kenneth A. and Pamela Paxton. 2000. "Subjective Measures of Liberal Democracy." *Comparative Political Studies* 33(1):58–86.

Bowman, Kirk, Fabrice Lehoucq and James Mahoney. 2005. "Measuring Political Democracy: Case Expertise, Data Adequacy, and Central America." *Comparative Political Studies* 38:939–70.

Brader, Ted. 2005. "Striking a Responsive Chord: How Political Ads Motivate and Persuade Voters by Appealing to Emotions." *American Journal of Political Science* 49(April):388–405.

Brady, Henry E. 2008. "Causation and Explanation in Social Science." In *The Oxford Handbook of Political Methodology*, eds. Janet M. Box-Steffensmeier, Henry E. Brady and David Collier. Oxford University Press.

Brady, Henry E. and David Collier, eds. 2004. *Rethinking Social Inquiry: Diverse Tools, Shared Standards.* Rowman and Littlefield and Berkeley Public Policy Press.

Braga, Anthony A., David L. Weisburd, Elin J. Waring, Lorraine Green Mazerolle, William Spelman and Francis Gajewski. 1999. "Problem-Oriented Policing in Violent Crime Places: A Randomized Controlled Experiment." *Criminology* 37(August):541–80.

Brambor, Thomas, William Roberts Clark and Matt Golder. 2006. "Understanding Interaction Models: Improving Empirical Analyses." *Political Analysis* 14:63–82.

Braumoeller, Bear F. and Gary Goertz. 2000. "The Methodology of Necessary Conditions." *American Journal of Political Science* 44:844–58.

Brewer, John and Albert Hunter. 2006. *Foundations of Multimethod Research: Synthesizing Styles.* Thousand Oaks, CA: Sage.

Brinkmann, Svend and Steinar Kvale. 2014. *InterViews: Learning the Craft of Qualitative Research Interviewing.* 3rd edn. Thousand Oaks, CA: Sage.

Burden, Barry C., Gregory A. Caldeira and Tim Groseclose. 2000. "Measuring the Ideologies of U.S. Senators: The Song Remains the Same." *Legislative Studies Quarterly* 25(2):237–58.

Burns, Nancy, Kay Lehman Schlozman and Sidney Verba. 2001. *The Private Roots of Public Action: Gender, Equality, and Political Participation.* Cambridge, Mass.: Harvard University Press.

Butler, Daniel M. and Matthew J. Butler. 2006. "Splitting the Difference? Causal Inference and Theories of Split-Party Delegations." *Political Analysis* 14(4):439–55.

Camerer, Colin F. 2003. *Behavioral Game Theory: Experiments in Strategic Interaction.* Princeton University Press.

Cameron, A. Colin and Pravin K. Trivedi. 2005. *Microeconometrics: Methods and Applications.* Cambridge University Press.

Cameron, Donald and Ian G. Jones. 1983. "John Snow, the Broad Street Pump and Modern Epidemiology." *International Journal of Epidemiology* 12(4):393–96.

Campbell, Donald T. 1975. "'Degrees of Freedom' and the Case Study." *Comparative Political Studies* 8:178–93.

Campbell, Donald T. and Duncan W. Fiske. 1959. "Convergent and Discriminant Validation by the Multitrait Multimethod Matrix." *Psychological Bulletin* 56:81–105.

Campbell, Donald T. and H. Laurence Ross. 1968. "The Connecticut Crackdown on Speeding: Time-Series Data in Quasi-Experimental Analysis." *Law and Society Review* 3(1):33–54.

Campbell, Donald T. and Julian C. Stanley. 1963. *Experimental and Quasi-Experimental Designs for Research.* Chicago, Ill.: Rand McNally College Publishing.

Caracelli, Valerie J. and Jennifer C. Greene. 1997. "Crafting Mixed-Method Evaluation Designs." *New Directions for Evaluation* 74:19–32.

Card, David. 1990. "The Impact of the Mariel Boatlift on the Miami Labor Market." *Industrial and Labor Relations Review* 43(January): 245–57.

Carroll, Royce, Jeffrey B. Lewis, James Lo, Keith T. Poole and Howard Rosenthal. 2009. "Comparing NOMINATE and IDEAL: Points of Difference and Monte Carlo Tests." *Legislative Studies Quarterly* 34(4):555–91.

Cartwright, Nancy. 1979. "Causal Laws and Effective Strategies." *Nous* 4:419–37.

Cartwright, Nancy. 1989. *Nature's Capacities and their Measurement.* Oxford University Press.

Cartwright, Nancy. 2007. *Hunting Causes and Using Them: Approaches in Philosophy and Economics.* Cambridge University Press.

Casper, Gretchen and Claudiu Tufis. 2003. "Correlation Versus Interchangeability: The Limited Robustness of Empirical Findings on Democracy Using Highly Correlated Data Sets." *Political Analysis* 11(2):196–203.

Caughey, Devin and Jasjeet S. Sekhon. 2011. "Elections and the Regression Discontinuity Design: Lessons from Close U.S. House Races, 1942–2008." *Political Analysis* 19(4):385–408.

Chatterjee, Abhishek. 2009. "Ontology, Epistemology, and Multi-Methods." *Qualitative and Multi-Method Research* 7(2):11–15.

Chhibber, Pradeep K. and Ken Kollman. 2004. *The Formation of National Party Systems: Federalism and Party Competition in Canada, Great Britain, India, and the United States.* Princeton University Press.

Chong, Dennis. 1993. "How People Think, Reason, and Feel about Rights and Liberties." *American Journal of Political Science* 37(3): 867–99.

Chong, Dennis and James N. Druckman. 2007. "Framing Theory." *Annual Review of Political Science* 10:103–26.

Clarke, Kevin A. 2005. "The Phantom Menace: Omitted Variable Bias in Econometric Research." *Conflict Management and Peace Science* 22:341–52.

Clarke, Ronald V. and David Weisburd. 1994. "Diffusion of Crime Control Benefits: Observations on the Reverse of Displacement." In *Crime Prevention Studies*, vol. 2, ed. R. V. Clarke. Monsey, NY: Criminal Justice Press.

Clinton, Joshua and Simon Jackman. 2009. "To Simulate or NOMINATE?" *Legislative Studies Quarterly* 34(4):593–621.

Clinton, Joshua, Simon Jackman and Douglas Rivers. 2004. "The Statistical Analysis of Roll Call Data." *American Political Science Review* 98(2):355–70.

Collier, David, Jason Seawright and Henry E. Brady. 2003. "Qualitative versus Quantitative: What Might This Distinction Mean?" *Qualitative Methods* 1:4–8.

Collier, David, Henry E. Brady and Jason Seawright. 2004. Sources of Leverage in Causal Inference: Toward an Alternative View of Methodology. In *Rethinking Social Inquiry: Diverse Tools, Shared Standards*, eds. Henry E. Brady and David Collier. Lanham, Md.: Rowman and Littlefield, 229–66.

Collier, David and James Mahoney. 1996. "Insights and Pitfalls: Selection Bias in Qualitative Research." *World Politics* 49(1):56–91.

Collier, Ruth Berins and David Collier. 1991. *Shaping the Political Arena: Critical Junctures, the Labor Movement, and Regime Dynamics in Latin America.* Princeton University Press.

Collier, Ruth Berins and David Collier. 2002. *Shaping the Political Arena: Critical Junctures, the Labor Movement, and Regime Dynamics in Latin America.* 2nd edn. South Bend, Ind.: University of Notre Dame Press.

Collier, David and Steven Levitsky. 1997. "Democracy with Adjectives: Conceptual Innovation in Comparative Research." *World Politics* 49(3):430–51.

Collier, David, James Mahoney and Jason Seawright. 2004. Claiming Too Much: Warnings about Selection Bias. In *Rethinking Social Inquiry: Diverse Tools, Shared Standards*, eds. H. E. Brady and D. Collier. Lanham, Md.: Rowman and Littlefield.

Cook, R. Dennis and Sanford Weisberg. 1982. *Residuals and Influence in Regression.* New York: Chapman and Hall.

Coppedge, Michael. 1999. "Thickening Thin Concepts and Theories: Combining Large N and Small in Comparative Politics." *Comparative Politics* 31(4):465–76.

Coppedge, Michael. 2005. Explaining Democratic Deterioration in Venezuela through Nested Inference. In *The Third Wave of Democratization in Latin America: Advances and Setbacks*, eds. Frances Hagopian and Scott P. Mainwaring. Cambridge University Press, 289–316.

Creswell, John W. and Vicki L. Piano Clark. 2011. *Designing and Conducting Mixed Methods Research*. Thousand Oaks, Calif.: Sage.

Cullen, Julie Berry, Brian A. Jacob and Steven Levitt. 2006. "The Effect of School Choice on Participants: Evidence from Randomized Lotteries." *Econometrica* 74:1191–1230.

Cunningham, William A., Kristopher J. Preacher and Mahzarin R. Banaji. 2001. "Implicit Attitude Measures: Consistency, Stability, and Convergent Validity." *Psychological Science* 12:163–70.

Cusack, Thomas R., Torben Iversen and David Soskice. 2007. "Economic Interests and the Origins of Electoral Systems." *American Political Science Review* 101(3):373–91.

Cusack, Thomas, Torben Iversen and David Soskice. 2010. "Coevolution of Capitalism and Political Representation: The Choice of Electoral Systems." *American Political Science Review* 104(2):393–403.

Cyr, Jennifer. 2016. "The Pitfalls and Promise of Focus Groups as a Data Collection Method." *Sociological Methods and Research* 45(May):231–59.

David, Paul A. 2007. "Path Dependence: A Foundational Concept for Historical Social Science." *Cliometrica* 1:91–114.

Deaton, Angus. 2010. "Understanding the Mechanisms of Economic Development." *Journal of Economic Perspectives* 24:3–16.

De La O, Ana L. 2013. "Do Conditional Cash Transfers Affect Electoral Behavior? Evidence from a Randomized Experiment in Mexico." *American Journal of Political Science* 57:1–14.

DeWalt, Kathleen M. and Billie R. DeWalt. 2011. *Participant Observation: A Guide for Fieldworkers*. Lanham, Md.: AltaMira Press.

Dion, Douglas. 1998. "Evidence and Inference in the Comparative Case Study." *Comparative Politics* 30:127–45.

Druckman, James N. and Thomas J. Leeper. 2012. "Learning More from Political Communication Experiments: Pretreatment and Its Effects." *American Journal of Political Science* 56:875–96.

Duflo, Esther, Rachel Glennerster and Michael Kremer. 2008. Using Randomization in Development Economics Research: A Toolkit. In *Handbook of Development Economics*, vol. 4, eds. T. Paul Schultz and John A. Strauss. Amsterdam: North-Holland, 3895–962.

Duncan, Otis Dudley. 1966. "Path Analysis: Sociological Examples." *American Journal of Sociology* 72:365–74.

Dunning, Thad. 2010. Design-Based Inference: Beyond the Pitfalls of Regression Analysis? In *Rethinking Social Inquiry: Diverse Tools, Shared Standards*, eds. Henry E. Brady and David Collier. 2nd edn. Rowman and Littlefield, 273–311.

Dunning, Thad. 2012. *Natural Experiments in the Social Sciences: A Design-Based Approach.* Cambridge University Press.

Dunning, Thad and Janhavi Nilekani. 2013. "Ethnic Quotas and Political Mobilization: Caste, Parties, and Distribution in Indian Village Councils." *American Political Science Review* 107:35–56.

Duran, Mauricio Garcia, Vera Grabe Loewenherz and Otty Patino Hormaza. 2008. "M-19's Journey from Armed Struggle to Democratic Politics: Striving to Keep the Revolution Connected to the People." *Technical Report*, Berghof Research Center for Constructive Conflict Management AltensteinstraSSe 48a, DŰ14195 Berlin, Germany.

Eid, Michael and Ed Diener, eds. 2006. *Handbook of Multimethod Measurement in Psychology.* Washington, DC: American Psychological Association.

Einhorn, Hillel J., Don N. Kleinmuntz and Benjamin Kleinmuntz. 1979. "Linear Regression and Process-Tracing Models of Judgment." *Psychological Review* 86(5):465–85.

Elster, Jon. 1989. *Nuts and Bolts for the Social Sciences.* Cambridge University Press.

Elster, Jon. 2007. *Explaining Social Behavior: More Nuts and Bolts for the Social Sciences.* Cambridge University Press.

Elwert, Felix and Christopher Winship. 2014. "Endogenous Selection Bias: The Problem of Conditioning on a Collider Variable." *Annual Review of Sociology* 40.

Fearon, James D. and David D. Laitin. 2003. "Ethnicity, Insurgency, and Civil War." *American Political Science Review* 96:75–90.

Fearon, James D. and David D. Laitin. 2008. Integrating Qualitative and Quantitative Methods. In *The Oxford Handbook of Political Methodology*, eds. Henry E. Brady, Janet Box-Steffensmeier and David Collier. New York, NY: Oxford University Press, 300–18.

Flyvbjerg, Bent. 2006. "Five Misunderstandings about Case-Study Research." *Qualitative Inquiry* 12(2):219–45.

Ford, J. Kevin, Neal Schmitt, Susan L. Schechtman, Brian M. Hults and Mary L. Doherty. 1989. "Process Tracing Methods: Contributions, Problems, and Neglected Research Questions." *Organizational Behavior and Human Decision Processes* 43:75–117.

Fourcade, Marion. 2009. *Economists and Societies: Discipline and Profession in the United States, Britain, and France, 1890s to 1990s.* Princeton University Press.

Fowler, Floyd J., Jr. 2013. *Survey Research Methods.* 5th edn. Thousand Oaks, CA: Sage.

Freedman, David A. 1991. "Statistical Models and Shoe Leather." *Sociological Methodology* 21:291–313.

Freedman, David A. 2005. "Linear Statistical Models for Causation: A Critical Review." In *Encyclopedia of Statistics in Behavioral Science*, eds. Brian S. Everitt and David Howell. Hoboken, NJ: John Wiley & Sons.

Freedman, David A. 2006. "Statistical Models for Causation: What Inferential Leverage Do They Provide?" *Evaluation Review* 30:691–713.

Freedman, David A. 2009. *Statistical Models: Theory and Practice, Revised Edition.* Cambridge University Press.

Gasking, Douglas. 1955. "Causation and Recipes." *Mind* 64(256):479–87.

Geddes, Barbara. 1990. "How the Cases You Choose Affect the Answers You Get: Selection Bias in Comparative Politics." *Political Analysis* 2(1):131–50.

Gelman, Andrew and Jennifer Hill. 2007. *Data Analysis Using Regression and Multilevel/Hierarchical Models.* Cambridge University Press.

George, Alexander L. 1979. Case Studies and Theory Development: The Method of Structued, Focused Comparison. In *Diplomacy: New Approaches in History, Theory, and Policy*, ed. Paul Gordon Lauren. New York, NY: Free Press.

George, Alexander L. and Andrew Bennett. 2004. *Case Studies and Theory Development in the Social Sciences.* Cambridge, Mass.: MIT Press.

Gerber, Alan S., Donald P. Green and Christopher W. Larimer. 2008. "Social Pressure and Voter Turnout: Evidence from a Large-Scale Field Experiment." *American Political Science Review* 102:33–48.

Gerring, John. 2004. "What Is a Case Study and What Is It Good For?" *American Political Science Review* 98(2):341–54.

Gerring, John. 2005. "Causation: A Unified Framework for the Social Sciences." *Journal of Theoretical Politics* 17(2):163–98.

Gerring, John. 2007a. "Is There a (Viable) Crucial-Case Method?" *Comparative Political Studies* 40(3):231–53.

Gerring, John. 2007b. "The Mechanismic Worldview: Thinking Inside the Box." *British Journal of Political Science* 38(1):161–79.

Giddens, Anthony. 1979. *Central Problems in Social Theory: Action, Structure, and Contradiction in Social Analysis.* Berkeley, Calif.: University of California.

Gilovich, Thomas, Dale Griffin and Daniel Kahneman, eds. 2002. *Heuristics and Biases: The Psychology of Intuitive Judgment.* Cambridge University Press.

Glynn, Adam N. and Nahomi Ichino. 2015. "Using Qualitative Information to Improve Causal Inference." *American Journal of Political Science* 59 (October):1055–71.

Glynn, Adam and Kevin M. Quinn. 2010. Combining Case Studies and Regression (or Other Large-N Techniques) for Population Causal Inference. In *ASPA Annual Meetings.*

Goertz, Gary and Jack S. Levy, eds. 2007. *Explaining War and Peace: Case Studies and Necessary Condition Counterfactuals.* New York: Routledge.

Goertz, Gary and James Mahoney. 2012. *A Tale of Two Cultures: Qualitative and Quantitative Research in the Social Sciences.* Princeton University Press.

Goertz, Gary and Harvey Starr, eds. 2003. *Necessary Conditions: Theory, Methodology, and Applications.* Lanham, Md.: Rowman and Littlefield.

Goldfrank, Benjamin. 2012. *Deepening Local Democracy in Latin America: Participation, Decentralization, and the Left.* University Park, Pa.: Pennsylvania State University Press.

Goldstone, Jack A. 1991. *Revolution and Rebellion in the Early Modern World.* Berkeley, Calif.: University of California Press.

Goldstone, Jack A. 1998. "Initial Conditions, General Laws, Path Dependence, and Explanation in Historical Sociology." *American Journal of Sociology* 104:829–45.

Gonzalez-Ocantos, Ezequiel, Chad Kiewiet de Jonge, Carlos Melendez, Javier Osorio and David W. Nickerson. 2012. "Vote Buying and Social Desirability Bias: Experimental Evidence from Nicaragua." *American Journal of Political Science* 56:202–17.

Good, Phillip. 2005. *Permutation, Parametric, and Bootstrap Tests of Hypotheses.* 3rd edn. New York, NY: Springer.

Granger, C. W. J. 1969. "e Models and Cross-Spectral Methods." *Econometrica* 36:424–38.

Granger, C. W. J. 1980. "Testing for Causality: A Personal Viewpoint." *Journal of Economic Dynamics and Control* 2:329–52.

Green, Donald P., Shang E. Ha and John G. Bullock. 2010. "Enough Already about 'Black Box' Experiments: Studying Mediation Is More Difficult Than Most Scholars Suppose." *The Annals of the American Academy of Political and Social Science* 628(1):200–8.

Green, Donald P., Mary C. McGrath and Peter M. Aronow. 2013. "Field Experiments and the Study of Voter Turnout." *Journal of Elections, Public Opinion and Parties* 23(1):27–48.

Greene, Jennifer C. 2007. *Mixed Methods in Social Inquiry.* San Francisco, Calif.: Jossey-Bass.

Greene, Jennifer C, Valerie J. Caracelli and Wendy F. Graham. 1989. "Toward a Conceptual Framework for Mixed-Method Evaluation Designs." *Educational Evaluation and Policy Analysis* 11(3):255–74.

Greene, William H. 2000. *Econometric Analysis.* 4th edn. Upper Saddle River, NJ: Prentice Hall.

Grimmer, Justin and Brandon M. Stewart. 2013. "Text as Data: The Promise and Pitfalls of Automatic Content Analysis Methods for Political Texts." *Political Analysis* 21:267–97.

Grofman, Bernard. 1999. SNTV, STV, and Single-Member-District Systems: Theoretical Comparisons and Contrasts. In *Elections in Japan, Korea, and Taiwan under the Single Non-Transferable Vote: The Comparative Study of an Embedded Institution*, eds. Bernard Grofman, Sung-Chull Lee, Edwin A. Winckler and Brian Woodall. Ann Arbor, Mich.: Univerity of Michigan Press.

Gross, James J. and Robert W. Levenson. 1995. "Emotion Elicitation Using Films." *Cognition and Emotion* 9:87–108.

Gross, Neil. 2009. "A Pragmatist Theory of Social Mechanisms." *American Sociological Review* 74:358–79.

Grossman, Guy and Delia Baldassarri. 2012. "The Impact of Elections on Cooperation: Evidence from a Lab-in-the-Field Experiment in Uganda." *American Journal of Political Science* 56:964–85.

Guest, Greg, Emily E. Namey and Marilyn L. Mitchell, eds. 2012. *Collecting Qualitative Data: A Field Manual for Applied Research.* Thousand Oaks, Calif.: Sage.

Haber, Stephen and Victor Menaldo. 2011. "Do Natural Resources Fuel Authoritarianism? A Reappraisal of the Resource Curse." *American Political Science Review* 105:1–26.

Hansen, Ben B. 2004. "Full Matching in an Observational Study of Coaching for the SAT." *Journal of the American Statistical Association* 99:609–18.

Harkness, Janet, Fons van de Vijver and Peter Ph. Mohler, eds. 2003. *Cross-Cultural Survey Methods.* Hoboken, NJ: Wiley.

Harrison, Glenn W. and John A. List. 2004. "Field Experiments." *Journal of Economic Literature* 42:1009–55.

Hausman, Daniel M. 1998. *Causal Asymmetries.* Cambridge University Press.

Heckman, James and James Snyder. 1997. "Linear Probability Models of the Demand for Attributes with an Empirical Application to Estimating the Preferences of Legislators." *Rand Journal of Economics* 28:142–89.

Hedström, Peter and Richard Swedberg. 1998. *Social Mechanisms: An Analytical Approach to Social Theory.* Cambridge University Press.

Henrich, Joseph, Robert Boyd, Samuel Bowles, Colin Camerer, Ernst Fehr, Herbert Gintis and Richard McElreath. 2001. "In Search of Homo Economicus: Behavioral Experiments in 15 Small-Scale Societies." *American Economic Review* 91:73–78.

Henrich, Joseph, Steven J. Heine and Ara Norenzayan. 2010. "The Weirdest People in the World?" *Behavioral and Brain Sciences* 33(June):61–83.

Hidalgo, Daniel. 2010. "Digital Democratization: Suffrage Expansion and the Decline of Political Machines in Brazil." Unpublished manuscript.

Hidalgo, F. Daniel and Neal P. Richardson. 2008. A Perfect Match? Verifying Statistical Assumptions with Case Knowledge. In *Annual Meeting of the American Political Science Association, Boston, Massachusetts.*

Hill, Kim Quaile, Stephen Hanna and Sahar Shafqat. 1997. "The Liberal-Conservative Ideology of U.S. Senators: A New Measure." *American Journal of Political Science* 41:1395–413.

Holland, Paul W. 1986. "Statistics and Causal Inference." *Journal of the American Statistical Association* 81:945–60.

Hume, David. 1748/1999. *An Enquiry concerning Human Understanding.* Oxford University Press.

Imai, Kosuke, Luke Keele, and Dustin Tingley. 2010. "A General Approach to Causal Mediation Analysis." *Psychological Methods* 15(December):309–34.

Imai, Kosuke, Luke Keele and Teppei Yamamoto. 2010. "Identification, Inference and Sensitivity Analysis for Causal Mediation Effects." *Statistical Science* 25(1):51–71.

Imai, Kosuke, Luke Keele, Dustin Tingley and Teppei Yamamoto. 2011. "Unpacking the Black Box of Causality: Learning about Causal Mechanisms from Experimental and Observational Studies." *American Political Science Review* 105(4):765–89.

Imbens, Guido W. and Thomas Lemieux. 2008. "Regression Discontinuity Designs: A Guide to Practice." *Journal of Econometrics* 142:615–35.

Imbens, Guido W. and Donald B. Rubin. 1997. "Bayesian Inference for Causal Effects in Randomized Experiments with Noncompliance." *The Annals of Statistics* 25:305–27.

Irzik, Gurol. 1996. "Can Causes Be Reduced to Correlation?" *British Journal for the Philosophy of Science* 47(2):249–70.

Jackman, Simon. 2001. "Multidimensional Analysis of Roll Call Data via Bayesian Simulation: Identification, Estimation, Inference, and Model Checking." *Political Analysis* 9:227–41.

Jaquette, Jane S. and Sharon L. Wolchik, eds. 1998. *Women and Democracy: Latin America and Central and Eastern Europe.* Baltimore, Md.: Johns Hopkins University Press.

Jick, Todd D. 1979. "Mixing Qualitative and Quantitative Methods: Triangulation in Action." *Administrative Science Quarterly* 24(4): 602–11.

Joreskog, Karl G. 2006. "LISREL." *Encyclopedia of Statistical Sciences* 7.

Jowell, Roger, Caroline Roberts, Rory Fitzgerald and Gillian Eva, eds. 2007. *Measuring Attitudes Cross-Nationally: Lessons from the European Social Survey.* Thousand Oaks, Calif.: Sage.

Kahneman, Daniel and Amos Tversky, eds. 2000. *Choices, Values, and Frames.* Cambridge: Cambridge University Press.

Kahneman, Daniel, Paul Slovic and Amos Tversky, eds. 1982. *Judgment under Uncertainty: Heuristics and Biases.* Cambridge University Press.

Kampwirth, Karen. 2004. *Feminism and the Legacy of Revolution: Nicaragua, El Salvador, Chiapas.* Athens, OH: Center for International Studies, Ohio University.

Kennedy, Peter. 2008. *A Guide to Econometrics.* Hoboken, NJ: Wiley-Blackwell.

Keyder, Caglar. 2005. "Globalization and Global Exclusion in Istanbul." *International Journal of Urban and Regional Research* 29:124–34.

King, Gary, Robert O. Keohane and Sidney Verba. 1994. *Designing Social Inquiry: Scientific Inference in Qualitative Research.* Princeton University Press.

Kiser, Edgar and Michael Hechter. 1998. "The Debate on Historical Sociology: Rational Choice Theory and Its Critics." *American Journal of Sociology* 104:785–816.

Kitschelt, Herbert. 2003. Accounting for Postcommunist Regime Diversity: What Counts as a Good Cause? In *Capitalism and Democracy in Central and Eastern Europe. Assessing the Legacy of Communist Rule*, eds. Grzegorz Ekiert and Stephen E. Hanson. Cambrige: Cambridge University Press, 49–86.

Kreuzer, Marcus. 2010. "Historical Knowledge and Quantitative Analysis: The Case of the Origins of Proportional Representation." *American Political Science Review* 104:369–92.

Kuehn, David and Ingo Rohlfing. 2009. "Does It, Really? Measurement Error and Omitted Variables in Multi-Method Research." *Qualitative and Multi-Method Research* 7(2):18–21.

Lachin, John M. 2000. "Statistical Considerations in the Intent-to-Treat Principle." *Controlled Clinical Trials* 21:167–89.

Lakoff, George and Mark Johnson. 1999. *Philosophy in the Flesh: The Embodied Mind and Its Challenge to Western Thought.* New York, NY: Basic Books.

Lazarsfeld, Paul F. 1958. "Evidence and Inference in Social Research." *Daedalus* 87:99–130.

Lebow, Richard Ned. 2010. *Forbidden Fruit: Counterfactuals and International Relations.* Princeton University Press.

LeCompte, Margaret D. and Judith Preissle Goetz. 1982. "Problems of Reliability and Validity in Ethnographic Research." *Review of Educational Research* 52:31–60.

LeGrand, Catherine C. 2003. "The Colombian Crisis in Historical Perspective." *Canadian Journal of Latin American and Caribbean Studies* 28(55/56):165–209.

Levy Paluck, Elizabeth. 2010a. "Is It Better Not to Talk? Group Polarization, Extended Contact, and Perspective Taking in Eastern Democratic Republic of Congo." *Personality and Social Psychology Bulletin* 36:1170–85.

Levy Paluck, Elizabeth. 2010b. "The Promising Integration of Qualitative Methods and Field Experiments." *The Annals of the American Academy of Political and Social Science* 628:59–71.

Lewis, David. 1973a. *Counterfactuals.* Cambridge, Mass.: Harvard University Press.

Lewis, David. 1973b. "Causation." *Journal of Philosophy* 70:556–67.

Lewis, David. 1979. "Counterfactual Dependence and Time's Arrow." *Nous* 13:455–76.

Lewis, David. 1986. Causation. In *Philosophical Papers II*. Oxford University Press, 159–213.

Lewis, David. 2000. "Causation as Influence." *Journal of Philosophy* 97:182–97.

Lieberman, Evan S. 2003. *Race and Regionalism in the Politics of Taxation in Brazil and South Africa*. Cambridge University Press.

Lieberman, Evan S. 2005. "Nested Analysis as a Mixed-Method Strategy for Comparative Research." *American Political Science Review* 99:435–52.

Lieberman, Evan S. 2010. "Bridging the Quantitative-Qualitative Divide: Best Practices in the Development of Historically Oriented Replication Databases." *Annual Review of Political Science* 13:37–59.

Lieberson, Stanley. 1992. Small N's and Big Conclusions: An Examination of the Reasoning in Comparative Studies Based on a Small Number of Cases. In *What Is a Case? Exploring the Foundations of Social Inquiry*, eds. Charles C. Ragin and Howard S. Becker. Cambridge University Press, 105–18.

Lijphart, Arend. 1971. "Comparative Politics and the Comparative Method." *American Political Science Review* 65:682–93.

Lijphart, Arend. 1975. "The Comparable-Cases Strategy in Comparative Research." *Comparative Political Studies* 8(July):158–77.

Lin, Jih-wen. 2011. "The Endogenous Change in Electoral Systems: The Case of SNTV." *Party Politics* 17:365–84.

Linz, Juan J. and Alfred Stepan. 1996. *Problems of Democratic Transition and Consolidation: Southern Europe, South America, and Post-Communist Europe*. Baltimore, Md.: Johns Hopkins University Press.

Mackie, J. L. 1974. *The Cement of the Universe: A Study of Causation*. Oxford University Press.

Mahoney, James. 1999. "Nominal, Ordinal, and Narrative Appraisal in Macrocausal Analysis." *American Journal of Sociology* 104(4):1154–96.

Mahoney, James. 2000. "Path Dependence in Historical Sociology." *Theory and Society* 29:507–48.

Mahoney, James. 2001. *The Legacies of Liberalism: Path Dependence and Political Regimes in Central America*. Baltimore, Md.: Johns Hopkins University Press.

Mahoney, James. 2004. "Comparative-Historical Methodology." *Annual Review of Sociology* 30:81–101.

Mahoney, James. 2008. "Toward a Unified Theory of Causality." *Comparative Political Studies* 41(4/5):412–36.

Mahoney, James. 2010. "After KKV: The New Methodology of Qualitative Research." *World Politics* 61(1):120–47.

Mahoney, James and Gary Goertz. 2006. "A Tale of Two Cultures: Contrasting Quantitative and Qualitative Research." *Political Analysis* 14(3): 227–49.

Mahoney, James and Kathleen Thelen, eds. 2009. *Explaining Institutional Change: Ambiguity, Agency, and Power.* Cambridge University Press.

Mahoney, James, Erin Kimball and Kendra L. Koivu. 2009. "The Logic of Historical Explanation in the Social Sciences." *Comparative Political Studies* 42:114–46.

McAdam, Doug, Sidney Tarrow and Charles Tilly. 2001. *Dynamics of Contention.* Cambridge University Press.

McDermott, Rose, Jonathan Cowden and Cheryl Koopman. 2002. "Framing, Uncertainty, and Hostile Communication in a Crisis Experiment." *Political Psychology* 23:133–49.

McKeown, Timothy J. 2004. Case Studies and the Limits of the Quantitative Worldview. In *Rethinking Social Inquiry: Diverse Tools, Shared Standards.* Lanham, Md.: Rowman and Littlefield, 139–68.

Mill, John Stuart. 1891/2002. *A System of Logic: Ratiocinative and Inductive.* Honolulu: University Press of the Pacific.

Mintz, Alex, Steven B. Redd and Arnold Vedlitz. 2006. "Can We Generalize from Student Experiments to the Real World in Political Science, Military Affairs, and International Relations?" *Journal of Conflict Resolution* 50:757–76.

Morgan, David L. 1996. *Focus Groups as Qualitative Research.* 2nd edn. Thousand Oaks, Calif.: Sage.

Morgan, Stephen L. and Christopher Winship. 2007. *Counterfactuals and Causal Inference: Methods and Principles for Social Research.* Cambridge University Press.

Munck, Gerardo L. 2009. *Measuring Democracy: A Bridge between Scholarship and Politics.* Baltimore, Md.: Johns Hopkins University Press.

Neyman, Jerzy Splawa. 1923/1990. "On the Application of Probability Theory to Agricultural Experiments. Essay on Principles. Section 9." *Statistical Science* 5(4):465–72.

Nisbett, Richard E. and Timothy D. Wilson. 1977. "Telling More Than We Can Know: Verbal Reports on Mental Processes." *Psychological Review* 84(3):231–59.

Patrick, John and Nic James. 2004. "Process Tracing of Complex Cognitive Work Tasks." *Journal of Occupational and Organizational Psychology* 77:259–80.

Payne, John W., Myron L. Braunstein and John S. Carroll. 1978. "Exploring Predecisional Behavior: An Alternative Approach to Decision Research." *Organizational Behavior and Human Performance* 22:17–44.

Pearce, Craig L., Henry P. Sims Jr., Jonathan F. Cox, Gail Ball, Eugene Schnell, Ken A. Smith and Linda Trevino. 2003. "Transactors, Transformers and Beyond: A Multi-Method Development of a Theoretical Typology of Leadership." *The Journal of Management Development* 22(4):273–307.

Pemstein, Daniel, Stephen A. Meserve and James Melton. 2010. "Democratic Compromise: A Latent Variable Analysis of Ten Measures of Regime Type." *Political Analysis* 18(4):426–49.

Persson, Torsten and Guido Tabellini. 2003. *The Economic Effects of Constitutions.* Cambridge, Mass.: MIT Press.

Pierson, Paul. 2000. "Increasing Returns, Path Dependence, and the Study of Politics." *American Political Science Review* 94:251–67.

Pierson, Paul. 2004. *Politics in Time: History, Institutions, and Social Analysis.* Princeton University Press.

Plumper, Thomas, Vera E. Troeger and Eric Neumayer. 2010. "Case Selection and Causal Inference in Qualitative Research." Unpublished Manuscript.

Poole, Keith T. and Howard Rosenthal. 1997. *Congress: A Political-Economic History of Roll-Call Voting.* New York, NY: Oxford University Press.

Powers, Donald E. and Donald A. Rock. 1999. "Effects of Coaching on SAT I: Reasoning Test Scores." *Journal of Educational Measurement* 36:93–118.

Prasad, Monica. 2006. *The Politics of Free Markets: The Rise of Neoliberal Economic Policies in Britain, France, Germany, and the United States.* University of Chicago Press.

Przeworski, Adam and Henry Teune. 1970. *The Logic of Comparative Social Inquiry.* Hoboken, NJ: John Wiley & Sons.

Rabkin, Rhoda. 1996. "Redemocratization, Electoral Engineering, and Party Strategies in Chile, 1989-1995." *Comparative Political Studies* 29:335–56.

Ragin, Charles C. 1987. *The Comparative Method: Moving Beyond Qualitative and Quantitative Strategies.* Berkeley, Calif.: University of California Press.

Ragin, Charles C. 2000. *Fuzzy-Set Social Science.* University of Chicago Press.

Ragin, Charles C. 2004. Turning the Tables: How Case-Oriented Research Challenges Variable-Oriented Research. In *Rethinking Social Inquiry:*

Diverse Tools, Shared Standards. Lanham, Md.: Rowman and Littlefield, 123–38.

Ragin, Charles C. 2006. "Set Relations in Social Research: Evaluating their Consistency and Coverage." *Political Analysis* 14:291–310.

Ragin, Charles C. 2008. *Redesigning Social Inquiry: Set Relations in Social Research.* University of Chicago Press.

Reppetto, Thomas A. 1976. "Crime Prevention and the Displacement Phenomenon." Crime and Delinquency 22(April):166–77.

Roberts, Kenneth M. 1996. "Neoliberalism and the Transformation of Populism in Latin America: The Peruvian Case." *World Politics* 48(1):82–116.

Robins, James M. and Sander Greenland. 1992. "Identifiability and Exchangeability for Direct and Indirect Effects." *Epidemiology* 3:143–55.

Rogowski, Ronald. 2004. How Inference in the Social (but Not the Physical) Sciences Neglects Theoretical Anomaly. In *Rethinking Social Inquiry: Diverse Tools, Shared Standards*, eds. Henry E. Brady and David Collier. Lanham, Md.: Rowman and Littlefield, 76–83.

Rosenbaum, Paul R. 1984. "The Consquences of Adjustment for a Concomitant Variable That Has Been Affected by the Treatment." *Journal of the Royal Statistical Society, Series A* 147(5):656–66.

Rosenbaum, P. and Donald B. Rubin. 1983. "The Central Role of the Propensity Score in Observational Studies for Causal Effects." *Biometrika* 70:41–55.

Rubin, Donald B. 1974. "Estimating Causal Effects of Treatment in Randomized and Non-Randomized Studies." *Journal of Educational Psychology* 66(5):688–701.

Rubin, Donald B. 1979. "Using Multivariate Matched Sampling and Regression Adjustment to Control Bias in Observational Studies." *Journal of the American Statistical Association* 74:318–28.

Rubin, Donald B. 1980. "Comment." *Journal of the American Statistical Association* 75:591–93.

Rubin, Donald B. 1986. "Statistics and Causal Inference: Comment: Which Ifs Have Causal Answers." *Journal of the American Statistical Association* 81:961–2.

Rubin, Donald B. 2006. *Matched Sampling for Causal Effects.* Cambridge University Press.

Schiffrin, Deborah, Deborah Tannen and Heidi E. Hamilton, eds. 2001. *The Handbook of Discourse Analysis.* Malden and Oxford: Blackwell.

Schneider, Carsten Q. and Claudius Wagemann. 2006. "Reducing Complexity in Qualitative Comparative Analysis (QCA): Remote and Proximate Factors and the Consolidation of Democracy." *European Journal of Political Research* 45:751–86.

Schuman, Howard and Stanley Presser. 1996. *Questions and Answers in Attitude Surveys: Experiments on Question Form, Wording, and Context.* Thousand Oaks, Calif.: Sage.

Schwartz-Shea, Peregrine and Dvora Yanow. 2012. *Interpretive Research Design: Concepts and Processes.* New York and London: Routledge.

Seawright, Jason. 2002. "Testing for Necessary and/or Sufficient Causation: Which Cases are Relevant?" *Political Analysis* 10(2):178–93.

Seawright, Jason. 2012. *Party-System Collapse: The Roots of Crisis in Peru and Venezuela.* Stanford University Press.

Seawright, Jason and David Collier. 2014. "Rival Strategies of Validation: Tools for Evaluating Measures of Democracy." *Comparative Political Studies* 47:111–38.

Seawright, Jason. 2016. "The Case for Selecting Cases That Are Deviant or Extreme on the Independent Variable." *Sociological Methods and Research,* forthcoming.

Seawright, Jason and John Gerring. 2008. "Case Selection Techniques in Case Study Research: A Menu of Qualitative and Quantitative Options." *Political Research Quarterly* 61:294–308.

Sherman, Lawrence W. and Heather Strang. 2004. "Experimental Ethnography: The Marriage of Qualitative and Quantitative Research." *The Annals of the American Academy of Political and Social Science* 595:204–22.

Siavelis, Peter. 1997. "Continuity and Change in the Chilean Party System: On the Transformational Effects of Electoral Reform." *Comparative Political Studies* 30:651–74.

Skocpol, Theda. 1979. *States and Social Revolutions: A Comparative Analysis of France, Russia, and China.* Cambridge University Press.

Skocpol, Theda and Margaret Sommers. 1980. "The Uses of Comparative History in Macrosocial Inquiry." *Comparative Studies in Society and History* 22:174–97.

Smith, Brian. 1982. *The Church and Politics in Chile.* Princeton University Press.

Smith, Allen G. and Karen Seashore Louis, eds. 1982. "Multimethod Policy Research: Issues and Applications." *American Behavioral Scientist* 26(1):6–144.

Snow, John. 1855. *On the Mode of Communication of Cholera*. 2nd edn. London: John Churchill.

Stewart, David W. and Prem N. Shamdasani. 2014. *Focus Groups: Theory and Practice*. 3rd edn. Thousand Oaks, Calif.: Sage.

Stigler, Stephen. 1986. *The History of Statistics: The Measurement of Uncertainty Before 1900*. Cambridge, Mass.: Harvard University Press.

Stinchcombe, Arthur. 1968. *Constructing Social Theories*. New York: Harcourt, Brace, and World.

Tarrow, Sidney. 1995. "Bridging the Quantitative-Qualitative Divide in Political Science." *American Political Science Review* 89(2): 471–74.

Tashakkori, Abbas and Charles Teddlie. 1998. *Mixed Methodology: Combining Qualitative and Quantitative Approaches*. Thousand Oaks, Calif.: Sage.

Tashakkori, Abbas M. and Charles B. Teddlie, eds. 2010. *SAGE Handbook of Mixed Methods in Social and Behavioral Research*. 2nd edn. Thousand Oaks, Calif.: Sage.

Teddlie, Charles and Abbas Tashakkori. 2009. *Foundations of Mixed Methods Research: Integrating Quantitative and Qualitative Approaches in the Social and Behavioral Sciences*. Thousand Oaks, Calif.: Sage.

Tetlock, Philip E. and Aaron Belkin. 1996. *Counterfactual Thought Experiments in World Politics: Logical, Methodological, and Psychological Perspectives*. Princeton University Press.

Thistlethwaite, Donald L. and Donald T. Campbell. 1960. "Regression-Discontinuity Analysis: An Alternative to the Ex Post Facto Experiment." *Journal of Educational Psychology* 51:309–17.

Thompson, Steven K. 2012. *Sampling*. 3rd edn. Hoboken, NJ: John Wiley.

Tourangeau, Roger, Lance J. Rips and Kenneth Rasinski. 2000. *The Psychology of Survey Response*. Cambridge University Press.

Treier, Shawn and Simon Jackman. 2008. "Democracy as a Latent Variable." *American Journal of Political Science* 52(1):201–17.

Van Evera, Stephen. 1997. *Guide to Methods for Students of Political Science*. Ithaca, NY: Cornell University Press.

Verba, Sidney, Kay Lehman Schlozman and Henry E. Brady. 1995. *Voice and Equality: Civic Voluntarism in American Politics*. Cambridge, Mass.: Harvard University Press.

Vicente, Pedro C. and Leonard Wantchekon. 2009. "Clientelism and Vote Buying: Lessons from Field Experiments in African Elections." *Oxford Review of Economic Policy* 25(2):292–305.

Ward, Andrew. 2009. "Causal Criteria and the Problem of Complex Causation." *Medicine, Health Care, and Philosophy* 12:333–43.

Ward, Dalston, Jeong Hyun Kim, Matthew Graham and Margit Tavits. 2015. "How Economic Integration Affects Party Issue Emphases." *Comparative Political Studies* 48(10):1227–59.

Webb, Eugene J., Donald T. Campbell, Richard D. Schwartz and Lee Sechrest. 1966. *Unobtrusive Measures: Non-Reactive Research in the Social Sciences.* Chicago, Ill.: Rand McNally.

Weller, Nicholas and Jeb Barnes. 2014. *Finding Pathways: Mixed-Method Research for Studying Causal Mechanisms.* Cambridge University Press.

Wong, Janelle S. 2005. "Mobilizing Asian American Voters: A Field Experiment." *The Annals of the American Academy of Political and Social Science* 601:102–14.

Woodward, James. 2003. *Making Things Happen: A Theory of Causal Explanation.* Oxford University Press.

Yakusheva, Olga, Kandice Kapinos and Marianne Weiss. 2011. "Peer Effects and the Freshman 15: Evidence from a Natural Experiment." *Economics and Human Biology* 9:119–32.

Yule, G. Udney. 1899. "An Investigation into the Causes of Changes in Pauperism in England, Chiefly During the Last Two Intercensal Decades (Part I)." *Journal of the Royal Statistical Society* 62(2):249–95.

Zinovyeva, Natalia and Manuel Bagues. 2010. "Does Gender Matter for Academic Promotion? Evidence from a Randomized Natural Experiment." http://papers.ssrn.com/sol3/papers.cfm?abstract_id=1618256.

Index